ANXIETY IN THE ELDERLY

Treatment and Research

Carl Salzman, MD, is Director of Psychopharmacology at the Massachusetts Mental Health Center in Boston, and an Associate Professor of Psychiatry at Harvard Medical School. He received his training in psychiatry at Harvard Medical School, at the Massachusetts Mental Health Center, and spent two years of post-graduate study at the National Institutes of Mental Health. Dr. Salzman is a Fellow of the American Psychiatric Association and the American College of Psychiatrists, and a member of the American College of Neuropsychopharmacology, and the American Association of Geriatric Psychiatrists. Dr. Salzman's primary interest is in psychopharmacology, in adults and in the elderly. He has served as chair of many national committees for both NIMH and the American Psychiatric Association, most recently the Task Force on Benzodiazepine Dependence, Toxicity, and Abuse. A recent co-winner of the American Psychiatric Association's Vestermark Award for Outstanding Contribution to Psychiatric Education, he is the author of over 120 original articles and reviews and is on the editorial boards of several professional journals. A second edition of Dr. Salzman's well regarded book *Clinical Geriatric Psychopharmacology* is being published.

Barry D. Lebowitz, PhD, is Chief of the Mental Disorders of the Aging Research Branch of the National Institute of Mental Health and a member of the adjunct faculty of the Department of Psychiatry of the Georgetown University School of Medicine. He is a graduate of McGill University and Cornell University and served on the faculties of Portland State University, the Catholic University of America, and George Washington University. Dr. Lebowitz is a Fellow of the Gerontological Society of America, and was elected as a founding member of the Council on Aging of the American Sociological Association. A frequent participant in public and scientific forums, Dr. Lebowitz serves on the editorial boards of a number of professional scientific journals and has made many published contributions to the literature of gerontology and geriatrics.

ANXIETY in the ELDERLY

Treatment and Research

Carl Salzman, MD
Barry D. Lebowitz, PhD

Editors

SPRINGER PUBLISHING COMPANY
New York

Springer Publishing Company, Inc.
536 Broadway
New York, NY 10012

91 92 93 94 95 / 5 4 3 2 1

Library of Congress Cataloging-in-Publication Data

Anxiety in the elderly / [edited by] Carl Salzman, Barry D. Lebowitz.
    p. cm.
    Papers presented at a workshop held in Boston in Jan. 1989.
    Includes bibliographical references and index.
    ISBN 0-8261-7090-0
    1. Anxiety in old age—Congresses. I. Salzman, Carl.
II. Lebowitz, Barry.
RC531.A616   1990
618.97'685223—dc20   90-10015
                                     CIP

Printed in the United States of America

Contents

Preface

Carl Salzman and Barry D. Lebowitz

This book began innocently enough with a telephone conversation between the editors inquiring about the presence of appropriate rating scales for the measurement of anxiety in older persons. After agreeing that no ideal rating scale or anxiety index was available, the discussion turned to the observation that little research into anxiety in the elderly was ongoing, despite the fact that clinicians were frequently called on to address problems of anxiety in the older patient. Over the next weeks and months we continued to discuss the lack of research into anxiety in the elderly and became increasingly convinced that research was necessary and should be encouraged. As a first step, we agreed that a "state of the art" conference on anxiety in the elderly should be convened. Although each of us was skeptical about the depth and quality of information that might be available, we became progressively more excited about the prospects for an important contribution that could be made in a systematic approach to anxiety in the older patient.

As is usual in such undertakings, the editors put together a rough outline of topics. Our approach to selecting topics for presentation at this conference was broad. We began with the nature of anxiety in older persons, in an attempt to synthesize the existing clinical definitions. From definition, we quickly moved to the clinical manifestation of anxiety, focusing on the relationship between this affective state and physical illness, atypical presentation (masked anxiety), and the relationship of anxiety in the elderly to depression, physical illness, and substance use and abuse. Each of these topics, of course, required redefinition of anxiety as an heuristic concept, and also required an epidemiologic survey into the incidence and prevalence of anxiety; consequently we decided to include a formal presentation of the existing data to answer the question: "How common is anxiety in the elderly?"

Having established the groundwork with attention toward diagnostic questions, as well as the frequency and multiple clinical presentations of anxiety in the elderly, we next sought to determine whether or not the aging process itself contributed to this affective state, or was responsible for the many ways in which it could present. Although reviews of the impact of aging of the CNS on depression and dementia were becoming increasingly common, there had never been a review of the role of the CNS in anxiety as people age, so this became our next focus. From this topic, we naturally moved into the pharmacological management of anxiety, and the impact of the aging process on the body's disposition of drugs, and the increasing sensitivity of the CNS to side effects.

Anxiety in old people is not treated exclusively with drugs. Although the conference was initially conceived from a biologically oriented research perspective, we decided that any conference on this topic would be remiss if it did not include both psychotherapeutic and behaviorally oriented therapeutic perspectives. So, the treatment section of the conference now included presentations of these two topics.

To conclude, we wished to look to the future, and ask how the field of geriatric diagnosis, treatment, and research can continue to move ahead. First, it was important to review the problems that had so far plagued the clinical and research communities, and then having discussed these problems, begin to explore solutions. Lastly, we asked for a peek into the future, particularly at pharmacology, to determine what an ideal treatment for an anxious older person would be, and what were the chemicals that were now under development that might approach such an ideal?

Perhaps in recognition of the importance of these many aspects of anxiety in the elderly or because of the excitement we were feeling about the project, or perhaps simply through good luck, outstanding, nationally recognized clinicians and investigators on the cutting edge of geriatric mental health enthusiastically agreed to participate. As they agreed to participate, there was remarkable consistency in their comments to us: "What a good idea, what an important issue, why has the field taken so long to get to discuss this problem?" Others were worried about participating: "I wish there were more data to present, but what can one say about anxiety in the elderly? . . . at least I can chart out the area and identify gaps in our knowledge." As it turned out, and as is evident by the content of this volume, much more data were presented than any of us ever anticipated. As a consequence, we decided to ask each of the participants to prepare a chapter for this volume with the hope that the resulting book, like the conference, would represent the "state of the art" and be useful to geriatric clinicians and researchers who wished to review what is known about anxiety in the elderly and then push the boundaries of our knowledge forward.

The chapters were prepared and presented at a small workshop in Boston in January 1989. We were blessed with fine weather, outstanding presentations, and truly stimulating discussion. We have tried to capture the highlights of the discussion at appropriate points in this volume. It was a marvelous intellectual exchange and was characterized by strongly held views graciously expressed and respectfully received. The interchange was substantive, good spirited, and witty; in all, it was the sort of meeting that is always planned but rarely takes place. The manuscripts that followed the conference and constitute this volume reflect the enthusiasm and intellectual inquiry of this conference.

The editors are grateful to each contributor for the remarkable quality and depth of their contributions and for their dedication and good humor in their approaches to their assigned tasks. We hope that each reader will gain useful information from this book, and thus, from the conference. There is much to be learned about anxiety in the elderly. Indeed, if there was one common theme that emerged from the meeting, and continues to emerge from the following chapters, it is the rudimentary and preliminary nature of our knowledge about anxiety in the elderly, especially as compared with other affective or cognitive states. Despite a volume of scholarship, it is still not clear whether the concept of anxiety, per se, is useful when referring to old people.

It is important to emphasize, however, that the chapters that comprise this volume are not simply the recorded proceedings of a scientific conference. Rather, each chapter according to its own theme, serves to summarize the experience and knowledge available to date regarding anxiety in older people. Taken together, the chapters thus form a compendium of the clinical and research experience that is available for use by future researchers, as well as by present-day clinicians. And, for both clinicians and researchers, the contributions as a whole point to the future by outlining the needs for both enhanced clinical experience with anxious older people as well as research goals, directions, and suggestions.

For all their contributions to the success of this project we acknowledge with gratitude the logistical aptitude of Janet Meleny, the wonderful support of the staff of the Massachusetts Mental Health Center, and especially of the Director, Miles F. Shore, M.D., whose assistance was invaluable, and of the National Institute of Mental Health, and its Director, Lewis L. Judd, M.D. This project was a collaborative endeavor in the best sense of the word and is faithfully represented as the Harvard–NIMH project on anxiety in the elderly.

Several pharmaceutical companies assisted with the support of this project. In particular, we are grateful for the contributions of: Bristol-Myers/Mead Johnson, Sandoz, Smith Kline and French Laboratories, Upjohn, and Wyeth/Ayerst. This partnership of academia, government, and industry constitutes a model for progress in our approach to the problems of sick old people and those who care for and about them.

As the project nears completion and the book goes to press, we want to acknowledge the special contributions of Kathleen O'Malley and Dr. Ursula Springer of the Springer Publishing Company. They have been responsive, supportive, and helpful throughout this process and we feel honored to have this book included in their important series of publications in the field of aging.

Contributors

George S. Alexopoulos, M.D.
Department of Psychiatry
New York Hospital-Cornell Medical
Center

Dan G. Blazer, M.D., Ph.D.
Department of Psychiatry
Duke University Medical Center

Gene D. Cohen, M.D., Ph.D.
National Institute on Aging

Jonathan O. Cole, M.D.
McLean Hospital
    and
Department of Psychiatry
Harvard Medical School

Dennis Deptula, Ph.D.
Nathan Kline Institute for Psychiatric Research
    and
Department of Psychiatry
New York University School of
Medicine

Edna Foa, Ph.D.
Department of Psychiatry
Medical College of Pennsylvania
at EPPI

Samuel Gershon, M.D.
School of Medicine
University of Pittsburgh

Linda K. George, Ph.D.
Department of Psychiatry
Duke University Medical Center

David G. Greenblatt, M.D.
Division of Clinical Pharmacology
Tufts-New England Medical Center

Bennett Gurian, M.D.
Massachusetts Mental Health
Center
    and
Department of Psychiatry
Harvard Medical School

Dana Hughes, Ph.D.
Department of Psychiatry
Duke University Medical Center

Frank A. Johnson, M.D.
Human Development and Aging
Program
University of California,
San Francisco

Ira R. Katz, M.D., Ph.D.
Department of Psychiatry
Medical College of Pennsylvania
at EPPI

Benjamin Liptzin, M.D.
McLean Hospital
and
Department of Psychiatry
Harvard Medical School

Paul McCarthy, Ph.D.
Department of Psychiatry
Medical College of Pennsylvania
at EPPI

John H. Miner, Psy.D.
Massachusetts Mental Health
Center
and
Department of Psychiatry
Harvard Medical School

Cherry Ann Monroy, M.D.
Nathan Kline Institute for Psychiatric Research
and
Department of Psychiatry
New York University School of
Medicine

Nunzio Pomara, M.D.
Nathan Kline Institute for Psychiatric Research
and
Department of Psychiatry
New York University School of
Medicine

Richard I. Shader, M.D.
Department of Psychiatry
Tufts-New England Medical Center

Charles A. Shamoian, M.D., Ph.D.
Department of Psychiatry
New York Hospital-Cornell Medical
Center

Rajkumar Singh, M.D.
Nathan Kline Institute for Psychiatric Research
and
Department of Psychiatry
New York University School of
Medicine

Trey Sunderland, M.D.
National Institute of Mental Health

Brian Taylor, B.A.
Department of Psychiatry and
Behavioral Sciences
Stanford University School of
Medicine

Jerome A. Yesavage, M.D.
Department of Psychiatry and
Behavioral Sciences
Stanford University School
of Medicine

Ben Zimmer, M.D.
Western Psychiatric Institute and
Clinic
University of Pittsburgh

Diagnosis, Description, and Prevalence of Anxiety in the Elderly

I

What Is Anxiety in the Elderly?

1

Charles A. Shamoian

Anxiety, a common human emotion, is experienced throughout all stages of the life cycle, including old age. Yet, it is a relatively undefined and poorly studied phenomenon in the elderly. To answer the question, what is anxiety in the elderly? requires prior to any discussion of any issue, a definition. The term anxiety signifies a "subjective state of inner distress with thoughts of dread, fear, foreboding or anticipation of imagined harm" and is accompanied by autonomic symptoms including palpitations, tachycardia, sweating, dry mouth, light headedness, etc. (Klerman, 1983). These cognitive and somatic symptoms occur without apparent external stimuli. In contrast, the state of fear which is accompanied by many of the cognitive and somatic symptoms of anxiety, is in fact a response to real external events. According to DSM-III-R, anxiety "may be focused on an object, situation or activity, which is avoided (phobia), or may be unfocused (free floating anxiety). It may be experienced in discrete periods of sudden onset and be accompanied by physical symptoms (panic attacks). When anxiety is focused on physical signs or symptoms and causes preoccupation with the fear or belief of having a disease, it is termed hypochondriasis" DSM-III-R (APA, 1987). The definition and

3

localization of the anxiety do not address the issue of origin of the emotion.

Current thinking about etiology derives from psychoanalytic, behavioral and psychobiologic theories with equivocal data supporting each. However, certain concepts frequently invoked in geriatrics to explain anxiety have their origins in psychoanalytic-psychodynamic theory. Yet, contrary to earlier Freudian thinking, anxiety in the elderly is viewed as arising from object losses and loss of external supplies, rather than its being a danger signal of an intrapsychic conflict (Verwoerdt, 1981). Depletion anxiety is such a concept and is thought to be analogous to separation anxiety and refers to the anticipation of loss of external supplies (Verwoerdt, 1980, 1981). The anxiety, which is progressive in nature, is due to essentially continuous overwhelming experiences, such as age specific losses of social status, physical aging, financial dependency, etc. which occur when internal and external resources are least available (Verwoerdt, 1981). There simply is no time for the elderly to adapt. This depletion is presumably at the basis of all anxiety experienced in old age. However, many elderly suffer similar losses and do not develop anxiety. Thus, some etiology other than that of depletion must be invoked. An explanation offered is that, many elderly, instead of developing anxiety, simply "freeze" (Jarvik & Russell, 1979).

Death anxiety, which has its origins in Erickson's theory of personality development (ego integrity vs. despair), has been thought to be common in the elderly and a source of anxiety for this age group (Erickson, 1950; Wagner & Lorion, 1984). However, this phenomenon is not unique to the elderly (Stevens et al., 1980), is not a general characteristic of this age group (Quinn & Reznikoff, 1985; Wagner, 1984), and is predicted by the presence or absence of past and present life experience (Tate, 1982). A sense of purposefullness in old age seems to be associated with the absence of death anxiety (Quinn & Reznikoff, 1985).

Is anxiety ever a positive emotional experience? In the relatively young, there is general agreement that a vague, equivocal demarcation exists between what is considered normal or abnormal in response to stimuli. In certain situations, at least in younger adults, a mild degree of anxiety may be a positive motivating force. In these individuals it would appear that the anxiety can be modulated such that it does not become incapacitating. Yet, learning studies have demonstrated a relationship between performance and anxiety (Klerman, 1983). Initially, with mild degrees of anxiety, learning is enhanced, whereas with higher degrees of anxiety, performance deteriorates. Does such a relationship exist in the elderly? One study has demonstrated decreased testing performance by the elderly in the presence of high levels of anxiety as compared to middle aged subjects (Cohen et al., 1980). Another relevant study clearly highlighted the importance of relaxation techniques in enhancing memory functions of anxious elderly (Yesavage et al., 1988). Contrary to these findings, another study did not demonstrate a performance decrement in the presence of anxiety in the elderly (La Rue et al., 1985). In fact, this study could not show an increase in anxiety with aging. Based on such reports, anxiety in the elderly as a positive motivating force cannot be said to exist, but rather its presence is a negative factor. However, this area requires additional studies in healthy elderly with "normal" degrees of anxiety.

Anxiety is frequently found as a symptom in a number of medical and psychiatric illnesses (Raj & Sheehan, 1988) (see Table 1.1). Of interest is that many of these have also been associated with depression, dementia or delirium. This emphasizes the need for a comprehensive medical and psychiatric evaluation prior to instituting treatment of anxiety to include or exclude specific illnesses so common to the elderly. Late onset, de novo anxiety may be the initial presentation of an occult disease.

The interaction of medical illness and anxiety is a critical and yet unclarified issue. Anxious patients are often told that although they may feel that they are dying, the anxiety won't kill them. Is this a valid statement? Earlier studies clearly demonstrated that elderly with anxiety and depression were twice as likely to be dead four years later as compared to a group of psychiatrically healthy individuals (Kay & Bergmann, 1966).

Table 1.1 Some Medical Disorders Commonly Associated with Anxiety as a Symptom

Cardiopulmonary	Neurologic
Asthma	Epilepsy
Cardiac Arrhythmias	Huntington's Disease
Chronic Obstructive Pulmonary Disease	Multiple Sclerosis
Congestive Heart Failure	Vestibular Dysfunction
Hypertension	Dementia
Hypoxia	Delirium
Pulmonary Emboli	

Endocrine	Toxic and withdrawal symptoms
Carcinoid Syndrome	Anticholinergic Drugs
Cushing's Syndrome	Caffeine
Hyper and Hypothyroidism	Cocaine
Menopause	Steroids
Pheochromocytoma	Sympathomimetics
Premenstrual Syndrome	Alcohol
	Narcotics
	Sedative-hypnotics

Adapted from: Raj, A. B. and Sheehan, D. V. (1988). *Psychiatric Annals* 18:176–181.

Others have stated that there is an increased morbidity and mortality associated with anxiety (Lader, 1982). These conclusions, however, are based on earlier literature, some of which are case reports, others with small numbers of patients and others without clear diagnostic criteria. However, catecholamine studies of anxious elderly clearly demonstrate an elevation of urinary epinephrine and heart rate during stress with a slower return of these parameters to baseline in the older subjects (Faucheux et al., 1983). The importance of catecholamines and amine receptors in cardiovascular disease states has been clarified (Kohn, 1972). It is conceivable that in high anxiety states in the elderly, with elevated catecholamine plasma levels, there is an increased risk for or morbidity from cardiovascular disease. This and similar issues such as the role of anxiety on the course of illness, on the cascading of medical illnesses in the elderly, on the immune system, etc., need to be clarified.

Table 1.2 lists some of the most common conditions in which anxiety occurs in the elderly (Corbett, 1983). Anxiety is frequently associated with narcissistic, schizoid, obsessive compulsive, and avoidant personality disorders in the elderly (Lader, 1982; Finlay-Jones, 1986). Although frequently denied or not remembered, anxiety probably has been experienced by these individuals prior to onset of old age. A comprehensive, in depth history will usually reveal a life long tendency to anxiety (Herman, 1984). Anxiety, not infrequently, is a prodromal or concomitant manifestation of dementia. Is the anxiety experienced by the demented patient similar to that of the nondemented patient with a lifelong history of a personality disorder? What is the mechanism underlying anxiety in the demented patient? These questions and others such as the association of depression and anxiety need clarification.

Clinically, anxiety and depression frequently co-exist and the differentiation as to which one is the major disorder is frequently difficult. In anxiety there is a loss of self confidence in

Table 1.2 Some of the More Common Causes of Anxiety in Late Life

 1. Major depressive episode
 2. Environmental stressors
 3. Medical illness (known or occult)
 4. True late onset neurotic disorder
 5. Life long recurrent anxiety
 6. Late onset acute phobic anxiety (in response to acute severe illness)
 7. Hypochondriasis
 8. Early dementia
 9. Episodic & self limiting anxiety due to bereavement or anniversary reaction
10. Paranoid psychotic state
11. Obsessional states
12. Withdrawal reactions
13. Medications & caffeine

performing daily tasks; autonomic hyperactivity; difficulty falling asleep; and a sense that something must be done. In depression however, there are feelings of guilt, worthlessness, loss of pleasure, interest and motivation, psychomotor retardation and decreased libido; early morning awakening; and a loss of energy and hopefulness (Klerman, 1983). At times, even with these differences, the differentiation is difficult. Studies have shown that approximately 80% of patients with a primary diagnosis of depression have a high degree of anxiety and that about 50% of patients with primary diagnosis of generalized anxiety disorder (GAD) have symptoms of depression (Zung, 1971). Thus the questions, are anxiety and depression separate entities or are they aspects of the same disease? These questions, especially in the elderly need to be addressed.

Anxiety, as a disorder, is based on the presence of a cluster of symptoms, with a characteristic course and treatment. DSM-III-R anxiety disorders are based on descriptive symptoms and do not address the issue of etiology (see Table 1.3). The criteria for GAD are listed in Table 1.4 and of note is that these do not take into consideration the unique and specific characteristics of old age. An elderly person living on the third floor of a

Table 1.3 Anxiety Disorders (DSM-III-R)

Characteristic features of this group of disorders are symptoms of anxiety and avoidance behavior

300.21	Panic Disorder with Agoraphobia
300.01	Panic Disorder without Agoraphobia
300.22	Agoraphobia without History of Panic Disorder
300.23	Social Phobia
300.29	Simple Phobia
300.30	Obsessive–Compulsive Disorder
309.89	Post-traumatic Stress Disorder
300.02	Generalized Anxiety Disorder
300.00	Anxiety Disorder Not Otherwise Specified

Reprinted with permission from the *Diagnostic and Statistical Manual of Mental Disorders, Third Edition, Revised.* Copyright 1987 American Psychiatric Association.

Table 1.4 Generalized Anxiety Disorder

A. Unrealistic or excessive anxiety and worry about 2 or more life circumstances for a period of 6 months or longer.
B. If another Axis I disorder is present, the focus of anxiety in A is unrelated to it.
C. Disturbance does not occur only during the course of a mood disorder or a psychotic disorder.
D. At least 6 of the following are often present when anxious

Motor tension
*1) trembling, twitching or feeling shaky
*2) muscle tension, aches or soreness
3) restlessness
*4) easy fatigability

Autonomic hyperactivity
5) shortness of breath
6) palpitations or tachycardia
7) sweating or cold clammy hands
8) dry mouth
*9) dizziness or lightheadedness
*10) nausea, diarrhea, or other abdominal distress
11) flushes or chills
*12) frequent urination
13) lump in throat

Vigilance and scanning
14) feeling on edge
15) exaggerated startle response
*16) difficulty concentrating
*17) trouble falling or staying asleep
18) irritability

Reprinted with permission from the Diagnostic and Statistical Manual of Mental Disorders, Third Edition, Revised. Copyright 1987 American Psychiatric Association.

walk-up building in a high crime area, constantly worried and anxious for the past two years about falling and being mugged would qualify for GAD. This same person would manifest many of the required symptoms of GAD as part of the normal aging process and might include the following from DSM-III-R: trembling or feeling shaky, muscle aches and soreness, easily tired, light-headedness, frequent urination, trouble falling asleep or staying asleep (DSM-III-R, 1987). Thus the inappropriate diagnosis of GAD would be applied to this patient and unnecessary pharmacological treatment probably instituted. This hypothetical patient clearly emphasizes the need for diagnostic criteria specific to the elderly. Even within the group designated as the elderly, specific age group criteria may be needed since there are marked differences between 65 and 85 years of age.

Does anxiety exist in the elderly? Based on clinical experience and the literature, there would be universal agreement among geriatric psychiatrists that anxiety does occur in the elderly both as a symptom and as a disorder. How prevalent anxiety is as a symptom or as a disorder in the elderly, how prevalent late onset is as compared to early onset anxiety in the elderly, and whether or not anxiety is age specific are questions and issues yet to be resolved. Some studies addressing these points are summarized in Table 1.5. Clearly the prevalence rates may vary from 5% to 68% depending upon the location and nature of patients, size of study sample and assessment scales used. The earlier studies utilized scales such as the Taylor (Taylor, 1953), Hamilton (Hamilton, 1959), or Spielberger (Spielberger et al., 1970) scales whereas the Epidemiological Catchment Area (E.C.A.) studies utilized the Diagnostic Interview Schedule/DSM-III Disorders (Robins et al., 1981). Conlin's study involved 22 ambulatory elderly (Conlin & Fennell, 1985) whereas those of Gurin (Gurin et al., 1963), Leighton (Leighton et al., 1963), Gaitz (Gaitz & Scott, 1972) and Regier (Regier et al., 1988) assessed large numbers of community residing elderly. Two of these (Gurin et al., 1963 and Himmelfarb & Murrell, 1984) reported that anxiety increased with age whereas the E.C.A. studies, although predominantly oversampled for elderly in three of its sites, showed the opposite (Regier et al., 1988). Leighton's study of 1963 revealed no difference between elderly and younger groups (Leighton et al., 1963). Clearly, additional studies are required to clarify the issues that arise from these seemingly contradictory findings.

Table 1.5 Some Anxiety Studies

Author	Site & type of Patient	Results & comments
Gurin, 1963	Nationwide: 2,460 adults living in private housing	10% of elderly anxious. Twice as prevalent as compared to younger. Age group prevalence of cognitive and somatic anxiety.
Leighton, 1963	1010 Residents of Canada	10.4% of elderly with Anxiety. Not different from younger age group.
Gaitz, 1972	1441 Residents of Houston	Tendency toward an age related prevalence of cognitive and somatic anxiety.
Himmelfarb, 1984	713 males, 1338 females Community residing 55 yrs. old and older	17% males and 22% females diagnosed as anxious. Anxiety inversely related to socioeconomic and educational levels, mean anxiety scores may increase with age group.
Magni, 1984	178 geriatric and 201 adult medical inpatients	40% of adult and 13% of geriatric patients had moderate to high levels of anxiety.
Conlin, 1985	22 Ambulatory elderly	68% rated clinically anxious.
Regier, 1988	E.C.A. Studies 5 sites	One month prevalence rates for anxiety disorders decrease with age in both sexes. Higher in elderly females as compared to males. Anxiety disorders approximately eight times more prevalent than major depressive episode in elderly.

SUMMARY

Anxiety exists in the elderly as a symptom and as a disorder. However, the studies available do not unequivocally answer such basic questions as the prevalence rates of trait vs. state or early vs. late onset anxiety disorders. Such information is urgently needed to clearly define appropriate mental health policy issues for ever increasing numbers of elderly. The etiology of anxiety also demands immediate attention since it may directly and indirectly increase morbidity and mortality rates. Its specific interactive role with medical illnesses and psychiatric disorders need clarification to avoid the debilitating effects of cascading mental and physical pathologies superimposed upon the aging process.

COMMENTARY

1. Concern was expressed that the old elderly may be underrepresented in community surveys (e.g., ECA survey) because of reluctance to answer personal questions. Community survey experience as indicated however, that older people tend to respond to these surveys at a higher rate than other populations, especially as compared with other groups that are more difficult to survey (middle aged males, single black males, homeless). There is no evidence that the elderly are less likely to respond to survey questions except for the subpopulation of the elderly who are severely physically ill. These persons tend to be screened from the interviewer by the family. The conclusion of surveyors is that in any community survey, the elderly response probably most approximates the truth of all age groups being surveyed.

2. There is considerable lack of clarity about the definitions of anxiety, the terms are used interchangeably. For example anxiety neurosis, anxiety state, and anxiety disorders all may mean the same thing, may mean different syndromes, or may overlap. Anxiety may not be differentiated from agitation, although agitated elderly patients may also be anxious and vise verse. Elderly patients who are anxious may also be manic, depressed, or schizophrenic. There has been no agreement as to whether such elderly people should be termed primarily anxious (and treated for their anxiety) rather than being categorized as having the other symptom with anxiety secondary.

3. To add to the semantic confusion, older people themselves may use the word "nervous" to describe their subjective experience. Nervousness may be associated with tremors, akathisia, restlessness, as well as true anxiety. It is common for old people to equate anxiety with nervousness.

4. Definitions of anxiety in the elderly are often based on rating scales and definitions developed in younger people. There is no agreement about the criteria for anxiety in the elderly. This is for the complicated by the heterogeneity of the older age sample. In many studies, subjects ages 55–65 are included, which may make the age range too broad and further confused definition but within the age range generally considered to the elderly, i.e., 65 and older there is also great variability in symptom presentation and treatment response. Patients who are over 85 may be substantially different from patients who are between 65 and 75. In addition to general agreement about the criteria for anxiety in the elderly, therefore, there needs to be consideration of subpopulations within the elderly, i.e., young old, middle old, and very old.

5. The literature on death anxiety suggest that it is actually less common in the elderly as compared with middle age. However, older people tend to talk more about death especially in the context of personal loss or physical illness. This is an illustration of a common misinterpretation of data collected from the elderly. Just talking more about death does not necessarily imply increased death anxiety, and if such data are not understood in the context of the older persons life and experience, they may be inappropriately skewed.

REFERENCES

American Psychiatric Association. (1987). *Diagnostic and statistical manual of mental disorders* (Third Edition-Revised) (DSM-III-R) Washington, D.C.: Author.

Cohen, D., Eisdorfer, C., Vitaliano, P. P., and Bloom, V. (1980). The relationship between age, anxiety and serum immunoglobulins with crystalized and fluid intelligence. *Biological Psychiatry, 15,* 699–709.

Conlin, M. M. and Fennell, E. B. (1985). Anxiety, depression and health locus of control orientation in an out-patient elderly population. *J. Florida Medical Assn., 72*(4), 281–288.

Corbett, L. (1983). Anxiety in the elderly: Current concepts. In J. Fawcett (Ed.) *Anxiety and anxiety in the elderly in contemporary psychiatry* (pp. 37–41). Chicago: Pragmaton Publications.

Erikson, E. H. (1950). *Childhood and society.* New York, N.Y.: Norton.

Facheux, B. A., Baulon, A., Poitrenaud, J., Lille, F., Moreaux, C., Dupuis, C., & Bourliere, F. (1983). Heart rate, urinary catecholamines and anxiety responses during mental stress in men in their fifties and seventies. *Age and Ageing, 12,* 144–150.

Finlay-Jones, R. (1986). Anxiety states in the elderly. In E. Murphy (Ed.). *Affective Disorders in the Elderly* (pp. 217–230). New York: Churchill Livingstone.

Gaitz, C. M., & Scott, J. (1972). Age and the measurement of mental health. *J. of Health and Social Behavior, 13,* 55–67.

Gurin, G., Veroff, J., & Feld, S. (1983). *Americans view their mental health.* New York: Basic Books.

Hamilton, M. (1959). The assessment of anxiety states by rating. *Brit. J. Medical Psychology, 32,* 50–55.

Herman, S. (1984). Anxiety disorder. In A. D. Whanger & A. C. Meyers (Eds.). *Mental health assessment and therapeutic intervention with older adults* (pp. 77–84). Rockville, M. D.: Aspen Publications.

Himmelfarb, S., & Murrell, S. A. (1984). The prevalence and correlates of anxiety symptoms in older adults. *J. of Psychology, 116,* 159–167.

Jarvik, L. F., & Russell, D. (1979). Anxiety, aging and the third emergency reaction. *J. of Gerontology, 341*(2), 197–200.

Kay, D. W. K., & Bergmann, K. (1966). Physical disability and mental health in old age. A follow-up of a random sample of people seen at home. *J. Psychosom. Res., 10,* 3–12.

Klerman, G. L. (1983). Classifying anxiety—The new nosology. In J. Fawcett (Ed.). *Anxiety and anxiety in the elderly in contemporary psychiatry* (pp. 7–10). Chicago: Pragmaton Publications.

Kohn, R. R. (1977). Heart and cardiovascular system. In C. E. Finch & L. Hayflick (Eds.) *Handbook of the biology of aging* (pp. 281–317). New York: Van Nostrand Rheinhold Co.

LaRue, A., & D'Elia, L. F. (1985). Anxiety and problem solving in middle-aged and elderly adults. *Experimental Aging Research, 11*(4), 215–220.

Lader, M. (1982). Differential diagnosis of anxiety in the elderly. *J. Clin. Psychiatry, 43*(9), 4–7.

Leighton, D. C., Harding, J. S., Macklin, D. B., MacMillan, A. M., & Leighton, A. H. (1963). *The Character of danger: Psychiatric symptoms in selected communities, III.* New York: Basic Books.

Magni, G., DeLeo, D. (1984). Anxiety and depression in geriatric and adult medical inpatients: A comparison. *Psychological Reports,* 55, 607–612.

Quinn, P. K., & Reznikoff, M. (1985). The relationship between death anxiety and the subjective experience of time in the elderly. *Int'l J. Aging and Human Development,* 21(3), 197–210.

Raj, B. A., & Sheehan, D. V. (1988). Medical evaluation of the anxious patient. *Psychiatric Annals,* 18(3), 176–181.

Regier, D. A., Boyd, J. H., Burke, Jr., J. D., Rae, D. S., Myers, J. K., Kramer, M., Robins, L. N., George, L. K., Karno, M., & Locke, B. Z. (1988). One month prevalence of mental disorders in the United States. *Arch. Gen. Psychiatry,* 45, 977–986.

Robins, L. N., Helzer, J. E., Croughan, J., & Ratcliff, K. S. (1981). National Institute of Mental Health Diagnostic Interview Schedule: Its history, characteristics, and validity. *Arch. Gen. Psychiatry,* 38, 381–389.

Stevens, S., Cooper, P., & Thomas, E. (1980). Age norms for Templer's death anxiety scale. *Psychological Reports,* 46, 205–206.

Spielberger, C. D., Gorusch, R. L., & Lushene, R. E. (1970). *State Trait Anxiety Inventory Manual.* Palo Alto: Consulting Psychologist Press.

Tate, L. A. (1982). Life satisfaction and death anxiety in aged women. *Int'l. J. Aging and Human Development,* 15(4), 299–306.

Taylor, J. A. (1953). A personality scale of manifest anxiety. *J. of Abnormal and Social Psychology,* 48, 285–290.

Verwoerdt, A. (1980). Anxiety, dissociative and personality disorders in the elderly. In E. W. Busse & D. G. Blazer (Eds.). *Handbook of geriatric psychiatry* (pp. 368–380). New York: Van Nostrand Rheinhold Co.

Verwoerdt, A. (1981). *Clinical geropsychiatry-Second Edition.* Baltimore, MD: Williams and Wilkins.

Wagner, K. D., & Lorion, R. P. (1984). Correlates of death anxiety in elderly persons. *J. Clinical Psychology,* 40(5), 1235–1241.

Yesavage, J. A., Sheikh, J., Tanke, E. D., & Hill, R. (1988). Response to memory training and individual differences in verbal intelligence and state anxiety. *Am. J. Psychiatry,* 145(5), 636–639.

Zung, W. W. K. (1971). The differentiation of anxiety and depressive disorders: A biometric approach. *Psychosomatics,* 12, 380–384.

The Epidemiology of Anxiety Disorders: An Age Comparison

2

Dan Blazer, Linda K. George, and Dana Hughes

The anxiety disorders are the most commonly reported psychiatric disorders in recent community-based epidemiologic surveys (Myers et al., 1984). There have been few studies, however, of the epidemiology of the anxiety disorders across the life cycle. Jane Murphy and her colleagues (1986) report the prevalence of both anxiety disorders and conversion disorders in those individuals less than 45 years of age vs. those 45 years of age and older from the Stirling County Study. The prevalence of generalized anxiety in males was 2.1% under the age of 45 but less than 1% in those individuals 45 years of age and greater. In contrast, the prevalence of generalized anxiety in females 45 years of age and older was 6% compared to 2.5% for those under the age of 45. Warheit (1986) reported the mean number of anxiety symptoms in a community sample of adults from the Florida Epidemiologic Study. Anxiety symptoms increased linearly with age, doubling from adolescence to late life. Recent reports from the Epidemiologic Catchment Area

17

Study, however (for current and lifetime prevalence of anxiety disorders) suggest that the current and lifetime prevalence of most anxiety disorders decreases with increased age for both sexes (Myers et al., 1984; Robins et al., 1984).

To explore the epidemiology of the anxiety disorders among older adults, we take advantage of the Piedmont Health Survey, part of the Epidemiologic Catchment Area Project. As an oversample of the elderly (60+) was included in this survey, individuals in mid life (45 to 64) were compared with late life distribution across demographic factors of the anxiety disorders, with special attention to generalized anxiety.

THE PIEDMONT HEALTH SURVEY

Data presented derive from the National Institute of Mental Health Epidemiologic Catchment Area (ECA) Project at Duke University Medical Center. The North Carolina sample, one of five ECA sites throughout the continental United States, contained the highest number of rural residents and was designed so that urban/rural comparisons as well as racial comparisons could be made. The sample was drawn into segments, the first complying with the original ECA project goal of obtaining 3,000 household interviews from subjects in the community 18 years of age and older and 500 institutional interviews. An additional sample was drawn to yield 900 interviews from the elderly (60+ years of age) within the community.

In the Wave I survey, administered in 1982–1983, 3,922 community subjects were interviewed (a 79% response rate) and 502 institutional subjects. One year later, 2,993 subjects were re-interviewed (Wave II). Data were weighted for both waves of the interview to distribute the attrition due to nonresponse (subjects who refused to participate, had moved beyond the tracking range, or were unlocatable) evenly across the demographic subgroups, i.e., sex, race, age, and residence.

Each participant in the survey underwent approximately a two hour interview, which included the Diagnostic Interview Schedule (DIS) (Robins et al., 1981) Wave I of the Piedmont

Health Survey assessed symptom data on panic disorders, phobic disorders, obsessive-compulsive disorders and psychotropic drug use. Only in Wave II were questions asked to determine the prevalence of generalized anxiety. The generalized anxiety section of the DIS screens for a series of symptoms associated with generalized anxiety. Symptoms from three of four categories—motor tension, autonomic hyperactivity, vigilance and scanning, and apprehensive expectation—lasting for one month or more constituted the DSM-III criteria for diagnosis (see Table 2.1).

Because the DSM-III criteria for generalized anxiety disorders were changed to DSM-III-R, we elected to use the term generalized anxiety syndrome to identify those individuals who report symptoms of generalized anxiety disorder on the DIS that correspond to DSM-III criteria (Blazer et al., 1987). DSM-III-R criteria were not available at the time these data were collected.

At Wave I of the survey, the weighed distribution by age of the sample was age 18 to 24 (18%), 25–44 (40%), 45–64 (27%), and 65+ (14%). Fifty-four percent of the sample was female and 38% was non-white (predominantly black). Fifty-seven percent of the sample were married. Thirty-eight percent of the sample had less than a high school education. For the purposes of this study of individuals in mid and late life, the age groups 45 to 64 and 65+ were compared.

When ECA data has been presented in previous studies, "hierarchies" have generally not been included. That is, if an individual suffers two disorders concurrently (regardless of which disorder preceded the other), both disorders are listed as current diagnoses. This approach, however, presents a problem to investigators of generalized anxiety disorder. The co-morbidity of generalized anxiety disorder with the depression disorders and panic disorder were of concern to the investigators. The prevalence of these disorders in the community at Wave II were as follows: dysthymia (80 cases were a prevalence of 2.8%), major depression (53 cases or 1.8%), panic disorder (12 cases, 0.4%). Of the subjects who suffered the generalized anxiety syndrome, seven women and no men also suffered dysthy-

Table 2.1 Comparison of DSM-III Diagnostic Interview Schedule Items for Generalized Anxiety

Symptom criteria
(Symptoms from three of the following four categories)

DSM-III Criteria	DIS Items
1. *Motor tension:*	
Shakiness	Eyelids twitched
Jitteriness	Jitteriness
Trembling	Body trembled
Fatigability	Tired very easily
Restlessness	Tenseness or jumpiness
Tension	Easily startled
	Trouble relaxing
2. *Autonomic hyperactivity:*	
Sweating	Sweating a lot
Heart pounding	Heart pounding
Dizziness	Dizziness
Paresthesias	Tingling in hands/feet
Upset stomach	Upset stomach
Diarrhea	Diarrhea
Frequent urination	Frequent urination
Flushing	Face flushing
Dryness in mouth	Dryness in mouth
High resting respiration rate	Breathing too fast
3. *Vigilance and scanning:*	
Hyperattentiveness	Trouble sleeping
Difficulty in concentrating	Trouble concentrating
Insomnia	Irritable/impatient
Irritability	
Impatience	
4. *Apprehensive expectation:*	
Anxiety	Anxious, afraid, worried
	1+ months
Fear	
Worry	
5. *Age criteria:*	
At least 18 years age	

mia, and nine women and three men suffered major depression. None suffered panic disorder. We operationally defined cases of the generalized anxiety syndrome as those individuals who did not suffer concurrent major depression or panic disorder.

RESULTS OF THE SURVEY

The six month and lifetime prevalence of the anxiety disorders are presented in Table 2.2. Middle age (45 to 64 years) is compared with late life (65+ years). For each of the anxiety disorders, the prevalence for the 45 to 64 age group is higher than that for the 65+ age group. The discrepancy is especially apparent with panic attack, but less so for the phobias and generalized anxiety. Lifetime prevalence is also lower for the 65+ age group. Problems with recall among the elderly may contribute to the lower lifetime prevalence. In addition, however, a cohort effect (as has been discussed frequently regarding depressive disorders) may impact upon lifetime as well as current prevalence rates. Regardless, the current and lifetime prevalence for the anxiety disorders is relatively high throughout the life cycle, especially when phobic disorders are included.

Table 2.2 Six-Month and Lifetime Prevalence of Anxiety Disorders by Age for the Duke ECA Community Sample

	Six-Month		Lifetime	
	45–64	65+	45–64	65+
Simple phobia	13.29	9.63	18.11	16.10
Social phobia	2.04	1.37	3.18	2.64
Agoraphobia	7.30	5.22	9.40	8.44
Panic disorder	1.10	0.04	2.04	0.29
Obsessive-compulsive disorder	2.01	1.54	3.33	1.98
Generalized anxiety syndrome*	3.10	1.90	6.70	4.60

*From Wave II

The remainder of this chapter focuses upon generalized anxiety. In the North Carolina data, generalized anxiety (see above) was only assessed at Wave II of the survey. In Table 2.3, generalized anxiety prevalence using three definitions are presented. As mentioned above, the operational definition which excludes panic and major depression is preferred by the investigators. Nevertheless, the prevalence by age and sex follow a similar pattern regardless of the exclusion criteria used. The vast majority of the non-blacks are Caucasian in the study. The highest prevalence of generalized anxiety is found among middle-aged black males. Older males and females, regardless of race, exhibit a lower prevalence.

Generalized anxiety is more prevalent among males in urban settings and females in rural settings (though the difference

Table 2.3 One Year Prevalence Rate (%) of Generalized Anxiety (Different Exclusionary Criteria) by Sex, Age, and Race for North Carolina

	Generalized anxiety (no exclusions)	Generalized anxiety (excluding panic and major depression)	Generalized anxiety (excluding all DSM-III disorders)
Male Nonblack			
45–64	1.4	1.1	0.0
65+	1.0	0.7	0.7
Male Black			
45–64	8.0	8.5	5.7
65+	0.3	0.3	0.0
Female Nonblack			
45–64	5.9	3.7	3.1
65+	2.9	2.7	1.3
Female Black			
45–64	3.2	1.2	1.1
65+	3.7	3.7	0.9

Table 2.4 Prevalence Rates (%) of Generalized Anxiety (No Panic or Major Depression) by Sex, Age, and Residence for North Carolina ECA Sites

	Urban	Rural
Male		
45–64	6.2	0.3
65+	0.9	0.2
Female		
45–64	2.5	3.3
65+	2.0	3.5

across urban/rural boundaries for females is minimal). Trends are similar regardless of age, as can be seen in Table 2.4.

In Table 2.5, the age of onset of generalized anxiety for all participants is presented. Age of onset is evenly distributed across the life cycle, except for individuals 65 years of age and older. Again, problems of recall and a tendency to deny symptoms of anxiety may contribute to the dramatic differences between the 45 to 64 age group and the 65+ age group. As would be expected (see Table 2.6), the average duration of

Table 2.5 Age of Onset of Generalized Anxiety (No Panic or Major Depression) in North Carolina ECA

Age	
18, 19	20.6%
20–24	19.5%
25–29	16.4%
30–44	23.0%
45–64	17.5%
65+	3.0%

Mean age of onset was 31.4

Table 2.6 Age Distribution of Generalized Anxiety (No Panic or Major Depression) by Duration of Symptoms for Current and Remitted Cases Duke Sample

	Current cases (%) 45–64	Current cases (%) 65+	Remitted cases 45–64	Remitted cases (%) 65+
Duration of symptoms				
< 1 year	20.9	14.8	43.8	36.2
1–5 years	33.8	36.8	18.5	27.2
6–10 years	5.3	9.0	5.9	7.2
11–20 years	9.3	0.0	9.4	8.5
21+ years	30.7	39.4	22.4	20.9
Number of cases	19	19	28	28
Mean years	11.2	16.84	7.87	9.39
Standard deviation	11.6	23.8	11.1	13.8

current anxiety disorders is greater for individuals 65 years and older than for the middle-aged group. The variation for the elderly is considerably increased. This suggests that some individuals experience long standing anxiety and perceive themselves to have been anxious much of their lives. Others experience the symptom for a much shorter duration. Nearly 50% of the 65+ age group reported duration of five years or less, suggesting that a considerable number of older adults do experience the first onset of generalized anxiety in late life, at least after the age of 60. There is little difference in remitted cases, for remission is reported by both the middle-aged and the elderly.

In Table 2.7, the use of general health services by patients suffering generalized anxiety is presented. Older adults are more likely to use inpatient physical health facilities than outpatient services if they report a current (one year) episode of generalized anxiety. In Table 2.8, the use of mental health services is presented. Older adults are more likely to use outpatient mental health services if they report that they suffered symptoms of generalized anxiety. This trend is not apparent for

Table 2.7 Age Distribution of the Use of Physical Health Services by Subjects Suffering Generalized Anxiety

	Outpatient physical health	
	45–64 years	65+ years
Overall Use—One Year	52.34%	60.66%
Overall Use— One Year Prevalence by Diagnosis		
No	52.83%	60.80%
Yes	37.00	53.53
	Inpatient physical health	
	45–64 years	65+ years
Overall Use—One Year (%)	5.86	12.46
Overall Use—One Year by Diagnosis		
No	5.72	11.95
Yes	10.32	38.36

Table 2.8 Age Distribution of Generalized Anxiety (No Panic or Major Depression) by Use of Mental Health Services (Weighted to Regional Demographic Distribution)

	Outpatient mental health	
	45–64 years	65+ years
Overall Use—One Year (%)	8.78	9.37
Overall Use—One Year by Diagnosis		
No	8.29	8.80
Yes	24.06	38.27
	Inpatient mental health	
	45–64 years	65+ years
Overall Use—One Year (%)	0.26	0.43
Overall Use—One Year by Diagnosis		
No	0.27	0.44
Yes	0.00	0.00

inpatient mental health services, though use of inpatient mental health services is minimal for this sample. In Table 2.9, benzodiazepine use is reported. As would be expected, older adults tend to use benzodiazepine more than those who are younger.

CONCLUSIONS

The results reported suggest that older adults do suffer relatively frequent generalized anxiety, compared with other psychiatric syndromes, though the prevalence is lower than for the middle-aged group. Nevertheless, under-reporting must be suspected. Specifically, if an older adult does report symptoms of generalized anxiety, they are more likely to use outpatient mental health facilities and are more likely to use anti-anxiety agents. A higher threshold of discomfort may be required for reporting these symptoms in late life. Once that threshold is crossed, however, the elder is likely to seek assistance for his or her symptoms.

The remaining anxiety disorders, i.e., phobic disorders, panic disorder, obsessive-compulsive disorder, are also less prevalent in late life, though the degree of variability between mid-life and late life varies for each disorder. For example, the prevalence of panic disorder in late life is rare compared to mid-life whereas the prevalence of obsessive-compulsive disorder and agoraphobia are similar for persons in mid-life and late life.

These epidemiologic data do not answer this question: whether generalized anxiety deserves recognition as a specific psychiatric disorder or rather is a constellation of residual symptoms from a number of other disorders, such as major depression, panic, or phobic disorders. Regardless, the condition contributes significantly to the use of health service. Though much attention has been directed in recent years to the psychobiologic etiology of psychiatric disorders, the role of chronic environmental stress has been neglected. Clinicians intuitively accept that internal unresolved psychological conflicts and external psychosocial stressors induce symptoms of

Table 2.9 Benzodiazepine Use from North Carolina ECA Study by Demographic Characteristics

Variable	Total	Number using drug	Percentage using drug
Sex			
Males	1489	104	6.9
Females	2309	310	10.6
Age			
18–34	1096	50	3.8
35–54	863	99	11.5
55–74	1414	208	14.0
75+	425	57	13.6
Marital Status			
Married	1953	197	9.3
Widowed	814	122	14.7
Separated/Divorced	480	70	11.4
Never married	551	25	3.6

*Remains significant in logistic regression analysis
**From Melville, et al. (unpublished manuscript)

anxiety. Yet our current conceptions of psychobiology have tended to ignore these less severe and less discrete disorders. Psychiatrists have tended to concentrate upon panic attacks or "anxiety attacks." Older adults appear to suffer these disorders less frequently than persons at earlier states of the life cycle.

If psychiatrists, on the other hand, focus upon the symptoms of psychopathology that lead to health service utilization and especially to the use of medications, then generalized anxiety is of the greater importance. General health services and mental health services are used by persons both in mid-life and late life suffering from DIS/DSM-III generalized anxiety. Though most of the care for these disorders is provided by primary care physicians, anxious individuals are often treated with benzodiazepines, which are among the most frequently prescribed by primary care physicians (Hasay & Karch, 1981).

In conclusion, anxiety—that distressing affect which is experienced as worry and thought to be the central emotional experience in modern society—has been relatively neglected in both clinical and epidemiologic studies of older adults. Symptoms of generalized anxiety and symptoms of the other anxiety disorders—phobias, obsessions, and compulsions—are among the more common experienced by older adults in a community population. Risk factors for these disorders and outcome need further study.

COMMENTARY

1. General medical illnesses that are accompanied by anxiety were not coded (unlike depression). In the community however, the likelihood of a medical illness contributing to an anxiety disorder is low. This likelihood increases markedly in psychiatric settings, hospital settings, or nursing home settings. In the community however, most elderly survey responders had no medical illness and therefore it was concluded that anxiety symptoms reported in the ECA data were not caused by medical illness.

2. It is this very lack of conclusion of medically ill patients that may lead to a significant under-reporting of anxiety in the community. This is especially true for institutionalized elderly. Although the number of physically ill elderly in the community is not higher in middle-aged respondents in the community, there is an increased number of elderly in psychiatric and nursing home settings.

3. ECA lifetime prevalence date for the elderly, like data for all age groups may have an under-reporting of anxiety symptoms. Older persons are much more likely to not report past episodes of anxiety than younger persons (There is no difference in reporting of current episodes of anxiety between young and elderly respondents). This under-reporting of anxiety symptoms among the elderly may contribute to the decline in lifetime prevalence with advance age that is seen in the ECA data.

4. The following clarifications of the ECA data were presented:
    a. Data presented in the preceding discussion include institutionalized elderly as well as community residents.
    b. Overall, only 4% of elderly are in institutions, so that even if there is an increased prevalence of symptoms in the institutionalized population, this may not add appreciably to the overall prevalence rate.

c. It should be noted that half the institutionalized elderly can't be interviewed because of cognitive impairment. Therefore, it is likely that prevalence rates of institutionalzed elderly patients will only represent 2% of the overall elderly population.

d. The ECA survey data used DIS questionnaires. The DIS is based on DIS-III criteria. This should be distinguished from surveys that use SADS which are based on RDC criteria. The DSM-III placed more emphasis on anxiety symptoms. The DSM-III-R places more emphasis on unrealistic and excessive worry as a core definition criteria.

e. The ECA survey data are six months prevalence data (the symptoms must have occurred within the prior six months). The duration of symptoms necessary for inclusion is one month. Therefore brief intermittent episodes of anxiety would not be recorded by this survey.

f. Like any survey data, there is not content or qualitative elaboration of symptoms. Compared with clinical description, survey data are superficial. It is possible, therefore, that many symptoms such as those of simple phobia which are not severe enough to interfere with function might not be recorded by the survey data.

g. The table illustrating benzodiazepine prescription represents only community residents and not patients in institutions. Different types of benzodiazepines are not described in this presentation. Overall, approximately 2–3% of the benzodiazepine use is hypnotics.

5. The overall conclusion—the elderly sample is generally similar to middle aged adults. The superficial survey data suggest that the similarities are far more striking than the differences.

REFERENCES

American Psychiatric Association. (1980). *Diagnostic and statistical manual of mental disorders* (Third Edition). Washington, DC: Author.

American Psychiatric Association. (1987). *Diagnostic and statistical manual of mental disorders* (Third Edition—Revised). Washington, DC: Author.

Balter, M. B., Levine, J., & Manheimer, D. I. (1974). Cross-national study of the extent of anti-anxiety sedative drug use. *New England Journal of Medicine, 290*, 769–774.

Blazer, D. G., & George, L. K. (1987). Stressful life events and the onset of a generalized anxiety syndrome. *American Journal of Psychiatry, 144*, 1178–1183.

Blazer, D. G., Hughes, D., George, L. K., Schwartz, M., & Boyd, J. (in press). Generalized anxiety disorders. In L. N. Robins & D. Regier (Eds.), *Psychiatric disorders in America.* New York: The Free Press.

Brickman, A. L., & Eisdorfer, C. (in press). Anxiety in the elderly. In E. W. Busse & D. G. Blazer (Eds.), *Geriatric psychiatry.* Washington, DC: American Psychiatric Press.

George, L. K., Hughes, D. C., & Blazer, D. G. (1986). Urban/rural differences and the prevalence of anxiety disorders. *American Journal of Social Psychiatry, 6*, 249–258.

Hasday, J. D., & Karch, F. E. (1981). Benzodiazepine prescribing in a family medical center. *JAMA, 246*, 1321–1325.

Myers, J. K., Weissman, M. M., Tischler, G. L., Holzer, C. E., Leaf, P. J., et al. (1989). Six-month prevalence of psychiatric disorders in three communities: 1980–1982. *Archives of General Psychiatry, 41*, 959–970.

Regier, D. A., Boyd, J. H., Burke, J. D., Rae, S., Myers, J. K., et al. (1988). One-month prevalence of mental disorders in the United States. *Archives of General Psychiatry, 45*, 977–986.

Robins, L. N., Helzer, J. E., Croughan, J., et al. (1981). National Institute of Mental Health Diagnostic Interview Schedule: Its history, characteristics, and validity. *Archives of General Psychiatry, 38*, 381–389.

Robins, L. N., Helzer, J. E., Weissman, M. M., Orvaschel, H., Gruenberg, E., Burke, J. D., et al. (1984). Lifetime prevalence of specific psychiatric disorders in three sites. *Archives of General Psychiatry, 38*, 381–389.

Warheit, G. J., Bell, R. A., Schwab, J. J., & Buhl, J. M. (1986). An epidemiologic assessment of mental health problems in the southeastern United States. In M. M. Weissman, J. K. Meyers, & C. E. Ross (Eds.), *Community surveys of psychiatric disorders* (191–208). New Brunswick: Rutgers University Press.

Clinical Presentation of Anxiety in the Elderly

3

Bennet S. Gurian and John H. Miner

In reviewing the records of geriatric patients seen in private practice over the last three years, very few seemed to meet all the criteria for any specific Anxiety Disorder as defined by DSM-III-R. Most anxious patients seemed to fall into other Axis I categories. Anxiety was found to be a very *common symptom* but an *uncommon syndrome*. Therefore, it seems reasonable to question whether the elderly manifest anxiety in the same way and with the same frequency as do younger patients, and whether DSM-III-R is appropriate for the classification of anxiety disorders as they appear in older persons.

There is little consensus whether there is a "classic" general clinical presentation of anxiety in older patients. For example, Salzman has written that "Anxiety may be experienced as cognitive apprehension, behavioral agitation, or somatic symptoms with hypochondriacal components" (1982). Busse underscored the somatic presentation: "Anxiety in the elderly may be displaced into high bodily concern and expressed as hypochondriacal symptoms" (1975). In contrast, Pfeiffer stated that "Among older persons ... the expression of anxiety is more commonly direct, appearing as overt fear, panic, worry of bewilderment, and without the intricate conversion mechanism customarily seen in younger persons" (Roche, p. 28). As seen in

clinical practice, many patients manifest symptoms in all of
these ways whether simultaneously or sequentially. In fact,
sub-classification within anxiety disorders may depend on
symptom emphasis at that moment when evaluation takes
place.

During a 1977 conference on anxiety in the elderly, many
questions were raised (Hoffmann-La Roche, 1979). For example: "Do the symptoms of anxiety differ in the old from those
seen in the young? Does the optimal management of anxiety
differ for the old and the young? Do related changes in
arousal or autonomic nervous system responsiveness influence
the relationship between stress and anxiety?" (Blumenthal,
p. 9)

In the decade that has elapsed since that conference, much
has been learned about neurochemical and neurophysiologic
mechanisms in anxiety disorders. New anxiolytic substances
have become clinically available and important epidemiologic
information concerning anxiety in the elderly has been obtained. Yet, as clinicians, we continue to struggle with differential diagnosis, with the persistence of symptoms despite our
therapeutic interventions, and with the difficulty in withdraw-
ing anti-anxiety medications.

DIAGNOSTIC DIFFICULTIES IN GEROPSYCHIATRY

The symptoms of anxiety are well-known and extensively
described in the literature (Klein & Rabkin, 1981; Klerman,
1983; Nakra & Grossberg, 1986; Rakel, 1981). Anxiety may be
defined as a subjective state of internal discomfort, dread, and
foreboding, accompanied by autonomic nervous system
arousal. Different from fear, anxiety tends to occur without
conscious or apparent stimulus. The physical symptoms include hyperventilation, palpitations, sweating, diarrhea, trembling, dizziness, headache, restlessness, and muscle aches. Certain cognitive changes are also associated with anxious states:
impaired attention, poor concentration, and memory problems.
For elderly patients, accurate diagnosis is complicated by "the

similarity between the somatic manifestations of anxiety and the presentation of common geriatric medical illnesses. Thus, headache is often the prime symptom of polymyalgia rheumatica or giant cell arteritis; palpitations may indicate paroxysms of rapid heart action and tremor may be familial, senescent or Parkinsonian" (Rowe, 1979, p. 9). Many patients with anxiety disorders are not seen in psychiatric practice because they seek treatment from their internist or family physician, especially when there is somatization of their anxiety, i.e., chest pain, headache, fatigue (Katon, 1986).

One difficulty in the identification of anxiety in older persons is the tendency for some elderly to attribute agitation, fears, or aches and pains to the normal process of aging, and therefore to deny and to under-report such symptoms.

The elderly tend to report anxiety as a feeling of nervousness and dread and present with heightened autonomic and central nervous system activity. On the other hand, they may not recognize their anxiety and may not attempt to ward it off by restricting their activities to only the most familiar and nontaxing. They may also be quite unable to make decisions (Eisdorfer et al., 1981).

In one large study of older people ($N = 2051$) physical health had the strongest linear relationship with anxiety for both men and women (Himmelfarb & Murrell, 1984). High anxiety was associated significantly with a number of general medical conditions commonly found in the elderly. There was low correlation between age and physical health, which reduced the likelihood that age alone mediated the health-anxiety relationship.

Little is known about the effects of age per se on Anxiety Disorders. A small number of older persons may be functionally impaired by anxiety for the first time in late life, or more likely, certain experiences in late life may activate or exaggerate a preexisting anxiety disorder. Panic may begin in the twenties and continue into old age as somatization or hypochondriasis, or mixed with depression. Being 85 is clearly different from being 35 because of 50 years of biological change; but the same 50 years can be described in terms of the life events experienced by the person in the aging body.

Traditionally, theory has held that anxiety in older persons may appear as a response to a compounding of losses, increasing dependency, loneliness and fear of isolation, increasing health problems, declining vigor, diminished sensory and functional capacities, change in economic or social status, feeling of uselessness, one's awareness of cognitive impairment early in dementia, and the approach of dying and death. No experimental studies have been done to substantiate that any of these variables are causally related to the more serious and persistent conditions described above as Anxiety Disorders.

Several psychological studies have focused on death as a significant source of anxiety in old age (Elkins & Fee, 1980; Myers, Wass, & Murphy, 1980; Quinn & Reznikoff, 1985; Roth, 1978; Sanders, Poole, Riveo, 1980; Tate, 1982; Wagner & Lorion, 1984).

Death anxiety varies with the individual and the sub-population examined and does not exist as a general characteristic of all elderly (Wagner & Lorion, 1984). The studies also suggest that black people tend to have more anxiety concerning death than whites. In addition, married people tend to fear death more possibly because of the fear of leaving their spouses behind. Interestingly, neither death anxiety nor anxiety in general was shown to correlate directly with age (Himmelfarb & Murrell, 1984; McAlpine & Wright, 1982; Wagner & Lorion, 1984), suggesting that death anxiety may be more an issue of the young-old person who is beginning to face but has not yet adapted to the "momento morri" of age-related health problems. The old-old may be less prone to anxiety in general by dint of their more extensive inoculating experience with stresses (Jarvik & Russell, 1979).

Various demographic correlates with anxiety were examined in the study by Himmelfarb & Murrell. Anxiety occurs more frequently and to a more severe degree in women than men, as measured on the Spielberger State-Trait Anxiety Scale. Marital status was found to have significant correlation. Widows had the most severe anxiety and divorcees had the next highest level. Among men, bachelors had the greatest anxiety, and those separated or divorced had the next highest level. Anxiety was inversely correlated with amount of education. Income was also inversely related to anxiety for both men and women, attesting to the buffering effect of financial security. Possibly related to reduced income, those elderly who lived in smaller quarters or in rural areas tended to experience more anxiety.

Beyond home size and rural location, the degree of independence in living situation appeared to exert an affect on level of anxiety. For example, nursing home residents were significantly more anxious than elderly residing in the community (Queen & Freitag, 1978). Anxiety was found to be related to lowered life satisfaction and loss of the sense of control over one's own life. The subjects of the study showed significantly elevated signs of anxiety on several MMPI scales (Hysteria, Depression, and Psychasthenia scales) that positively correlate with external locus of control.

The feeling of being controlled by others, in addition to social introversion, are two critical personality factors in chronic anxiety (Hoehn-Saric, 1981) The authors found that introverted and passively dependent people experience considerable demoralization due to a number of associated factors: fewer social skills, less self-confidence, helpless self-perception, tendency toward pessimism, excessive rumination and indecisiveness. Such characteristics undermine the anxious person's ability to cope with stressful or conflictive situations.

Some miscellaneous, but still very important conditions have been found to correlate strongly with anxiety in the elderly. Those people who have sleep disturbance—and presumably greater autonomic arousal—tend to be more anxious, suggesting that sympathetic tonus heightens in evening hours (Davis et al., 1982; Wagner & Lorion, 1984). Hearing loss has been found to correlate significantly with anxiety of an interpersonal nature, particularly in group settings. Hearing handicap accounted for 74% of the variation in this type of anxiety (Salerno, 1981). Anxiety can be related to dementia, where an anxiety attack is expressed as an exacerbation of both physical and psychiatric symptoms.

The subcategories of anxiety disorders may overlap with each other and with depression (Marx, 1986). Low morale, life dissatisfaction, and feeling of helpless dependency are critical components of the psychiatric picture of older people presenting with mixed anxiety and depression. This dual presentation has been frequently observed, particularly in the demented elderly (Eisdorfer et al., 1981). In a recent review, (Folgelson et al., 1988), the interrelationships between major depression and the anxiety disorders were explored, but without special attention to the aged.

CASE PRESENTATIONS

The following two case histories were selected because of their complicated nature and overlapping diagnoses. They are intended as examples of the more usual clinical presentations of anxiety encountered in geropsychiatry. The first case is an older patient with anxiety whose history is one of chronicity and episodic recurrence. There is lack of clarity regarding the contribution to his symptoms made by medical problems and their somatic treatments. He is also sensorially impaired and there is an apparent recent precipitant to his current episode.

Mr. A. is an eighty-three-year old, white, twice married man, referred by his son because of agitation of two months duration following the death of his older brother in a nursing home. This brother was said to have been "strange" all of his life, socially inappropriate and abusive. The patient's only other sibing, a twin brother, committed suicide many years earlier by overdose with Doriden. Neither of Mr. A.'s brothers ever married. Their father died when Mr. A. was ten years old and his mother was said to have threatened suicide at that time. After a marriage of forty-three years, his first wife died and he then married one of their best friends who was also recently widowed.

Mr. A. described himself as anxious and fearful. Periodically he had been overcome by feelings of insecurity especially around his finances although he understood that he was quite wealthy. During these periods he would often wake up and go immediately to his check book to be sure of his bank balance. He used the word "churning" to describe his frequent ruminations about slights and insults he has experienced from a particular brother-in-law. He avoided social situations when he knew this person would be there. He described himself as cowardly, inadequate, and unable to stand up to this person. When "nervous and depressed" he felt "twinges in different parts of his body." He recalled having several similar episodes in the past and thought of them more as depression than anxiety. He saw another psychiatrist one time eight years ago but chose not to enter treatment.

Mr. A. had several major complaints including indecisiveness, sleep disturbance, and impotence. He was so ambivalent about commitment that he could not agree to marry his fiancée until she threatened to break the engagement. His awakening after four hours of sleep could only be improved with the use of a sedative. Finally, he was embarrassed by his inability to sustain an erection.

His sexual history is pertinent: From ages six to eight he was the victim of sodomy by his older brother. He described his first wife as, "very naive, built small, and as one who performed her wifely duty, but not because she enjoyed it." He had one extramarital affair in 1966 that made him very guilty and he told his wife about it. From that time on he has not been able to sustain an erection. From 1966 until her death in 1980, he and his wife did not have intercourse. He remarried in 1982, two years after a prostatectomy, and has not had intercourse with his current wife, though he described her as "warm, loving and willing." Though he sometimes feels desire he denied waking with an erection or having erections during sleep. He felt his marriage is missing this intimacy and would like to be potent once more.

His other medical problems include hiatus hernia for which he takes Ranitidine; hypertension treated with Nifedipine; and arthritis for which he takes Sulindac. He has been deaf in one ear since age seventeen and uses a hearing aide in his other ear. He was treated with Orinase 1960–1972 because of one abnormal Glucose Tolerance Test.

Mr. A. meets DSM-III-R criteria for several disorders illustrating the mixed symptomatic picture of anxiety in the elderly. According to DSM-III-R, he meets the criteria for an Obsessive Compulsive Disorder with anxiety and depression and a mild phobic reaction as associated features. "Many people who develop Obsessive Compulsive Disorder have first suffered a major depression and about half become depressed afterward. Irrational guilt and obsessional ruminations are common to both disorders . . . " (Obsessive-Compulsive Disorder, 1985).

He also has a Male Erectile Disorder which, according to DSM-III-R, may be accompanied by anxiety, depression, and somatic symptoms as associated features. It is unclear whether it is due to psychological issues alone or whether there is also an organic etiology. He is also suffering from an Adjustment Disorder with Mixed Emotional Features, i.e., anxiety and depression, following the death of his brother and all that it stirred up from his past. Mr. A. does not meet all criteria for a Major Depressive Episodes, showing only three or four of the required five symptoms.

He was treated with weekly visits for insight oriented psychotherapy for three months with the adjunctive use of alprazolam 0.25 mg bid. His wife attended one session that focused on their sexual life. He made rapid progress with significant relief of his anxiety and with improved sleep, but there was no change with regard to his impotence.

> With an older patient, confusion may exist between an Axis I and Axis II Diagnosis, as illustrated by Mr. B. An eighty-nine-year old white, widowed male referred by his cardiologist because of his fear of dying, Mr. B. had been making frequent calls at all hours of the night to his doctor and to his children stating "I am dying, take me to the hospital."
>
> Mr. B. carries diagnoses of coronary artery disease, congestive heart failure, and atrial fibrillation with a pacemaker in place for several years. He had made many visits to the Emergency Room with complaints of dizziness, stomach upset, and chest discomfort for which antacids and acetaminophen (but not nitroglycerine) were occasionally helpful. Other medical conditions include cataracts, hearing impairment, and duodenal ulcer.
>
> He stated that he has always had sleep problems; trouble falling asleep, waking up frequently, getting up early, then taking

naps during the day. He reported no change in appetite or weight, or in bowel habits.

The patient was furious that none of his seven children took him into their home after his wife died of heart disease in 1983. He said he had taken total care of her for several years before her death as he had done for his own parents. This has made him very disappointed in his children; in fact he was critical towards every one and feels a responsibility to point out people's failings to them. He missed his wife and missed work.

Mr. B. was a very engaging man: smart, proud, articulate, and willing to share many reminiscences. He complained of some memory failure, but showed little evidence of cognitive impairment with the exception of retelling the same anecdote at different sessions without remembering that he had already done so. He was angry, disappointed, irritated with people, and somatizing. He was worried about his failing health, fearful of his increasing dependency, and angry at his loss of physical strength and abilities and scared of dying.

On each of his three visits he was brought and picked up by his youngest daughter. She seemed agitated and irritated with him. I asked Mr. B. if he thought it might be helpful if I met with his family. He agreed and I invited all seven children to the next session. Only the daughter came, stating that none of his other children wanted anything to do with him. In dramatic contrast to Mr. B.'s perception of his role in the family, his daughter described him as "sadistic, egocentric, insensitive, impossible to please, and constantly critical." Their mother had served as a buffer between Mr. B. and his children. After her death only his daughter was willing to remain involved and has become his "constant care giver, chauffer, cook, and laundress," despite her heavy responsibilities to her own family.

Mr. B. was unwilling to continue in treatment stating nothing would be helpful. He was very help-rejecting especially if any of the options we reached interfered with his need to manipulate or to instill guilt in his children. His lack of empathy, his need for attention and control, his entitlement and manipulation of others all point to an Axis II Narcissistic Personality Disorder, even though at first blush he appeared to be having an Axis I Anxiety Disorder, i.e., Panic Disorder. The picture is made more complicated by the presence of life-threatening cardiovascular disease.

CONCLUSION

As is true in many other areas within psychiatry, we are beginning to learn more about the genetic/biological determinants as well as the importance of life experience in the etiology of anxiety. Though much of what has been studied in younger adults can be stretched to an imperfect fit with elderly patients, little research has been directed at the impact of aging on the course of these anxiety disorders. Not only are there all the problems inherent in following a large sample of anxious adults into their later years in a longitudinal fashion, but the diagnostic criteria themselves undergo continual modification as the result of our evolving body of knowledge.

It is not enough to theorize about correlative relationships between a host of variables and the emergence of an anxiety disorder; each variable must be evaluated in a rigorous way. To do this, some form of diagnostic "gold standard" must be agreed upon against which all investigative instruments may be compared for validity in this age group. We have to work toward improving our ability to differentiate among anxiety as a manifestation of underlying medical disorders, as a consequence of a somatic therapy, as related to substance abuse, or from those clinical situations when it can not be shown that any of these are related to the development of symptoms. Until we have better data, our skills in differential diagnosis remain too much art and too little science, and the task of describing the "usual" clinical presentation of anxiety in the elderly will remain elusive.

COMMENTARY

There were two major themes to this discussion. First, there was general agreement that the definition of anxiety is difficult for older patients, and may actually add confusion when selecting a treatment. Secondly, clinicians tended to try to organize symptoms into categories, and then treat the category that caused the most dysfunction to the older patient. The selection of treatment for the category of anxiety symptoms was not generally agreed upon, but reflected individual clinicians' own experience and treatment bias.

1. The diagnosis of anxiety as a state of subjective distress was particularly difficult in three areas.
a. Anxiety and depression overlap, and coexist.
b. Anxiety is very common in personality disorders. Anxiety is commonly seen, for example, in patients with narcissistic personality disorders, paranoid personality disorders, and obsessive compulsive personality disorders. The question of whether this anxiety is an integral part of the personality disorder or whether it is a singnal that the adaptive functions of the personality style are failing, cannot be answered.
c. There are no generally agreed upon clinical criteria to determine when a patient is anxious. It was noted that DSM-III-R was not helpful for older patients since symptoms must be present for six full months and this may indicate a personality disorder rather than general anxiety disorder.
2. It was suggested that the concept of anxiety itself in the elderly may be outmoded and not helpful. Most clinicians, understanding the overlap between anxiety, depression, agitation, fear, worry, etc., may prefer terms such as dysphoria or subjective distress.
3. Because of the diagnostic confusion it may be logically more useful to define clinical criteria that correlate with specific treatment and response. Thus there would be antianxiety, subjective distress syndromes, antidepressant responsive subjective distress syndromes, etc. Linking diagnosis to treatment response would also provide a basis for research studies with greater agreement between researchers.
4. The diagnosis of anxiety is further complicated by the development of secondary symptoms such as disordered sleep and agitation as the anxiety worsens.
5. Not only must the clinical manifestations of anxiety, or subjective distress, be carefully characterized, but their intensity and duration must also be considered in any overall diagnostic scheme.
6. When evaluating the older patient with subjective distress, there was agreement that clinicians tended to organize their observations following a computer-like category model. Thus symptoms might be

organized into the category of cognitive dysfunction, the category of affective disturbance especially depression, and the category of anxiety, phobia, panic, etc. A "threshold of suffering" for each category is developed based on clinical interview. The category with the highest threshold is then chosen as the primary diagnosis and the symptoms requiring treatment first. For most elderly patients with anxiety, the choice is between depression and anxiety; impaired cognition is not a frequent factor in this group of patients.

   7. There is no general agreement about the first choice pharmacologic treatment for relief of subjective distress, regardless of the diagnostic label that is used. Even when the term anxiety is applied to the older patient's symptoms, there is no general agreement regarding selection of drug. Some clinicians prefer to start with a benzodiazepine anxiolytic, fearing that antidepressant toxicity is too great among the elderly. Others think the reverse and worry more about the potential problem of addiction and withdrawal using benzodiazepines and therefore choose an antidepressant as the first choice of drug treatment.

   8. It is important to remember that the older patient, especially outpatients who are residing in the community, may ask for a particular form of treatment. It was noted that patients who describe themselves as anxious and wanting anxiolytic drug treatment are the patients who tend to respond best to anxiolytic drugs. When older patients visit a psychiatrist's office, it may be useful to ask them what they want and what form of treatment they envision. In a general practitioner, family practitioner, or internist office this approach is less useful since anxiety may not be the presenting symptom, but may be just contributing to medical problems.

REFERENCES

Blumenthal, M. (1979). Anxiety in the elderly: Problems and promises. *Diagnosis and treatment of anxiety in the elderly, part I*, (pp. 9–27). Hoffmann-La Roche Inc.

Busse, E. (1975). Aging and psychiatric diseases in late life. M. Reiser (Ed.), *American handbook of psychiatry, 4*. New York: Basic Books.

Davis, M. R., Cohen, D., Eisdorfer, C., Breen, A., & Wright, R. G. (1982). Anxiety and depression in the aged with sleep disturbances.

Journal of Clinical and Experimental Gerontology, 4, 239–248.

Eisdorfer, C., Cohen, D., & Keckich, W. (1981). Depression and anxiety in the cognitively impaired aged. In D. F. Klein & J. G. Rabkin (Eds.), *Anxiety: New research and changing concepts* (pp. 415–430). New York: Raven Press.

Elkins, G. R., & Fee, A. F. (1980). Relationship of physical anxiety to death anxiety and age. *Journal of Genetic Psychology, 137,* 147–148.

Fogelson, D., Bystritsky, A., & Sussman, N. (1988). Interrelationships between major depression and the anxiety disorders: clinical relevance. *Psychiatric Annals, 18,* 158–167.

Hoffman-La Roche, (1979). Diagnosis and treatment of anxiety in the elderly.

Himmelfarb, S., & Murrell, S. A. (1984). Prevalence and correlates of anxiety symptoms in older adults. *Journal of Psychology, 116,* 159–167.

Hoehn-Saric, R. (1981). Characteristics of chronic anxiety patients. In D. F. Klein & J. G. Rabkin (Eds.), *Anxiety: New research and changing concepts* (pp. 399–409). New York: Raven Press.

Jarvik, L. F., & Russell, D. (1979). Anxiety, aging, and the third emergency reaction. *Journal of Gerontonology, 34,* 197–200.

Katon, W. et al. (1986). Panic disorder: Epidemeology in primary care. *Journal of Family Practice, 23,* 233–239.

Klein, D. F. & Rabkin, J. G. (1981). *Anxiety: New research and changing concepts.* New York: Raven Press.

Klerman, G. L. (1983). Classifying anxiety: The new nosology. In J. Fawcett (Ed.), *Anxiety and anxiety in the elderly in contemporary psychiatry: A report from a symposium on anxiety* (pp. 7–9). Chicago: Upjohn Company.

Marks, I. (1986). The Epidemeology of anxiety. *Social Psychiatry, 21,* 167–171.

McAlpine, C. J., & Wright, Z. J. (1982). Attitudes and anxieties of elderly patients on admission to a geriatric assessment unit. *Age and Aging, 11,* 35–41.

Myers, J. E., Wass, H., & Murphey, M. (1980). Ethnic differences in death anxiety among the elderly. *Death Education, 4,* 237–244.

Nakra, B. R., & Grossberg, G. T. (1986). Management of anxiety in the elderly. *Comprehensive Therapy, 12,* 53–60.

Obsessive-Compulsive Disorder, (1985). *Harvard Medical School Mental Health Letter, 2,* 1–4.

Pfeiffer, E. (1979). Interviewing the anxious patient. *In Diagnosis and Treatment of Anxiety in the Elderly, part II,* (pp. 23–33). Hoffmann-La Roche Inc.

Queen, L., Freitag, C. B. (1978). A comparison of externality, anxiety, and life satisfaction in two aged populations. *Journal of Psychology, 98,* 71–74.

Quinn, P. D., & Reznikoff, M. (1985). Relationship between death anxiety and the subjective experience of time in the elderly. *International Journal of Aging and Human Development, 21,* 197–210.

Rakel, R. E. (1981). Differential diagnosis of anxiety. *Psychiatric Annals, 11,* 11–14.

Roth, N. (1978). Fear of death in the aging. *American Journal of Psychotherapy, 32,* 552–560.

Rowe, J. (1979). Anxiety: A geriatritions perspective. *In Diagnosis and Treatment of Anxiety in the Elderly, part III,* (pp. 5–13). Hoffmann-La Roche Inc.

Salerno, M. (1981). Interpersonal anxiety as a function of hearing handicap in the elderly. Unpublished dissertation, Catholic University of America, Washington D.C.

Salzman, C. (1982). A primer on geriatric psychopharmacology. *American Journal of Psychiatry, 139,* 67–74.

Sanders, J. F., Poole, T. E., & Rivero, W. T. (1980). Death anxiety among the elderly. *Psychological Reports, 46,* 53–54.

Spielberger, C. D., (1966). Theory and research on anxiety. In C. D. Spielberger (Ed.), *Anxiety and behavior* (pp. 3–20). New York: Academic Press.

Tate, L. A. (1982). Life satisfaction and death anxiety in aged women. *International Journal of Aging and Human Development, 15,* 299–306.

Wagner, K. D., & Lorion, R. P. (1984). Correlates of death anxiety in elderly persons. *Journal of Clinical Psychology, 40,* 1235–1241.

Co-morbidity of Anxiety with Other Common Problems of the Elderly

II

Anxiety and General Medical Disorders

4

Gene D. Cohen

While the overall scientific literature on anxiety and aging has been limited, particular attention to relationships between anxiety and general medical disorders in older patients has been even more sparse. The following review will focus on the role of anxiety or anxiety-like clinical manifestations in the onset, diagnoses, natural history, treatment, and prognosis of general medical and surgical conditions in older adults.

PREVALENCE OF ANXIETY-LIKE SYMPTOMS IN GENERAL MEDICAL PATIENTS

Most studies of the prevalence of anxiety or anxiety-like symptoms in general medical and surgical patients have inadequately taken age into consideration (Levenson & Hall, 1981; Raj & Sheehan, 1988). For example, in one study of 4,097 patients referred from general medical and specialty clinics for psychiatric consultation, 200 (5%) received a primary or secondary diagnosis of anxiety reaction (Clancy & Noyes, 1976), but age-specific frequencies were not stated. Moreover, the assessment of anxiety was only on referred patients as opposed to on a random sample of all the patients in those clinics. Other

47

similar studies suffer from a lack of clarity about diagnostic criteria.

DIFFERENTIATING ANXIETY FROM PHYSICAL ILLNESS AS THE CAUSE OF SOMATIC SYMPTOMS

Anxiety's somatic symptoms (e.g., respiratory restriction, palpitations, feeling shaky, dizziness, headache, chest pains) and signs (e.g., sighing and rapid breathing, trembling, diarrhea, vomiting, coughing, rapid pulse, sweating) may be difficult to distinguish from similar clinical manifestations of various physical illnesses. In the elderly, the diagnosis of anxiety may be obscured because anxiety and physical illness commonly co-exist, and in some cases anxiety may be the presenting symptom of occult physical illness. Some signs and symptoms of anxiety in the elderly may resemble specific physical disorders and phenomena as illustrated in Table 4.1 (Gurland & Myers, 1988).

Anxiety is commonly associated with hypochondriasis or high bodily concern (Kay, Beamish, & Roth, 1964; Pfeiffer, 1977; Busse & Blazer, 1980) although less common than depression. For example, a psychogenic explanation is commonly given as the explanation for gastrointestinal (GI) complaints in elderly patients. However, some of these so-called psychogenic GI complaints may be due to real illness. For example, Sklar (1978) studied 300 patients over age 65 who presented with complaints at the outpatient department of a medical center. The patients were evaluated comprehensively and followed for at least a year. The various diagnoses that were established and the percentage of patients possessing each diagnosis were as follows:

   10% had gastrointestinal malignancy
   8% had bladder disease
   6% had duodenal ulcer
   3% had gastric ulcer
   3% had diverticulosis of the colon

Table 4.1 Physical Disorders and Phenomena Associated with Varied Clusters of Anxiety-like Signs & Symptoms*

Conditions Producing Trembling, Tachycardia, or Hyperexcitability
• Hypoglycemia
• Pheochromocytoma
• Hyperthyroidism
Conditions Producing Dread, Bewilderment, Weakness, Dizziness, Respiratory Distress or Sweating
• Silent myocardial infarct
• Pulmonary embolism
• Small stroke or cerebral ischemic attack
• Excess intake of caffeine
• Sympathomimetic medications in nonprescription drugs
• Withdrawal symptoms of sedatives, hypnotics, or alcohol

*Adapted from Gurland & Meyers, 1988.

14% had a wide variety of problems with other organic bases
56% had gastrointestinal distress associated with psychogenic factors, with no anatomical changes to account for them.

Thus, both psychogenic (56%) and physical factors (44%) assume major roles in different older patients with GI problems, in a ratio of almost 50:50. Hence, a comprehensive differential diagnostic evaluation should nearly always be considered in such patients, and a psychogenic cause, or hypochondriasis should not be assumed.

ANXIETY AS A SIDE-EFFECT OF MEDICATIONS

The Physicians' Desk Reference 1988 Drug Interactions And Side Effects Index lists well over 150 medications (Table 4.2) with "anxiety" or "paradoxical anxiety" as a potential side-effect; approximately 90 medications are also listed as having the potential side-effect of "agitation" (Sifton, 1988). Special

Table 4.2 Drugs with Anxiety as a Potential Side Effect*

Anxiety

Actifed with Codeine cough Syrup	• Adrenalin Chloride Sol	AeroBid Inhaler
Alurate Elixir	Amipaque	Amitriptyline HCI
Ana-Kit Insect Sting Treatment Kit	Android	Apresazide
Apresoline	Arm-a-Med Isoetharine	Asendin
Astramorph	Atrohist Sprinkle Tabs	Azo Gantrisin Tabs
BAL in Oil Ampules	Bancap HC Caps	Brethine Ampules
Bretylol Injection	Brevibloc Injection	Brevital Sodium
Bronkosol	Butisol Sodium	Catapres
Cesamet Pulvules	Cinobac Pulvules	Co-Gesic Tabs
Colestid Granules	Combipres Tabs	Danocrine
Deconamine	Deconsal Sprinkle Caps	Demser Caps
Deprol Tabs	Diazepam Tabs	Dilaudid
Dopamine	Duramorph	Elavil
Emcyt Caps	Endep Tabs	EpiPen
Etrafon	Fedahist	Flexeril Tabs
Haldol (all forms)	Halotestin Tabs	Hycomine
Hycotuss Expectorant Syrup	Hydrocet	Hyperstat I.V.
Hy-Phen Tabs	Hytrin	Inapsine
Indocin	Indomethacin	Innovar
Intron A	K-Lyte	Larodopa
• Lozol	• Ludiomil Tabs	• Lupron Injection
Marcaine	• Marinol Caps	Maxzide
Mebaral Tabs	Metandren	Nardil
Nembutal	Nesacaine	Nodudar
Norpramin	Novafed	Novahistine
Octamide	Omnipaque	Orap Tabs
Oreton Methyl	Pamelor	Parlodel
Parnate Tabs	Pepcid	Pertrofane Caps
Phenergan	Pondimin Tabs	Premarin
• Proglycem	Questran	Relefact
Retrovir Caps	Roferon-A Injection	Sandimmune
Sectral Caps	Sensorcaine Injection	Ser-Ap-Es Tabs
Serax	Serpasil-Apresoline Tabs	Sinemet Tabs
• Symmetrel Caps	Tagemet	Tambocor Tabs
Tegison Caps	Tenuate	Testred Caps
Thypinone	Timoptic in Ocudose	Tefranil
Tonocard Tabs	Trental	• Trexan
Triavil	Trinalin Repetabs	Tussend
Tympagesic Otic Solution	Valium	Valrelease Caps
Vasoxyl Injection	VERSED Injection	Vicodin Tabs
• Visken Tabs	Vivactil	Wytensin Tabs
• Yotopar	Zydone	

(continued)

Table 4.2 Continued

Anxiety, Paradoxical

Demi-Regroton Tabs	Diupres	Diutensen-R Tabs
Hydropres	Metatensin	Moderil
Raudixin Tabs	Rauzide Tabs	Regroton Tabs
Renese-R Tabs	Salutensin/Salutensin-Demi	Ser-Ap-Es Tabs
Serpasil	Serpasil-Apresaline Tabs	Vivactil Tabs

• Indicates incidence of 3% or more.
*Adapted from the 1988 PDR Side Effects Index (Sifton, 1988).

attention is focused on which among the medications cause agitation in the elderly, although not for the anxiety-causing drugs.

IMPACT OF ANXIETY ON PHYSICAL MORBIDITY AND MORTALITY

There have been various reports in the scientific literature of increased mortality rates in anxious, neurotic, physically older patients—especially among men (Kay & Bergman, 1966). In particular, an association of anxiety in later life with cardiac disease and with the pathogenesis of atherosclerotic pathology has been described (Bergmann, 1978). In younger adult patients, excess mortality has been associated with panic disorder (Coryell, Noyes, & Clancy, 1982).

The explanation for apparent increased vulnerability to physical morbidity and mortality resulting from psychosocial stress is unknown. Current theories suggest alterations in the neuroendocrine and immune systems (Besedovsky, Del Ray, & Sorkin, 1985; Calabrese, Kling, & Gold, 1987; Pert et al., 1985; Stein, Keller, & Schleifer, 1985). Although the role of depression in relation to physical health has been examined more closely than that of anxiety, the adverse impact of stress on neuroendocrine and immune system functioning appears to be greater in older individuals as compared to younger adults (Schleifer et al., 1989).

IMPACT OF *TREATING* ANXIETY ON CLINICAL COURSE OF MEDICAL ILLNESS

While the adverse effect of anxiety on the course of physical health is suggested by the above reports, positive effects on the course of physical illness by treating concomitant anxiety are suggested in another series of investigations. In a review of 34 controlled studies of patients of all ages, the impact of psychological intervention on recovery from heart attacks and surgery was examined (Mumford, Schlesinger, & Glass, 1982). Patients who received such intervention did better than those who did not. Further analysis of 13 of the studies revealed an average reduction in length of stay of 20% in the intervention group as compared to the controls. Though not explicit, the role of anxiety as an aggravating factor that is mitigated through psychological intervention, may be inferred from these studies. A later revealed study showed that cardiac arrythmias, as assessed by electrophysiologic studies, improved when associated anxiety was treated with supportive psychotherapy (Menza, Stern, & Cassem, 1988). Similar studies have not been conducted in the elderly patients.

ANXIETY-LIKE SYMPTOMS ASSOCIATED WITH CLINICAL PROBLEMS IN VARIOUS SYSTEMS OF THE BODY AN SPECIFIC DISEASES

Throughout virtually every system of the body, clinical disorders can develop that produce anxiety-like symptoms (Levenson & Hall; Raj & Sheehan, 1988). The frequency of these symptoms varies with different syndromes, and, as indicated, the nature of these symptoms or symptom clusters varies with different problems (Table 4.1). Just as the Eskimos have many different words for snow to better understand different contexts in which it exists, the body offers a number of ways in which anxiety-like symptoms manifest themselves. To the extent that clinicians examine anxiety-like manifestations the way the Eskimos examine snow, i.e., by improved discriminating ability to better recognize hidden disorders with many subtle variations, improved diagnostic acumen is likely to follow. Some of the systems of the body and the specific associated clinical conditions are discussed below.

Anxiety and the Cardiovascular System

The implicated role of anxiety in the pathogenesis or aggravation of heart disease has been mentioned. Among 441 consecutive admissions, many elderly, to a coronary care unit, 145 (approximately one-third): 47% received a diagnosis of anxiety, 44% depression (Cassem & Hackett, 1971). Thus, more than 15% of the total patient population of this coronary care unit were diagnosed with anxiety. Following myocardial infarction, anxiety-like symptoms commonly appear because of rising levels of catecholeamines which overstimulate the body, causing anxiety-like symptoms of dread, bewilderment, weakness, dizziness, respiratory distress, and/or sweating. These same symptoms also accompany silent myocardial infarcts, providing the initial signal of this disease event (Gurland & Myers, 1988), indicating the importance of differential diagnosis between anxiety and cardiac disease.

Anxiety and the Pulmonary System

A higher degree of psychiatric morbidity—especially anxiety—is found in breathing impaired patients (as compared to nonphysically ill controls); this is particularly the case with severe asthma and chronic obstructive pulmonary disease (Renfroe, 1988; Yellowlees, Haynes, Potts, & Ruffin, 1988). Chronic heavy smoking has been a significant risk factor for the development of COPD by later life. Rehabilitative strategies for COPD focus both on the dyspnea and the associated state anxiety, since the latter compounds the former. Among the interventions utilized that alleviate dyspnea and anxiety alike in

COPD patients are progressive muscle relaxation techniques (Renfroe, 1988), an approach also used to treat anxiety found with other conditions as well in older adults (see McCarthy et al., this volume).

Anxiety can also have an indirect adverse affect on the pulmonary system—a negative effect that is magnified in later life. For example, when excess alcohol is used by older persons as an attempt to alleviate feelings of anxiety, an insidious sequence of events involving the pulmonary system can follow, and have potentially serious consequences in altering normal bodily mechanisms of defense against infection along the respiratory tract (Cohen, 1988; Freeman, 1978). Four basic pulmonary defense mechanisms may be challenged:

1. Alcohol may impair the cough reflex, thereby reducing the elimination of infected material along the upper respiratory tract (nasopharynx) (Berkowitz, Reichel, & Shim, 1973).

2. Alcohol's dehydrating properties can lead to a drying of mucus along the respiratory tract. Reduced amounts of mucus are less effective in capturing inhaled pathogens for removal via swallowing or coughing.

3. Macrophages can be found along the respiratory tract in specialized bacterial cells. How these macrophages are affected by aging is not clear, but alcohol excess has been shown to have a toxic effect on macrophages, rendering them no longer bactericidal (Freeman, 1978).

4. Cilia, the microscopic finger-like projections lining the respiratory tract, facilitate the upward and outward expulsion of pathogens. There is some suspicion that alcohol excess retards ciliary movement.

Hence, by interfering with the cough reflex, mucus level, macrophage activity, and ciliary movement, alcohol excess can place an older person at greater risk for respiratory tract infections. Since smaller amounts of alcohol may cause toxicity in the elderly than in earlier adulthood, the potential for this insidious sequence of events involving the pulmonary system may be greater among older alcohol abusers.

Anxiety and the Endocrine System

Hyperthyroid conditions and anxiety

In a study of 33 patients of varying ages with newly diagnosed untreated hyperthyroidism (Kathol & Delahunt, 1986), ten were found to have depression, fifteen (45%), anxiety using DSM-III (Diagnostic and Statistical Manual of the American Psychiatric Association, Third Edition) criteria were used to evaluate the frequency of anxiety and depression. The number of anxiety symptoms corresponded to the number of hyperthyroid symptoms, whereas the depressive symptoms did not. Neither prior history of psychiatric disease nor family history of mental disorder predicted either anxiety or depression in these patients with hyperthyroidism. More research must now be done, particularly with older patients, to determine (a) the relationship between the magnitude of thyroid dysfunction and the magnitude of anxiety symptomatology and (b) the relationship between the sequence of onset of the respective clinical manifestations. Such relationships are especially important in cases where anxiety-like symptoms are found to be associated with incipient or latent pathophysiological conditions.

In the case of depressive symptomatology and thyroid dysfunction, either hypothyroidism or hyperthyroidism can be the pathogenic factor. When hypothyroidism causes a depression-like picture, the condition is referred to as *apathetic hyperthyroidism*, a paradoxical form of the disease more commonly seen in the elderly (Gregerman, 1985). Does a corresponding situation exist where hypothyroidism is sometimes accompanied by anxiety-like symptoms in older adults? The following case example illustrates how much might occur.

Case Example

An emergency consultation was requested for a 72-year-old woman described as being "extremely anxious," who complained of being so "nervous inside" that she was ready to jump off the roof of her apartment building. This nervousness was described as having built up over the past two months and was associated with increased trouble concentrating and remembering things. The visiting nurse who requested the consultation had searched for recent psychosocial crisis that may have precipitated an acute anxiety reaction, and she also wondered whether the memory trouble and agitation signalled early Alzheimer's disease with compounding catastrophic reactions in response to increased stress.

The patient was evaluated in her home, and during a careful history it was learned that two years earlier she had been diagnosed as being hypothyroid and had since then been treated with thyroid tablets. An immediate laboratory test revealed that she was in a hyperthyroid state, apparently from over-medication. The medication was halted and over the next two months the anxiety-like symptoms subsided while thyroid function tests returned to normal. Her difficulties with concentration and memory also disappeared.

Hyperparathyroidism, pancreatic carcinoma, and anxiety

Anxiety is common in endocrine disorders in general, and a number of these disorders increase in frequency with age (Lavis, 1981). Hyperparathyroidism, for example, is more common in older than younger adults; the majority of patients with this illness manifest anxiety-like symptoms, displaying irritability and restlessness in relation to low calcium levels (Eliel, 1985). Similarly, pancreatic cancer is eight to ten times more common in males over age 75 than the general population; symptoms of depression and anxiety are often the presenting symptoms (Mezey, 1985), at times related to hypoglycemia resulting from excess production of insulin.

Anxiety and Vitamin Deficiencies

Though not common in developed nations, vitamin deficiencies can still occur, and in the elderly may be less well recognized due to many symptoms being dismissed as concomitants of normal aging. Nearly all the vitamin deficiency states are accompanied by irritability, feelings of nervousness, and other anxiety-like signs and symptoms. This applies to deficiencies of thiamine, niacin, Vitamin B-12, folic acid, and a number of other nutritional substances (Gershell, 1981; Gross, 1987).

Anxiety and Brain Disease

Alzheimer's disease

Anxiety-like symptoms are common in dementing disorders, particularly Alzheimer's disease (Merriam et al., 1988; Teri, Larson, & Reifler, 1988). These are discussed in Chapter 4, this volume.

Parkinson's disease

While depression is commonly associated with Parkinson's disease, anxiety has more recently been described in this disorder. In one study, 12 of 16 Parkinson's disease patients met the criteria of a present or past diagnosis of either generalized anxiety disorder or panic disorder; only 2 of 20 multiple sclerosis controls did (Schiffer, Kurlan, Rubin, & Boer, 1988). In 7 of the 8 Parkinson's patients with panic disorder, the clinical onset of panic occurred after the onset of neurological symptoms and following the initiation of treatment with dopamine agonist medication. The suggestive relationship of these symptoms to dopamine changes—caused by both the disease and drug treatment—may offer additional clues about the pathophysiology of panic and anxiety disorders independent of neurological disorder.

Anxiety and Sensory Impairment

Hearing loss and visual disturbances both occur with considerable frequency in later life, and both can precipitate anxiety-like symptoms. Irritability, for example, is quite common with hearing loss, making a number of such individuals appear chronically anxious. Sensory deprivation phenomena appear to be playing a role.

Anxiety-like symptoms can also accompany visual impairments due to a range of ocular diseases and disorders, including cataracts. Improved management of cataract surgery has reduced the frequency of major psychological sequelae, with one large series finding 33% with manifestations of anxiety and motor restlessness; typically, this is reversible within two days (Mamelok, 1985). In general, sensory deprivation phenomena appear to underlie these symptoms, as in the case of hearing impairment.

Bed Rest, Anxiety, and Exercise

The amount of time in bed is of clinical concern with a number of frail older persons, particularly the nursing home population. Here, too, anxiety-like symptoms have been systematically described, in what appears to be another form of sensory deprivation (Harper & Lyles, 1988). Behavioral interventions, e.g., exercise regimens, can alleviate the problem, anxiety suggesting an interactive relationship between the brain, body, and behavior.

Exercise may also be a helpful treatment for anxiety. In a study comparing older men (average age 66 ± 5.85) to younger ones (26.1 ± 2.52), exercise was found to reduce modest anxiety levels in the older group, with constant levels found in the younger men (Hatfield, Goldfarb, Sforzo, & Flynn, 1987). Exercise was not found to aggravate anxiety in these subjects.

CONCLUSION

The above survey reflects only the limited observations to date looking for and describing anxiety-like symptoms in relation to physical health. More careful attention to the systems of the body and their age-associated problems will undoubtedly provide yet further data on the frequency, recognition, nature, magnitude, variation, and response to treatment of anxiety-like symptoms in later life. Through studying this mental health/ physical health interface in later life, anxiety in general, in all age groups, might become better understood and managed. Further research must be encouraged!

COMMENTARY

1. Characteristics of the Charles Bonet Syndrome.
a. Not an illusion, a true form visual hallucination.
b. Often hallucinations of little creatures.
c. Accompanied by low levels of anxiety.
d. May be associated with mild cognitive impairment. Some question whether it is a dementing illness with visual hallucinations.
e. Initially appears as an isolated hallucination.
2. Older patients with medical illness often have mixtures of anxiety and depressive disorders which are difficult to diagnostically separate. Some clinicians prefer treating these mixed dysphoric states with antidepressants and some prefer to use short-term interventions with benzodiazepines. Clinicians must be careful not to label an affective state as depression even if it responds to an antidepressant.
3. Factor analytic studies using rating scales to attempt to discriminate between subjective symptoms and anxiety verses subjective symptoms of depression have found that the interpretation of these symptoms is dependent on their context. In non ill community residents elderly patients, anxiety was easily discriminated from depression. In hospitalized or residentially ill older patients however the discrimination or symptoms separation was impossible. Therefore the interpretation of symptoms in the elderly may be context dependent.
4. Anxiety may be associated with a number of physical illnesses or the treatment of these illnesses. For example, the anxiety is commonly associated with pulmonary disease, or with the use of broncho dilators. Treatment of Parkinson's disease with dopamine agonists may also cause anxiety.

REFERENCES

Bergmann, K. (1978). Neurosis and personality disorder in later life. In A. D. Isaacs & F. Post (Eds.), *Studies in geriatric psychiatry* (pp. 41–75). New York: Wiley.

Berkowitz, H., Reichel, J., & Shim, C. (1973). The effect of ethanol on the cough reflex. *Clinical Science and Molecular Medicine, 45,* 527–531.

Besedovsky, H. O., Del Ray, A. E., & Sorkin, E. (1985). Immune-endocrine interactions. *The Journal of Immunology, 135,* 750s–754s.

Busse, E. W., & Blazer, D. (1980). Hypochondriasis. In E. W. Busse & D. Blazer (Eds.), *Handbook of geriatric psychiatry* (pp. 403–405). New York: Van Nostrand Reinhold.

Calabrese, J. R., Kling, M. A., & Gold, P. W. (1987). Alterations in immunocompetence during stress, bereavement, and depression: Focus on neuroendocrine regulation. *The American Journal of Psychiatry, 144,* 1123–1134.

Cassem, N. H., & Hackett, T. P. (1971). Psychiatric consultation in a coronary care unit. *Annals of Internal Medicine, 75,* 9–14.

Clancy, J., & Noyes, R. (1976). Anxiety neurosis: A disease for the medical model. *Psychosomatics, 17,* 90–93.

Cohen, G. D. (1988). *The brain in human aging.* New York: Springer Publishing.

Coryell, W., Noyes, R., & Clancy, J. (1982). Excess mortality in panic disorder. *Archives of General Psychiatry, 39,* 701–703.

Eliel, L. P. (1985). Primary hyperparathyroidism. In R. Andres, E. L. Bierman, & W. Hazzard (Eds.), *Principles of geriatric medicine* (pp. 776–780). New York: McGraw Hill.

Freeman, E. (1978). The respiratory system. In J. C. Brocklehurst (Ed.), *Textbook of geriatric medicine and gerontology* (433–451). New York: Churchill Livingstone.

Gershell, W. J. (1981). Psychiatric manifestations and nutritional deficiencies in the elderly. In A. J. Levenson & R. C. W. Hall (Eds.), *Neuropsychiatric manifestations of physical disease in the elderly* (pp. 119–131). New York: Raven Press.

Gregerman, R. I. (1985). Thyroid diseases. In R. Andres, E. L. Bierman, & W. Hazzard (Eds.), *Principles of geriatric medicine* (pp. 727–749). New York: McGraw Hill.

Gross, L. S. (1987). Neuropsychiatric aspects of vitamin deficiency states. In R. E. Hales & S. C. Yudofsky (Eds.), *Textbook of neuropsychiatry* (327–338). Washington, DC: The American Psychiatric Press.

Gurland, B. J., & Meyers, B. S. (1988). Geriatric psychiatry. In J. A. Talbott, R. E. Hales, & S. C. Yudofsky (Eds.), *Textbook of psychiatry* (1117–1139). Washington, DC: The American Psychiatric Press.

Harper, C. M., & Lyles, Y. M. (1988). Physiology and complications of bed rest. *Journal of the American Geriatrics Society, 36,* 1047–1054.

Hatfield, B. D., Goldfarb, A. H., Sforzo, G. A., & Flynn, M. G. (1987). Serum beta-endorphin and affective responses to graded exercise in young and elderly men. *Journal of Gerontology, 42,* 429–431.

Kathol, R. G., & Delahunt, J. W. (1986). The relationship of anxiety and depression to symptoms of hyperthyroidism using operational critera. *General Hospital Psychiatry, 8,* 23–28.

Kay, D. W. K., Beamish, P., & Roth, M. (1964). Old age mental disorders in Newcastle upon Tyne, Part I: A study of psychological. *British Journal of Psychiatry, 110,* 146–158.

Kay, D. W. K., & Bergmann, K. (1966). Physical disability and mental health in old age. *Journal of Psychosomatic Research, 10,* 3–12.

Lavis, V. R. (1981). Psychiatric manifestations of endocrine disease in the elderly. In A. J. Levenson & R. C. W. Hall (Eds.), *Neuropsychiatric manifestations of physical disease in the elderly* (pp. 59–81). New York: Raven.

Levenson, A. J., & Hall, R. C. W. (1981). *Neuropsychiatric manifestations of physical disease in the elderly.* New York: Raven Press.

Mamelok, A. E. (1985). Psychiatry and ophthalmology. In H. I. Kaplan & B. J. Sadock (Eds.), *Comprehensive textbook of psychiatry/IV* (pp. 1298–1301). Baltimore: Williams & Wilkins.

Menza, M. A., Stern, T. A., & Cassem, N. H. (1988). Treatment of anxiety associated with electrophysiologic studies. *Heart & Lung, 17,* 555–560.

Merriam, A. E., Aronson, M. K., Gaston, P., Wey, S., & Katz, I. (1988). The psychiatric symptoms of Alzheimer's disease. *Journal of the American Geriatrics Society, 36,* 7–12.

Mezey, E. (1985). Disorders of the pancreas. In R. Andres, E. L. Bierman, & W. Hazzard (Eds.), *Principles of geriatric medicine* (pp. 692–696). New York: McGraw Hill.

Mumford, E., Schlesinger, H. J., & Glass, G. V. (1982). The effects of psychological intervention on recovery from surgery and heart attacks: An analysis of the literature. *American Journal of Public Health, 72,* 141–151.

Pert, C. B., Ruff, M. R., Weber, R. J., et al. (1985). Neuropeptides and their receptors: A psychosomatic network. *The Journal of Immunology, 135,* 820s–826s.

Pfeiffer, E. (1977). Psychodynamics of hypochondriasis. In J. E. Birren & K. W. Schaie (Eds.), *Handbook of the psychology of aging* (p. 657). New York: Van Nostrand Reinhold.

Raj, A. B., & Sheehan, D. V. (1988). Medical evaluation of the anxious patient. *Psychiatric Annals, 18,* 176–181.

Renfroe, K. L. (1988). Effect of progressive relaxation on dyspnea and state anxiety in patients with chronic obstructive pulmonary disease. *Heart & Lung, 17,* 408–413.

Schiffer, R. B., Kurlan, R., Rubin, A., & Boer, S. (1988). Evidence for atypical depression in Parkinson's disease. *American Journal of Psychiatry, 145,* 1020–1022.

Schleifer, S. J., Keller, S. E., Bond, R. N., Cohen, J., & Stein, M. (1989). Major depressive disorder and immunity. *Archives of General Psychiatry, 46,* 81–87.

Sifton, D. W. (Ed.). (1988). *PDR drug interactions and side effects index.* Oradell, N.J.: Medical Economics Company Inc.

Sklar, M. (1978). Gastrointestinal diseases in the aged. In W. Reichel (Ed.), *Clinical aspects of aging.* Baltimore: Williams & Wilkins.

Stein, M., Keller, S. E., & Schleifer, S. J. (1985). Stress and immunomodulation: The role of depression and neuroendocrine function. *The Journal of Immunology, 135,* 827s–833s.

Teri, L., Larson, E. B., & Reifler, B. (1988). Behavioral disturbance in dementia of the Alzheimer type. *Journal of the American Geriatrics Society, 36,* 1–6.

Yellowlees, P. M., Haynes, S., Potts, N., & Ruffin, R. E. (1988). Psychiatric morbidity in patients with life-threatening asthma: Initial report of a controlled study. *Medical Journal of Australia, 149,* 246–249.

Anxiety and Depression in the Elderly

5

George S. Alexopoulos

The relationship between anxiety and depressive disorders is complex. Psychiatric nosological classification usually depends on differences in clinical manifestations, course and outcome, family history, response to treatment, and evidence of biological dysfunction (Andreasen, 1982). Despite recent expansion of knowledge concerning clinical and biological aspects of anxiety and depression, considerable nosological ambiguity remains. The overlap of symptoms and signs of anxiety and depression often makes it difficult to distinguish the two syndromes (Tyrer, 1983; Derogatis et al., 1972). Furthermore, a significant percentage of depressed and anxious patients do not retain their original diagnosis over time (Kendell, 1974). In addition to phenotypical similarities, some genetic studies suggest a nonspecific genetic predisposition to anxiety and depressive symptomatology (Kendler et al., 1987). Another source of diagnostic complexity is the relative lack of specificity of antianxiety and antidepressant drugs (Johnstone et al., 1980; Paykel et al., 1982). Finally, central monoaminergic abnormalities have been postulated in both anxiety (Shear and Fyer, 1988) and depressive disorders (Alexopoulos, 1985) suggesting that related brain abnormalities are responsible for their pathogenesis.

63

Various clinical and biological characteristics distinguish geriatric depression from depressive syndromes occurring in
younger adulthood (Alexopoulos et al., 1988). Therefore, descriptions of anxious-depressed younger adults cannot be
generalized to the elderly. This chapter focuses on the relationship between depression and anxiety and addresses three
areas: concepts and findings in mixed-age populations; findings
on comorbidity of anxiety and depressive disorders in the elderly; and the significance of anxiety symptoms in geriatric
depressives.

ANXIETY AND DEPRESSION IN
MIXED-AGE POPULATIONS

Historically two positions have been taken in dealing with
the differentiation of anxiety and depression syndromes. The
first was advocated by Sir Aubrey Lewis (1934) who viewed
anxiety and depression as part of a continuum and believed
that the marked overlap between anxiety and depression manifestations makes any differentiation artificial. This unitarian
position is supported by studies showing that tricyclic antidepressants (Paykel et al., 1982; Johnstone et al., 1980), monoamine oxidase inhibitors (Paykel et al., 1980), and minor tranquilizers (Johnstone et al., 1980) are almost equally effective
for various anxiety and depressive syndromes. The diagnosis of
either primary depression or anxiety disorder does not appear
to predict response to pharmacological treatment (Johnstone
et al., 1980; Ancill et al., 1984).

Longitudinal studies investigating the stability of psychiatric
diagnosis over time offer support to the unitarian view. In a
position paper, Tyrer (1985) found evidence that only a minority of anxiety and depressive syndromes retain the same diagnosis over time. Fewer than 40 percent of patients with anxiety
or neurotic depression were found to maintain the same diagnosis on two consecutive psychiatric hospitalizations (Kendell,
1974). It has been reported that anxiety disorders often change

to depressive disorders (Kendell, 1974) and episodes of depression occur frequently in agoraphobics (Mathews et al., 1981).

Personality abnormalities were found to predict better the outcome of patients with neurotic disorders than manifestations of anxiety or depression (Tyrer et al., 1983). Based on this observation, Tyrer (1985) extended Eliot and Slater's (1944) views and proposed that a "general neurotic syndrome" exists which is strongly influenced by a coexisting personality disorder, and its symptomatology changes over time depending on the presence or absence of life events.

Recent genetic research supports Tyrer's view. Kendler et al., (1987) examined symptom self-reports of twins, and found that genetic factors act in a non-specific wy to influence the overall level of psychiatric symptoms. However, certain features of the environment were found to influence strongly symptoms of anxiety while having little impact on symptoms of depression. Although Kendler's study has the limitation of using self-reports, it suggests that environmental factors determine whether a predisposed individual will develop anxiety or depression.

On a biological level, the unitarian position is supported by evidence of limbic abnormalities in both anxiety and depression syndromes (Shear and Fyer, 1988). If the function of the limbic system is the integration of many disparate brain functions into an orderly whole, then qualitatively different abnormalities may not be confined to limbic subsystems and therefore can be expressed with relatively homogeneous symptomatology.

The opposite of the unitarian position suggests that anxiety disorders are independent and can be segregated into a class totally apart from depressive disorders. This syndromic view of anxiety disorders is supported by follow-up studies which observed that anxiety and depression syndromes have a different course and outcome (Roth et al., 1972; Gurney et al., 1972; Kerr et al., 1972; Shapira, 1972). In a cross-sectional study, rating scores of several anxiety and depression scales were able to separate into two groups patients with the tentative diagnosis of anxiety, depression or phobia (Roth et al., 1982). A second analysis showed that symptomatology recorded according to the Present State Examination (Wing et al., 1974) differentiated the population into anxiety and depressive disorders. Use of personality inventories identified patients with anxiety disorders as shy, introverted, and anxiety prone, while those from the depressive group were characterized as outgoing, emotionally stable, and tender minded. These personality characteristics identified correctly 84 percent of patients with anxiety or depressive disorder. Roth et al. (1982) concluded that anxiety and depression syndromes are distinct but related phenomena and are separated by a limited area of diagnostic overlap.

If anxiety and depression are considered separate syndromes then the comorbidity of the two syndromes can be studied. The Epidemiologic Catchment Area Study showed that 2 to 7 percent of community residents with anxiety disorders met criteria for major depression (Boyd et al., 1984). In a study of mixed-age outpatients with unipolar or bipolar major depression, 58 percent of the sample also had an anxiety disorder (Leckman et al., 1983a). The onset of the anxiety and the depressive disorder occurred within a year. Approximately one-third of the patients with anxiety and depression in this sample met criteria for an anxiety disorder even during the periods between depressive episodes (Leckman et al., 1983a).

Differences in family history between depressed and anxious-depressed patients have been noted. First-degree relatives of patients with both major depression and an anxiety disorder appear to be at a greater risk for major depression as well as anxiety disorders than are relatives of individuals with major depression alone (Leckman et al., 1983a). This was especially true for patients with major depression and a panic disorder (Leckman et al., 1983b). In a longitudinal investigation, depressed patients with phobic symptoms or panic attacks have a chronic course of illness twice as frequently as depressives with generalized anxiety (Katschnig et al., 1986). The family history and outcome findings raise the question whether depression combined with some anxiety syndromes constitutes an entity nosologically distinct from depression without anxiety. This hypothesis can be tested with biological and clinical studies including investigations of the adrenergic system and of the response to antidepressant treatment.

ANXIETY AND DEPRESSION
IN GERIATRIC PATIENTS

Epidemiologic data suggest that anxiety syndromes have onset in young age. Most phobic disorders emerge during childhood up to the mid-twenties, and the mean age onset for panic disorder is in the mid-thirties (Weissman, 1988). In a mixed-age study, patients with major depression and anxiety disorders had illness onset at a younger age than patients with major depression alone (Leckman et al., 1983b). In this study, the mean age of onset of patients with both anxiety and depressive disorders was 27 years as opposed to 34 years of patients with major depression alone.

In addition to early age of onset, the Epidemiologic Catchment Area Study observed that the prevalence of anxiety disorders declines after the age of 65 years (Regier et al., 1988). While epidemiologic investigations found that anxiety syndromes have onset in early life and decreased prevalence in old age, clinical studies suggest that considerable comorbidity of anxiety and depression exists in geriatric patients. A robust overlap of symptoms of depression, anxiety and hypochondriasis was observed in psychiatrically hospitalized elderly men (Hyer et al., 1987). We examined the comorbidity of anxiety and depressive disorders in 45 patients consecutively admitted to the Geriatric Psychiatry Specialty Clinic of New York Hospital—Westchester Division. This clinic has a training and research orientation and focuses on geriatric affectic disorders and related conditions. Only 2 percent of the Clinic's population had an anxiety disorder alone. This low percentage may be due to a selection bias, but is in agreement with recent epidemiologic data indicating that older persons with anxiety disorders rarely seek help (Thompson et al., 1988). In our sample, 38 percent of patients with major depression also met DSM-III criteria for an anxiety disorder. This degree of comorbidity was only a little lower than that (58%) reported by Leckman et al. (1983a) in a younger sample.

In our sample, many patients first met criteria for depression and anxiety disorders in late life, and therefore complex psychobiological processes relating to aging or medical disorders may have contributed to the development of psychopathology. A clinical vignette illustrates this point.

Mrs. A., a 74-year-old widowed woman, was referred to the Geriatric Psychiatry Specialty clinic by an internist because of symptoms of anxiety, depression and poor compliance to treatment for bronchial asthma. She had a family history of alcoholism in her father, two brothers, and one sister and a traumatic childhood characterized by verbal and physical abuse. Mrs. A. left her family home after she graduated high school, came to New York and worked as a waitress and a domestic. She married a much older man who died four years after their marriage. Mrs. A's only child, a daughter, had a chaotic lifestyle and was estranged from Mrs. A.

Mrs. A. had features of avoidant personality disorder perceiving most people as aggressive, critical, and unable to offer affection. She had very few relationships throughout her life. Mrs. A. first developed mild fear of inability to breathe at age 17 years during a bronchial asthma attack. Since then she experienced this fear intermittently but never asked for help nor appeared to meet criteria for a psychiatric disorder prior to the age of 70 years. At that time, and after an exacerbation of her bronchial asthma, Mrs. A developed depressed mood, anhedonia, inability to fall asleep or sustain her sleep, anorexia, weight loss, lack of energy, and feelings of worthlessness and hopelessness. She saw unsurmountable difficulties everywhere and often said that she would be better off dead. In addition, Mrs. A. had episodes of fear, dyspnea, sensation of choking, discomfort in the chest, and shakiness. Even when free of these attacks she was anxious and apprehensive about having another attack. Since age 70, she met DSM-III criteria for both major depression and panic disorder. She sought help for her respiratory disease in several medical clinics but was rarely compliant to a regimen of steroids and theophylline. She did not comply to any of two successive trials of nortriptyline and alprazolam given in the Geriatric Psychiatry Specialty Clinic.

This case illustrates several points: The patient had a family history of alcoholism, traumatic early childhood, and a personality dysfunction similar to those observed by Tyrer et al. (1983) and Roth et al. (1982) in patients with anxiety disorders. She had a propensity towards anxiety and phobic symptomatology since adolescence, but finally met criteria for an anxiety and depression syndrome in old age during an exacerbation of a medical illness with which she coped throughout her life. Increasing disability, social isolation, and treatment with steroids and theophylline may have contributed to the development of her psychiatric syndrome. As expected from the epidemiologic literature (Thompson et al., 1988), this patient did not seek psychiatric help. The comorbidity data on anxiety and depression, the observation that anxiety and depression syndromes can first develop or be excerbated in late life, and the contribution of various factors that are particularly important in late life suggest that depression and anxiety syndromes should be examined afresh in the elderly.

ANXIETY SYMPTOMS IN GERIATRIC MAJOR DEPRESSION

The presence of anxiety symptoms in symptoms of major depression has long been recognized and most instruments for the assessment of depression include symptoms of anxiety (Hamilton, 1960; Zung, 1965; Carroll et al., 1973). We studied a population of depressed geriatric patients in order to identify the prevalence of anxiety symptoms and examine their relationship with demographic and clinical characteristics.

The subjects were 184 patients consecutively hospitalized in the geriatric psychiatric service of New York Hospital–Westchester Division who agreed to participate in a series of clinical research studies. All patients met DSM-III criteria for depression and were older than 60 years (mean age: 74.1 years, SD:7).

Depressive symptomatology was quantified with the 24-item Hamilton Depression Rating Scale (HDRS) (Hamilton, 1960), and cognitive dysfunction was rated with the Cognitive Capacity Screening Examination (CCSE) (Jacobs et al., 1977). Subjects who met DSM-III criteria for dementia and had a CCSE score lower than 24 were considered demented. Of the 184 subjects, 107 had no significant cognitive impairment, and 77 met DSM-III criteria for both major depression and dementia on admission to the hospital. The 0 to 4 scales of the HDRS were used to rate psychic and somatic anxiety. Psychic anxiety is defined as subjective tension, apprehension, fear, irritability, and excessive concern about minor matters. Somatic anxiety consists of bodily experiences including dry mouth, indigestion, diarrhea, belching, abdominal cramps, cardiac palpitations, hyperventilation, urinary frequency, and perspiration not attributable to warm environment or effort.

Psychic anxiety was similarly distributed in depressed patients with and without dementia. Sixty-one percent of the whole sample had moderate or severe psychic anxiety. The sample was divided into reversible and irreversible dementia after amelioration of depressive symtomatology. Subjects with major depression and dementia were classified as having depression with reversible dementia if their cognitive dysfunction improved by three or more points in the CCSE and achieved a total CCSE score of 24 or greater when symptoms of depression was ameliorated (change in HDRS score > 9 or final HDRS score < 12). Subjects with a total CCSE lower than 24 even after improvement of depression were considered to have both major depression and irreversible dementia. Psychic anxiety was differently distributed among depressives without dementia ($N = 106$), reversible dementia ($N = 30$), and irreversible dementia ($N = 21$) (chi square 13.98, $df = 6$, $p < 0.03$). Severe psychic anxiety was observed in 40% of depressives with reversible dementia, 19% of depressives with irreversible dementia, and 26% of subjects with major depression alone.

Somatic anxiety was similarly distributed in geriatric depressed patients with and without dementia. Fifty-three percent of the sample had mild somatic anxiety, and 13% had moderate or severe somatic anxiety. There was no significant difference in somatic anxiety between depressives with reversible and irreversible dementia.

There was a trend towards lower psychic anxiety in patients with chronic depression in both depressed (chi square: 9.88, $df = 6$, $p < 0.15$) and depressed-demented patients (chi square: 9.57, $df = 6$, $p < 0.15$). However, there was no relationship between somatic anxiety and duration of depressive episodes in depressed or depressed-demented patients.

Psychic anxiety had no significant relationship with age of depression onset in depressed or depressed-demented patients. However, there was a trend towards a different distribution of somatic anxiety in late—compared to early-onset (< 61 years) geriatric depressed-demented patients (chi square: 6.63, $df = 3$, $p < 0.07$). Neither psychic or somatic anxiety were associated with response to antidepressant treatment.

Psychic anxiety refers to the perception of anxious mood, while somatic anxiety refers to the perception of bodily symptoms related to autonomic hyperactivity. Although both symptoms occur in depression, intense somatic anxiety (13% of the sample) was rarer than severe psychic anxiety (61% of the sample). The difference in the prevalence of psychic and somatic anxiety in depressed geriatric patients led to the hypothesis that psychic and somatic anxiety are independent clinical characteristics in major depression.

The hypothesis was first tested by examining the association between psychic and somatic anxiety in depressed and in depressed-demented patients. There was no significant linear or quadratic relationship between psychic and somatic anxiety (Table 5.1).

The second step in testing the hypothesis that psychic and somatic anxiety are relatively independent symptoms was pursued by examining the relationship of psychic and somatic anxiety to other clinical characteristics of depressed patients. We used multiple regression to evaluate the association between psychic or somatic anxiety with a set of variables hypothesized to predict anxiety. The set of predictors was determined after a review of the literature (Paykel et al., 1971;

**Table 5.1 Relationship Between Psychic and Somatic Anxiety in
Geriatric Patients with Major Depression and/or Dementia**

	Somatic anxiety			
	Major Depression ($N = 106$)		Depression-Dementia ($N = 77$)	
Psychic	Linear	Quadratic	Linear	Quadratic
anxiety	r	r	r	r
Linear	0.17	0.17	0.09	0.26
Quadratic	0.16	0.15	0.07	0.005

Downing and Rickels, 1974; Roth et al., 1982; Prusoff and Klerman, 1974) which resulted in a relatively long list of clinical and
demographic variables. The list was presented to nine geriatric
psychiatrists of New York Hospital who were asked to shorten
it by identifying the items that in their experience had a strong
association with anxiety. This process resulted in a list of seven
predictors of anxiety.

The model had a significant association with psychic anxiety
but not with somatic anxiety (Table 5.2). The same model was
tested in depressed-demented patients. Again, a significant association was found between psychic anxiety and the overall
model ($F = 3.63$, $p < 0.001$), but there was no significant relationship with somatic anxiety ($F = 1.05$, $p < 0.42$).

The relationship of somatic anxiety and another two models
was examined. There was no significant association between
somatic anxiety and the melancholic syndrome (diurnal variation, late insomnia, agitation, retardation, weight loss, guilt) or
the set of bodily symptoms and preoccupations of the HDRS
(gastrointestinal symptoms, general somatic symptoms, hypochondriasis).

Data for this study were prospectively obtained. However,
hypotheses on anxiety were retrospectively formed after review of the literature. Studies are needed to examine whether
depressed geriatric patients with psychic or somatic anxiety

Table 5.2 Relationship of Psychic and Somatic Anxiety to Clinical and Demographic Variables in 106 Cognitively Intact Geriatric Patients with Major Depression

Variable	Psychic anxiety t	Somatic anxiety t
Age	−0.51	0.52
Sadness	2.25**	−0.72
Early Insomnia	2.50*	−0.39
Agitation	3.09*	0.36
Middle Insomnia	−1.85	−0.49
Late Insomnia	0.89	−0.29
Retardation	−2.39**	−2.81
Chronicity	−2.22**	0.38
Whole Model $F = 5$, $p < 0.0001$ $F = 1.68$, $p < 0.11$		

*$p < 0.001$
**$p < 0.002$

have differences in family history, prospective course of illness, or biological parameters than nonanxious depressives.

CONCLUSIONS

Review of the literature as well as our own observations suggest that anxiety syndromes occur frequently in elderly patients with major depression. The high comorbidity and the observation that some anxiety-depression syndromes first develop or become exacerbated in late life indicate the need for studies to evaluate the role of medical morbidity, pharmacotherapy, disability, personality factors, and family history in the development of geriatric anxiety-depression syndromes.

Anxiety symptoms develop in a high proprotion of non-demented and demented geriatric patients with major depression. Psychic anxiety consisting of tension, apprehension, fear, irritability and excessive worries is more frequent than symptoms of autonomic hyperactivity (somatic anxiety) in geriatric

depressives. Severe psychic anxiety appears to be more frequent in depressives with reversible dementia than in non-
demented or irreversibly demented depressed patients. It is
likely that psychic anxiety interferes with test performance and
leads to the erroneous diagnosis of dementia in anxious depressed patients. However, another possibility may be that cognitive disturbance and anxiety result from dysfunction of related brain systems in geriatric depressed patients.

In our sample of geriatric depressives, psychic anxiety
seemed independent of somatic anxiety and correlated with
different clinical characteristics. While further confirmation is
needed, these findings suggest that research is needed to examine whether patients with prominent somatic or psychic
anxiety have biological abnormalities that distinguish them
from the remaining group of geriatric depressives.

COMMENTARY

The discussion of overlapping symptoms and comorbidity
continued.

1. In the clinic population described, there was a low incidence of
primary diagnosis of anxiety in inpatients. But in the clinic population
of outpatients who make criteria for major depressive disorder, there
is a 38% incidence of patients who also met criteria for an anxiety
diagnosis.

2. Patients with reversible dementia were the same people who
also had the most severe anxiety (40%). There were three possible
explanations: a. anxiety interferes with cognitive testing; b. anxiety
and cognitive dysfunction are regulated by related biologic systems;
c. anxiety in cognitive dysfunction are regulated by saying psychological symptoms. Considerable controversy about the independence
of syndromes of pure anxiety versus pure depression in non geriatric
populations. One point of view suggests that overlap is relatively
infrequent and is limited to a small subpopulation. In all others a
meaningful discrimination can be made between anxiety and depressive states. The second point of view represents the opposite end of
the spectrum. In this point of view, there is no meaningful discrimina-

tion between anxiety and depressive states—there is such overlap between the two states, that independent diagnostic categories make little sense. It may be, that for the geriatric population, meaningful diagnostic classification is in the middle. Some older patients have mixed anxious depressive states and cannot be further subtyped, but others can be meaningfully subtyped.

3. The discussion continued to point out that clinicians may not be able to distinguish meaningfully between the two states in terms of deciding whether to treat anxiety or treat depression. Surveys suggest that internists prefer to use benzodiazepines whereas psychiatrists prefer to use tricyclic antidepressants.

4. The choice of antianxiety drugs versus antidepressant drugs may be based more on severity of symptoms rather than on type of symptoms. Benzodiazepines may be chosen as the first treatment for the less severe symptoms pictures.

REFERENCES

Alexopoulos, G. S. (1985). Psychobiology of affective disorders. In V. D. Volkan (Ed.), *Depressive States and Their Treatment* (pp. 337–358). Northvale, NJ: Jason Aronson.

Alexopoulos, G. S., Young, R. C., Meyers, B. S., Abrams, R. C., & Shamoina, C. A. (1988). Late-onset depression. *Psychiatr Clin North Am, 11,* 101–115.

Ancill, J. R., Poyser, J., Davey, A., et al. (1984). Management of mixed affective symptoms in primary care: A critical experiment. *Acta Psychiatr Scand, 70,* 463–469.

Andreasen, N. C. (1982). Concepts diagnosis and classification. In E. S. Paykel (Ed.), *Handbook of Affective Disorders* (pp. 24–44). New York: Guilford Press.

Boyd, J. H., Burke, J. D., Gruenberg, E. et al. (1984). Exclusion criteria of DSM-III: A study of cooccurrence of hierarchy-free syndromes. *Arch Gen Psychiatry, 41,* 983–989.

Carroll, B. J., Fielding, J. M., & Blashki, T. G. (1973). Depression rating scales: A critical review. *Arch Gen Psychiatry, 28,* 361–366.

Derogatis, L. R., Klerman, G. L., & Lipman, R. S. (1972). Anxiety states and depressive disorders. *J Nerv Ment Dis, 155,* 392–403.

Downing, R. W., & Richels, K. (1974). Mixed anxiety-depression: Fact or myth? *Arch Gen Psychiatry, 30,* 312–317.

Gurney, C., Roth, M., Garside, R. F., Kerr, T. A., & Schapira, K. (1972). Studies in the classification of affective disorders: The relationship between anxiety states and depressive illness—II. *Br J Psychiatry, 121*, 162–166.

Hamilton, M. (1960). A rating scale for depression. *J Neurol Neurosurg Psychiatry, 23*, 56–62.

Hyer, L., Gonveia, I., Harrison, W. R., et al. (1987). Depression, anxiety, paranoid reactions, hypochondriasis, and recognitive decline of later-life inpatients. *J Gerontology, 42*, 92–94.

Jacobs, J. W., Bernhardt, M. R., Delgrado, A., et al. (1977). Screening for organic mental syndromes in the elderly. *Ann Intern Med, 86*, 40–46.

Johnstone, E. C., Cunningham, O. D. G., Frith, C. D., et al. (1980). Neurotic illness and its response to anxiolytic and antidepressant treatment. *Psychol Med, 10*, 321–328.

Katschnig, H., Nutzinger, D., David, H. P., et al. (1986). Anxiety and the clinical course of depression. *Clin Psychopharm, 9* (Suppl. 4), 146–148.

Kendler, K. S., Heath, A. C., Martin, W. G., et al. (1987). Symptoms of anxiety and symptoms of depression: Same genes, different environments? *Arch Gen Psychiatry, 122*, 451–457.

Kendell, R. E. (1974). The stability of psychiatric diagnoses. *Br J Psychiatry, 124*, 352–356.

Kerr, T. A., Roth, M., Schapira, K., & Gurney, C. (1972). The assessment and prediction of outcome in affective disorders. *Br J Psychiatry, 121*, 162–174.

Leckman, J. F., Merikangas, K. R., Pauls, D. L., et al. (1983a). Anxiety disorders and depression: Contradictions between family study data and DSM-III conventions. *Am J Psychiatry, 140*, 880–882.

Leckman, J. F., Weissman, M. M., Merikangas, K. R., et al. (1983b). Panic disorder and major depression. *Arch Gen Psychiatry, 40*, 1055–1060.

Lewis, A. J. (1934). Melancholia: A clinical study of depressive states. *J Psychiatry, 109*, 451–463.

Mathews, A. M., Gelder, M. G., & Johnson, D. W. (1981). *Agoraphobia: Nature and treatment.* London: Tavistock.

Paykel, E. S. (1971). Classification of depressed patients: A cluster analysis derived grouping. *Br J Psychiatry, 118*, 275–288.

Paykel, E. S., Rowan, P. R., Rao, B. M., & Bhat, A. (1982). Atypical depression: Nosology and response to antidepressants. In P. Clayton & J. Barrett (Eds.), Treatment of depression: Old controversies and new approaches (pp. 237–263). New York: Raven Press.

Prussoff, B., & Klerman, G. L. (1974). Differentiating depressed from anxious neurotic outpatients: Use of discriminant function analysis for separation of neurotic affective states. *Arch Gen Psychiatry, 30,* 302–309.

Regier, D. A., Boyd, J. H., Burke, J. D., et al. (1988). One-month prevalence of mental disorders in the United States. *Arch Gen Psychiatry, 45,* 977–986.

Roth, M., Gurney, C., Garside, R. F., & Kerr, T. A. (1972). Studies in classification of affective disorders: The relationship between anxiety states and depressive illness. *Br J Psychiatry, 121,* 147–161.

Roth, M., Mountjoy, C. Q., & Caetano, D. (1982). Further investigations into the relationship between depressive disorders and anxiety state. *Pharmacopsychiat, 15,* 135–141.

Schapira, K., Roth, M., Kerr, T., & Gurney, C. (1972). The prognosis of affective disorders: The differentiation of anxiety states from depressive illness. *Br J Psychiatry, 121,* 175–181.

Shear, M. K., & Fyer, M. R. (1988). Biological and psychopathologic findings in panic disorder. In A. J. Frances & R. E. Hales (Eds.), *Review of Psychiatry* (pp. 29–53). Washington, DC: American Psychiatric Press.

Slater, E., & Slater, P. (1944). A heuristic theory of neurosis. *J Neurol Psychiatry, 7,* 49–55.

Thompson, J. W., Burns, B. J., Bartko, J., et al. (1988). The use of ambulatory services by persons with and without probia. *Med Care, 26,* 183–198.

Tyrer, P. (1985). Neurosis divisible? *Lancet, i,* 685–688.

Tyrer, P., Casey, P., & Gall, J. (1983). Relationship between neurosis and personality disorder. *Br J Psychiatry, 142,* 404–408.

Weissman, M. M. (1988). The epidemiology of panic disorders and agoraphobia. In A. J. Frances & R. E. Hales (Eds.), *Review of Psychiatry* (pp. 54–66). Washington, DC: American Psychiatric Press.

Wing, J. K., Cooper, J. E., & Sartorius, N. (Eds.). (1974). Measurement and Classification of Psychiatric Symptoms: An Instruction Manual for the PSE and Catego Program. Cambridge: Cambridge University Press.

Zung, W. W. K. (1965). A self-rating depression scale. *Arch Gen Psychiatry, 12,* 63–70.

Anxiety and Dementia　6

Jerome A. Yesavage and Brian Taylor

The purpose of this chapter is to review the conceptual issues and diagnosis of anxiety in elderly demented patients. Several studies in the past have documented anxious-agitated behaviors as a major problem in demented nursing-home residents (Barnes, 1980, 1982; Chandler et al., 1988; Lader, 1982; Morgan, 1987; Swearer, 1988; Zimmer, 1984). This chapter will include both a review of theoretical and research issues and an evaluation of clinical studies.

DEFINITION OF ANXIETY IN DEMENTED PATIENTS

Any definition of anxiety includes worry or mental anxiety as well as tension or physical anxiety. A separation between the psychic and physical manifestations of anxiety has been made by Liebert and Morris. They chose the words "worry" versus "emotionality" to describe the distinction and have developed a

This research was supported in part by the Medical Research Services of the Veteran's Administration, NIMH Grant MH 40041 for the Clinical Research Center for the Study of Senile Dementias and the Henry Golobic Memorial Fund.

rating scale to quantify these two concepts (1967). The concept of "worry" or mental anxiety in the elderly must include ruminations about cognitive performance. This can be quantified using the cognitive interference questionnaire (Sarason, 1980). One might expect that dementia patients would "worry" early in their illness and not necessarily show any physical manifestations of their concerns. Later one could expect that "emotionality" would be observed as cognitive coping mechanisms fade.

In a recent review of agitated behaviors in the elderly, Cohen-Mansfield and Billig (1986) carefully discuss related concepts. Their own literature review provides an exhaustive survey of the different types of agitated behaviors in the elderly. They point out that the word is often linked to a variety of additional concepts in the elderly. These include "dementias, senility, depression, anxiety, sleep disturbances, tension, irritability, phobic reactions, assaultiveness, disruptive or self-injurious behaviors, hostility, uncooperativeness, excessive confused walking through the wards, trying doors, tearing clothes, over-talkativeness, loudness, repetitious mannerisms, wandering, aggressiveness, motor restlessness, and excitability." Their empirical work includes a survey of such behaviors in a nursing home and a factor analysis to determine the presence of any underlying concepts to such behavior (Cohen-Mansfied & Billig, 1986). The analysis suggested three factors corresponding to physically aggressive behavior, verbal assault, and inappropriate motor behavior, such as pacing. There was no "anxiety" factor, so it remains unclear whether anxiety is a separate entity from agitation in the demented elderly.

DIAGNOSIS

Given the rich variety of anxiety-related syndromes, it is possible that one could be very specific about formal diagnosis. However, the terms that are used in DSM-III and DSM-III-R apply only to a segment of the adult neurotic population. Thus nuances of the variety of agitated-anxious behaviors seen in elderly demented patients are not taken into account in current psychiatric diagnosis. Perhaps these considerations will appear in DSM-IV.

This problem is further complicated by the lack of appropriate scales for use with the elderly and demented. Most behavioral rating scales have not been validated for use in such populations while the few scales that have been validated may assess different symptoms than the syndrome observable in younger adults. For example, scales to diagnose depression in the elderly may be more successful if they do not rely on somatic complaints, whereas somatic complaint in scales for younger depressed patients may be quite helpful (Yesavage et al., 1983). Furthermore, such scales may not be equally sensitive to the clinical phenomena along the entire range of severity of dementia (Yesavage et al., 1988). This can lead to certain artifacts during assessment. If, for example, an anxiety scale is more sensitive in early stages of the disease than in later stages, one might be falsely led to the conclusion that over the course of the illness anxiety declines.

In addition, separation of anxiety and depression is complicated. A study of 200 inpatients suggested that in the mildly and moderately depressed elderly, symptoms of anxiety predominated (Good et al., 1987). Are such patients really manifesting anxiety disorders with secondary depression? Current diagnostic criteria do not suggest means to separate these entities in spite of the obvious therapeutic implications.

Despite these problems, one study by Swearer and associates (1988) carefully studies the interaction between various problem behaviors including anxiety and dementias. Although they found that 63% of demented patients exhibited anxiety, this symptom was not related to the degree of dementia. A significant but low (.26) correlation was found between measures of anxiety and angry outbursts. In turn, angry outbursts were highly (.54) correlated with assaultive behavior. They found no difference in behavioral symptoms among degenerative, vascular or mixed dementias. They concluded that emotional disturbances (both depression and anxiety) appear to form a distinct grouping from other behavior disturbances and conceivably represent different pathological processes. This study has important implications in that the anxious demented patient may represent a distinct clinical syndrome, diagnostic entity, and treatment challenge.

CONCLUSION

Although attempts such as that of Swearer and associates have shed some light on the concept of anxiety in dementing illness, the numerous psychopharmacologic studies reviewed elsewhere in this volume suggest cause for concern. The term agitation is often interchanged with anxiety in these studies. What is the relation between these concepts? Is anxiety merely a milder form of agitation which becomes primarily manifest as nonverbal anxiety or "emotionality" as the patient loses their ability to communicate? Or are there really two different phenomena such as a mild to moderate cognitive "worry" about lost mental abilities in early stages of dementia which later changes to a psychotic state of agitation with delusional thinking in later stages? Could it also be that as demented patients live longer with their illness their anxiety is reduced by developing various coping strategies, then, perhaps, as their cognitive resources fade, they develop a more generalized motoric agitation.

Such questions might be answered with properly constructed psychometric studies and pharmacologic experiments. Future pharmacologic studies of anxiety in demented subjects, however, could be complicated by side-effects of medications which themselves mimic anxiety and agitation. The tremor of lithium toxicity or the akathesia associated with neuroleptic use could be mistaken for either phenomena.

It is likely that treating any anxiety associated with dementia can only bring an improvement in cognitive function, well-being as well as reduce "excess disability." Unfortunately, effective treatment in this area is handicapped by linguistic and diagnostic confusions. Furthermore, psychological interventions in the area are poorly explored and medications often have serious side-effects (Thackrey, 1987). Future studies should include newer agents such as pimozide (Salzman, 1988) as well as careful examination of pharmacokinetic factors relating to drug efficacy and side-effects in this frail population. Further exploration of behavioral interventions is clearly indicated given the downside to many pharmacologic interventions in elderly debilitated populations.

COMMENTARY

Rating the anxious elderly patient is beset by several fundamental problems.

1. There exists considerable confusion between anxiety and agitation. The literature and all outcome studies confuse these two states. These concepts are likely to be strongly inter-related. Furthermore, as cognitive impairment increases, personality characters sometimes become more prominent and may take precedence over other symptoms in some elderly patients. In other elderly patients, personality characteristics may actually diminish and the patient may become less anxious or behaviorally disordered.

2. Anxiety may contribute to the emergence of other symptoms such as paranoia and aggression. However this is not true for every patient, and is not reliably predictable.

3. The problem of rating the elderly patient who cannot describe his symptoms dominates the field. Can you have subjective anxiety in someone who cannot tell you how they feel? If an elderly individual cannot express his symptoms then how do we decide what we are treating, what drugs to use, and what is the outcome? This question is easy to answer for agitation objective behavioral impairment, but may be impossible to answer for the inner subjective state.

4. In elderly patients with cognitive impairment, subjective affective symptoms do not cluster together as they do in the cognitively nonimpaired. Therefore, rather than talking about anxiety that is secondary to a dementia, clinicians and researchers should develop an empirically based classification of anxiety symptoms that depend on careful clinical evaluation. We must be very careful about how we label symptoms in the elderly, especially in the cognitively impaired elderly.

5. For patients with mild to moderate impairment, the BPRS may be a useful scale. The tension anxiety ratings, however, become less reliable as impairment increases.

6. Although rating scales may be necessary for research, clinical sensitivity may be more accurate for some older patients. It was pointed out that some demented patients can be assessed by clinically sensitive clinicians who know the patient well. Using a variety of subtle clues, and changes over time, it may be possible to accurately determine the presence and severity of anxiety. However, such clinical sensitivity does not lend itself to rating scale instruments.

7. There is disagreement about the predictable presence or absence of anxiety as part of the Alzheimer's dementia. Some workers have noted that early Alzheimer's patients may not be more anxious than other elderly patients, and may even be less anxious than depressed elderly patients. Others have noted that early Alzheimer's patients may not be able to express their anxiety because of decrease in self-observation powers.

8. In the absence of a reliable biologic test for the presence of anxiety, the field is left with the crude empirical state of the art that relies on imperial trials of drugs from different classes. Elderly patients should be labeled as responsive to a particular from a particular class rather than labeled at the presence of anxiety or other specific affective state.

REFERENCES

Barnes, R., & Raskind, M. (1980). Strategies for diagnosing and treating agitation in the aging. *Geriatrics*, March, 111–119.

Barnes, R., Veith, R., Okimoto, J., Raskind, M., & Gumbrecht, G. (1982). Efficacy of antipsychotic medications in behaviorally disturbed dementia patients. *Am J Psychiatry, 139*, 9.

Chandler, J. D., & Chandler, J. E. (1988). The prevalence of neuropsychiatric disorders in a nursing home population. *Journal of Geriatric Psychiatry and Neurology, 1*, 71–76.

Cohen-Mansfield, J. (1986b). Agitated behaviors in the elderly: II. Preliminary results in the cognitively deteriorated. *J Am Geriat Soc, 34*, 722–727.

Cohen-Mansfield, J., & Billig, N. (1986a). Agitated behaviors in the elderly: I. A conceptual review. *J Am Geriat Soc, 34*, 711–721.

Good, R., Vlachonikolis, I., Griffiths, P., & Griffiths, R. A. (1987). The structure of depressive symptoms in the elderly. *Br J Psychiatry, 150,* 463–470.

Greendyke, R. M., Kanter, D. R., Schuster, D. B., Verstreate, S., & Wooton, J. (1986). Propranolol treatment of assaultive patients with organic brain disease. *Nervous and Mental Dis, 174,* 290–294.

Lader, M. (1982). Differential diagnosis of anxiety in the elderly. *J Clin Psychiatry, 43,* 9 [Sec. 2], 4–7.

Liebert, R. M., & Morris, L. W. (1967). Cognitive and emotional components of test anxiety: A distinction and some initial data. *Psychology Reports, 20,* 975–978.

Morgan, K., Dallosso, H. M., Arie, T., Byrne, E. J., Jones, R., & Waite, J. (1987). Mental health and psychological well-being among the old and very old living at home. *Br J Psychiatry, 150,* 801–807.

Salzman, C. (1988). Treatment of agitation, anxiety, and depression in dementia. *Psychopharmacology Bull., 24,* 49–53.

Sarason, I. W. (1980). Introduction to the study of test anxiety. In I. W. Sarason (Ed.), Test anxiety: Theory, research and applications (pp. 3–14). Hillsdale, NJ: Lawrence Erlbaum Associates.

Swearer, J. M., Drachman, D. A., O'Donnell, B. E., & Mitchell, A. J. (1988). Troublesome and disruptive behaviors in dementia: Relationships to diagnosis and disease severity. *J Am Geriat Soc, 36,* 784–790.

Thackrey, M. (1987). *Therapeutics for aggression.* New York: Human Sciences Press.

Yesavage, J. A., Brink, T. L. Rose, T. L., Adey, M. B., Lum, O., Huang, V., & Lierer, V. O. (1983). Development of a geriatric depression rating scale: A preliminary report. *J Psychiatric Res, 17,* 37–49.

Yesavage, J. A., Poulsen, S. L., Sheikh, J. I., & Tanke, E. (1988). Rates of change of common measures of impairment in senile dementia of the Alzheimer's type. *Psychopharm. Bull., 24,* 531–534.

Zimmer, J. G., Watson, N., & Treat, A. (1984). Behavioral problems among patients in skilled nursing facilities. *Am J Public Health, 74,* 1118–1121.

Masked Anxiety— Alcohol and Drug Use

7

Benjamin Liptzin

Does anxiety contribute to problems with drinking or drugs, and conversely, do drinking or drugs contribute to anxiety? To what extent does alcohol or drug use constitute a symptom of anxiety, a self-treatment for anxiety, or a masking of anxiety? In order to address these issues, this chapter will first review some of the definitions and epidemiological data regarding symptoms or behaviors that constitute "anxiety" or "alcohol/substance use." Unique aspects of the relationship between anxiety and alcohol/substance use in the elderly will then be considered followed by suggestions for future research.

DEFINITIONS

In addition to alcohol, the sedative/hypnotic/anxiolytic drugs are most likely to be used as well as abused by older persons. Prescription analgesic drugs are also widely used by

Revised version of chapter presented at a Harvard-NIMH Conference on Anxiety in the Elderly, Boston, MA January 9–10, 1989, supported by the National Institute of Mental Health.

the elderly, and may also be abused. The elderly narcotic addict is usually the younger addict grown old, with a mean
length of opiate abuse of 36 years in one study and 44 addicts
over age 50 (Atkinson & Schuckit, 1983). Although the elderly
are often in pain, narcotic use nevertheless may be treating an
underlying dysphoria or anxiety rather than pain, and continued use may be necessary to avoid or treat withdrawal
symptoms. The older addict uses drugs less frequently and
generally takes prescription drugs such as morphine, codeine,
meperidine (Demerol) or paregoric, and obtains them legally
from physicians. Other important definitions that need to be
kept in mind are shown in Table 7.1 for alcohol induced, and in
Tables 7.2 and 7.3 for sedative/hypnotic/anxiolytic, and for
opioid-induced organic mental disorders (American Psychiatric Association, 1987). Table 7.4 shows the criteria for delirium
due to any cause. Drug discontinuance, with or without delirium, can be associated with anxiety. In addition, the behavioral
changes associated with intoxication can lead to anxiety at the
time or, more likely, the next morning.

EPIDEMIOLOGY

What is the prevalence of alcohol and drug use in relation to
anxiety disorders in the elderly? Two recent reports (Regier,
Boyd, Burke, et al., 1988; Blazer, 1989) indicate that for persons
aged 65 years and older, the overall rate for anxiety disorders
was 5.5% including 4.8% with phobias, 0.1% with panic disorder,
and 0.8% with obsessive–compulsive disorder. The rates for
older men were 3.6% overall and 2.9% for phobias, 0 for panic
disorder and 0.7% for obsessive–compulsive disorders. For
older women, the rates are 6.8% overall and 6.1%, 0.2%, and 0.9%
respectively. For both older men and women, these rates were
somewhat lower than that found in younger age groups. As
with all younger age groups, older women were more likely
than older men to be diagnosed with anxiety disorders. With
respect to substance use disorders, the sex ratios were reversed. Older men had a 1.8% rate of substance use disorder all

of which involved alcohol. Older women had a 0.3% rate of substance use disorder which also involved only alcohol. There was virtually no drug abuse/dependence identified in the population over age 65 and only 0.1% in persons 45–64 years old in contrast to rates of 3.5% in persons 18–24 and 1.5% in persons 25–44 with men having higher rates than women at all ages. Similarly, the rate for alcohol abuse and dependence was higher for men than women at all ages and overall the rate was 4.1% in persons 18–24, 3.6% in persons 25–44, 2.1% in persons 45–64, and 0.9% in persons over 65.

These data suggest that anxiety disorders are less common in older than younger persons. For alcohol abuse and dependence, the lower rates may reflect a developmental change for men who "settle down" or learn to drink responsibly by a certain age. The decline in alcoholism after 65, may be due to higher mortality among alcoholic men. Older women were much less likely to drink than men when they were younger, and are even less likely to admit it when interviewed in later life.

A U.S. Bureau of the Census survey (1986), found that nearly half (45%) of the 55 and older population completely abstained from alcohol compared to 28% of the 35 to 54 years olds and 22% of the 20 to 34 year olds. Meyers (1982) found that 53% of those 60 and over surveyed in Boston were nondrinkers and a national survey (Wilsnack and Cheloha, 1987) found 66% of women 65 and older reported themselves to be nondrinkers. In contrast to these abstinence rates, the rate of "problem drinking" has been estimated as high as 15% in the elderly (Osborne, 1979). Atkinson and Schuckit (1983) indicate that it has been difficult to determine the prevalence of alcoholism but report that community surveys estimate a rate of 2 to 10% for alcoholism in the older population. Other reports indicate that the percentage of heavy drinkers decreases with advancing age as does the prevalence of health, work, and police-related problems. They also point out that some elderly alcoholics had alcohol problems when young but managed to survive until age 65 while others start having alcohol problems late in life and continue drinking past age 65.

Table 7.1 DSM-III-R Criteria for Alcohol-Induced Organic Mental Disorders

303.00 Alcohol Intoxication
   A. Recent ingestion of alcohol (with no evidence suggesting that the amount was insufficient to casue intoxication in most people).
   B. Maladaptive behavioral changes, e.g., disinhibition of sexual or aggressive impulses, mood lability, impaired judgment, impaired social or occupational functioning.
   C. At least one of the following signs:
      (1) slurred speech
      (2) incoordination
      (3) unsteady gait
      (4) nystagmus
      (5) flushed face
   D. Not due to any physical or other mental disorder.
291.40 Alcohol Idiosyncratic Intoxication
   A. Maladaptive behavioral changes, e.g., aggressive or assaultive behavior, occurring within minutes of ingesting an amount of alcohol insufficient to induce intoxication in most people.
   B. The behavior is atypical of the person when not drinking.
   C. Not due to any physical or other mental disorder.
291.80 Uncomplicated Alcohol Withdrawal
   A. Cessation of prolonged (several days or longer) heavy ingestion of alcohol or reduction in the amount of alcohol ingested, followed within several hours by coarse tremor of hands, tongue, or eyelids, and at least one of the following:
      (1) nausea or vomiting
      (2) malaise or weakness
      (3) autonomic hyperactivity, e.g., tachycardia, sweating, elevated blood pressure.
      (4) anxiety
      (5) depressed mood or irritability
      (6) transient hallucinations or illusions
      (7) headache
      (8) insomnia
   B. Not due to any physical or other mental disorder such as Alcohol Withdrawal Delirium

(continued)

Table 7.1 Continued

291.00 Alcohol Withdrawal Delirium
   A. Delirium (p. 77) developing after cessation of heavy alcohol
      ingestion or a reduction in the amount of alcohol ingested
      (usually within one week).
   B. Marked autonomic hyperactivity, e.g., tachycardia, sweating.
   C. Not due to any physical or other mental disorder.

Reprinted with permission from the *Diagnostic and Statistical Manual of Mental Disorders, Third Edition, Revised.* Copyright 1987 American Psychiatric Association.

In considering the relationship of alcohol use and abuse to social factors, Alexander and Duff (1988) surveyed 260 residents of three retirement communities. In contrast to the Bureau of the Census (1986) data, they found only 21.5% nondrinkers compared to 45% in the general population and found 46% who were regular drinkers compared to 28% in the general population. Alexander and Duff also reported that higher levels of alcohol consumption were positively associated with higher levels of social interaction as measured by an Index of Social Interaction. They hypothesized that the relatively high level of alcohol use may reflect the middle and upper-middle class background of people who move to retirement communities as well as the importance of alcohol in the social class of such communities. It is significant that the majority of heavy drinkers in these retirement communities admitted that they drank alone as well as socially.

The relationship between life events and alcohol consumption and problem drinking was examined in an important study by LaGreca, Akers, and Dwyer (1988). These authors noted a prior study (Dupree et al., 1984) indicating that "the geriatric problem drinker . . . develops an abusive use of alcohol to the stress of aging. [This] later-life onset abuser's reasons for drinking are hypothesized to be more in response to fairly recent age-related events rather than a reflection of long-term, well-defined psychological problems." La Greca et al. then interviewed 1410 adults age 60 and over in two retirement com-

Table 7.2 DSM-III-R Criteria for Sedative-, Hypnotic-, or Anxiolytic-Induced Organic Mental Disorders

305.40 Sedative, Hypnotic, or Anxiolytic Intoxication
  A. Recent use of a sedative, hypnotic, or anxiolytic.
  B. Maladaptive behavioral changes, e.g., disinhibition of sexual or aggressive impulses, mood lability, impaired judgment, impaired social or occupational functioning.
  C. At least one of the following signs:
     (1) slurred speech
     (2) incoordination
     (3) unsteady gait
     (4) impairment in attention or memory
  D. Not due to any physical or other mental disorder.
292.00 Uncomplicated Sedative, Hypnotic, or Anxiolytic Withdrawal
  A. Cessation of prolonged (several weeks or more) moderate or heavy use of a sedative, hypnotic or anxiolytic, or reduction in the amount of substance used, followed by at least three of the following:
     (1) nausea or vomiting
     (2) malaise or weakness
     (3) autonomic hyperactivity, e.g., tachycardia, sweating
     (4) anxiety or irritability
     (5) orthostatic hypotension
     (6) coarse tremor of hands, tongue, and eyelids
     (7) marked insomnia
     (8) grand mal seizures
  B. Not due to any physical or other mental disorder, such as Sedative, Hypnotic, or Anxiolytic Withdrawal Delirium.
292.00 Sedative Hypnotic, or Anxiolytic Withdrawal Delirium
  A. Delirium (p. 77) developing after the cessation of heavy use of a sedative, hypnotic or anxiolytic, or a reduction in the amount of substance used (usually within one week).
  B. Autonomic hyperactivity, e.g., tachycardia, sweating.
  C. Not due to any physical or other mental disorder

Reprinted with permission from the *Diagnostic and Statistical Manual of Mental Disorders, Third Edition, Revised.* Copyright 1987 American Psychiatric Association.

munities and two age-integrated communities. The four communities were selected to represent community settings typical of the living situations of the noninstitutionalized older adult population. They found that 38.2% of their sample had abstained from alcohol in the past year while 21.1% reported having some alcoholic beverage nearly daily or almost every day. Of the total sample, 3.1% experienced a drinking-related

Table 7.3 DSM-III-R Criteria for Opioid-Induced Organic Mental Disorders

305.50 Opioid Intoxication
  A. Recent use of an opioid.
  B. Maladaptive behavioral changes, e.g., initial euphoria followed by apathy, dysphoria, psychomotor retardation, impaired judgment, impaired social or occupational functioning.
  C. Pupillary constriction (or pupillary dilation due to anoxia from severe overdose) and at least one of the following signs:
     (1) drowsiness
     (2) slurred speech
     (3) impairment in attention or memory
  D. Not due to any physical or other mental disorder.
292.00 Opioid Withdrawal
  A. Cessation of prolonged (several weeks or more) moderate or heavy use of an opioid, or reduction in the amount of opioid used (or administration of an opioid antagonist after a brief period of use), followed by at least three of the following:
     (1) craving for an opioid
     (2) nausea or vomiting
     (3) muscle aches
     (4) lacrimation or rhinorrhea
     (5) pupillary dilation, piloerection, or sweating
     (6) diarrhea
     (7) yawning
     (8) fever
     (9) insomnia
  B. Not due to any physical or other mental disorder

Reprinted with permission from the *Diagnostic and Statistical Manual of Mental Disorders, Third Edition, Revised.* Copyright 1987 American Psychiatric Association.

Table 7.4 DSM-III-R Criteria for Delirium

A. Reduced ability to maintain attention to external stimuli (e.g., questions must be repeated because attention wanders) and to appropriately shift attention to new external stimuli (e.g., perseverates answer to a previous question).

B. Disorganized thinking, as indicated by rambling, irrelevant, or incoherent speech.

C. At least two of the following:
  (1) reduced level of consciousness, e.g., difficulty keeping awake during examination.
  (2) perceptual disturbances: misinterpretations illusions, or hallucinations.
  (3) disturbance of sleep-wake cycle with insomnia or daytime sleepiness.
  (4) increased or decreased psychomotor activity
  (5) disorientation to time, place, or person.
  (6) memory impairment, e.g., inability to learn new material, such as the names of several unrelated objects after five minutes, or to remember past events, such as history.

D. Clinical features develop over a short period of time (usually hours to days) and tend to fluctuate over the course of a day:

E. (1) or (2):
  (1) evidence from the history, physical examination, or laboratory or tests of a specific organic factor (or factors) judged to be etiologically related to the disturbance
  (2) in the absence of such evidence, an etiologic organic factor can be presumed if the disturbance cannot be accounted for by any non-organic mental disorder, e.g., Manic Episode accounting for agitation and sleep disturbance.

Reprinted with permission from the *Diagnostic and Statistical Manual of Mental Disorders, Third Edition, Revised.*

problem in the past year and 6.3% were rated as heavy consumers in the previous year. Most of the elderly survey respondents continued the pattern of drinking behavior that had been established before age 60 although 3.9% decreased their drinking. However, 5% began drinking for the first time, increased their drinking, or became heavy drinkers. Nearly three-fourths

(73.6%) experienced at least one significantly upsetting life event in the past year, commonly, the death of a family member or close friend (40%), personal health problems (22.3%), or family members with health problems (26.4%). In this study of older people there was no association between the occurrence of life events and the frequency, quantity or problems of drinking behavior. Apparently this survey population coped well with "stressful" life events so that increased alcohol use or abuse did not result.

There are no studies that examine the presence of anxiety disorders in conjunction with alcohol or substance abuse in the elderly. Two studies of younger substance abusers seeking treatment however, (Weiss and Rosenberg, 1985; Ross, Glaser, and Germanson, 1988) suggest that alcoholism or other drug abuse may begin as a form of self medication for anxiety.

SPECIAL ISSUES FOR GERIATRIC PATIENTS

A number of special issues arise in considering the relationship of anxiety to alcohol or other substance use/abuse in the elderly (Atkinson & Schuckit, 1983). With normal aging there is decreased hepatic metabolism which may lead to higher blood levels of drugs and alcohol in an older person. Furthermore, the aging brain is more sensitive to the effects of alcohol and drugs so that at the same blood level, an older person may be more likely than a younger person to become intoxicated. Older persons are also more likely than younger persons to have some cognitive deficit that is aggravated by alcohol-associated memory problems.

The identification of older persons with substance abuse is hampered by public and professional misconceptions of an older abuser. Families tend to hide or protect their afflicted older relatives and the police are less likely to press alcohol-related charges against an older person. Measures of amounts or frequency of use ignore the fact that older persons may be sensitive to relatively small amounts of drugs and these may have prolonged effects in the body. Criteria using social prob-

lems to identify older substance abusers are difficult to apply
since the elderly are less likely than younger persons to be
arrested, or to have job problems because they are retired, or
to have marital problems because they are widowed. The effects of alcohol on the physical health of the older person may
be difficult to distinguish from pre-existing or coexisting physical problems. For all these reasons, Atkinson and Schuckit
recommend using diagnostic criteria as guidelines rather than
as rigid diagnostic rules. In considering etiologic factors including comorbid psychiatric disorders, they argue "what matters
most is identifying factors that affect the course of substance
use. One must help the patient deal with these factors and
provide the best opportunity for treatment and rehabilitation."

Atkinson and Schuckit (1983) also discussed the misuse and
abuse of sedative/hypnotic and anxiolytic drugs in the elderly.
According to a survey of community physicians, clinics, hospitals and nursing homes, patients over age 65 who comprised
10% of the U.S. population, accounted for over 21% of all pre-
scriptions of diazepam (Valium®), over 23% of chlordiazepoxide (Librium®), over 27% of phenobarbital, and over 30% of
flurazepam (Dalmane®). A household survey of medication use
by persons age 60 to 74 years old found that 11% of the men
and 25% of the women used "antianxiety" agents (benzodiazepines, propanediols, barbiturates) while 7 to 8% of both men
and women used prescription sleeping medications (short-act-
ing barbiturates, glutethimide, chloral hydrate, and others).
These percentages were slightly greater than those found in
younger age groups. A third survey of 242 older people living in
the community found that 34.3% used CNS depressants (barbiturates, benzodiazepines, propanediols).

In a fourth survey, 1.3% of 2,278 older persons living in a
community in Florida were found to be taking meprobamate
(Hale, May, Moore, et al., 1988). Over one-third of the
meprobamate users began taking meprobamate after 1979 despite the availability of more effective benzodiazepines. All of
the patients using meprobamate had the medication prescribed by a primary care physician. Almost all patients reported taking the same dose of the drug in 1987 that was

prescribed initially, and there was no evidence of tolerance or of oversedation in this group of patients from age 72 to 91 years. Most older users indicated that it calmed their anxiety or promoted more restful sleep than when the drug was not used, including those who used it on a daily basis for many years.

CLINICAL ISSUES

This section will address some of the clinical issues involved in the assessment and management of elderly patients with anxiety and concomitant alcohol or substance use or abuse.

Any older patient who presents to a health or mental health professional with symptoms of anxiety must be asked tactfully but directly about use of alcohol or other drugs. It is important to know whether anxiety symptoms preceded or followed the drug use. Even patients with other complaints such as "depression" or "nothing to do" or "loneliness" should be asked about their use of drugs. In addition, it is often helpful to ask about behavior that may be alcohol or drug related such as auto accidents, arrests or other interpersonal difficulties. Information from family members or other knowledgeable informants should also be obtained. The following case illustrates these points.

A 72-year-old man was referred to a psychiatrist for "talking too much" which antagonized his family and supervisors at his part-time job. The history included a previous episode of depression for which he was hospitalized as well as frequent complaints about having nothing to do, mild memory impairment, and difficulty concentrating. As an example of the latter, he mentioned an accident in which he had turned his car into the wrong lane of a divided highway because he was "not paying attention." In response to a direct question he indicated that he would usually drink 2–3 beers/day including some at lunch or before driving. His wife hesitantly corrected him and pointed out that he sometimes drank 2 cases (48 cans) of beer in a week. However, he denied having a problem with alcohol saying "I grew up around Milwaukee where everyone develops a taste for beer." When his daughter took him to meetings of Alcoholics Anonymous (AA) he was unable to identify with "those people." However, he agreed that his symptoms required a gradual reduction of alcohol use or even abstinence since at his age he would only become more sensitive to the effects of alcohol.

Another case illustrates the importance of careful history taking.

A 77-year-old man was admitted to a general hospital for an elective cholecystectomy. By the second hospital day he was restless, irritable and not sleeping well at night. By the third day he was frightened, hiding under the covers, and had visual hallucinations of frightening animals or people in his room. In the face of a severe delirium, the treating physicians then obtained a history from his wife that the patient had been taking 10mg of diazepam at bedtime every night for years but hadn't thought to mention it when the admitting doctor asked if he was taking any medication.

Past history of drug or alcohol use is important even in patients who are not currently using or abusing alcohol or drugs.

For example, a 69-year-old married woman with a history of severe depression and anxiety was hospitalized. She was known to have had a long history of alcohol abuse but had been abstinent for 20 years and an active participant in AA. However, a more detailed history indicated that many years previously she had been hospitalized for detoxification from Valium. Her present anxiety was compounded by fear of again having benzodiazepine withdrawal symptoms in the event that such drugs were prescribed.

The proper role of anxiolytic medication is particularly challenging when an anxious elderly patient has a history of alcohol or substance use or abuse. Other nonpharmacological psychotherapies including individual, group, marital, family and behavioral approaches may also help anxious elderly patients. For older patients with a history of alcohol abuse, the support and encouragement available through AA may be vital. For anxious older patients with a primary depressive disorder or with panic disorder or agoraphobia, tricyclic antidepressants or monamine oxidase inhibitors can be effective and used safely without a risk of abuse. If drug treatment for anxiety is necessary, drugs that are not as subject to abuse as benzodiazepines should be considered first such as beta-blockers, antihistamines, antidepressants, or buspirone. If a benzodiazepine is chosen, one with less abuse potential, oxazepam or halazepam is preferred because of low abuse potential (Ciraulo, Sands, and Shader, 1988). A limited number of pills should be prescribed, and careful follow-up, which may include urine toxicology screens for other drugs of abuse, should be done. To determine continued need, the physician should periodically taper the patient's medication and observe the patient for recurrence of anxiety symptoms. If there is evidence of coexisting alcohol and benzodiazepine abuse, detoxification should be undertaken only under close medical supervision.

SUGGESTIONS FOR FUTURE RESEARCH

1. More epidemiologic studies are needed to clarify the differences between anxiety in the elderly and in younger persons. What is the natural history of anxiety disorders? Do anxiety disorders persist unchanged into late life or do biological or psychosocial changes mitigate or enhance anxiety symptoms in late life?

2. What are the underlying physiological or genetic relationships between anxiety and the predisposition to alcohol or substance abuse?

3. How do older people cope with anxiety symptoms? Which symptoms are most likely to be reported to health professionals?

4. Is the long-term use of anxioloytic drugs appropriate or not for elderly patients who report continued benefit and are not showing signs of abuse? Are certain benzodiazepines preferable for the elderly?

5. What nonpharmacologic treatments are useful in elderly patients with anxiety symptoms, especially those with a past history of alcohol or substance use?

6. Will newer anxiolytic drugs prove to be safe, effective, and non-addicting in elderly patients?

COMMENTARY

1. Most of the studies of benzodiazepines are not conducted in a population of elderly patients but in mixed age populations.
2. Actual prevalence rates of long term benzodiazepine use in the elderly is small and limited to a subpopulation with physical illness and depression.
3. There is not a large amount of outpatient benzodiazepine use in the elderly but there is a much higher long term use rate in inpatients and residential facilities.
4. In the elderly, anxiolytic benzodiazepines are also used for hypnotic purposes. They may also be used for muscle relaxant purposes, but data suggest that neither benzodiazepine nor meprobamate are impressive muscle relaxants.
5. Older patients especially inpatients and nursing home residents may be reluctant to discontinue benzodiazepines. This may represent a psychological as well as a physical dependence.
6. The toxicity of all anxiolytic drugs increases with age.

REFERENCES

Alexander, F., & Duff, R. W. (1988). Social interaction and alcohol use in retirement communities. *The Gerontologist, 28,* 632–636.
American Psychiatric Association (1987). *Diagnostic and statistical manual for mental disorders* (3rd edition, revised). Washington, D.C.: Author.
Atkinson, Jr., J. H., & Schuckit, M.A. (1983). Geriatric alcohol and drug misuse and abuse. *Advances in Substance Abuse, 3,* 195–237.
Blazer, D. G. Epidemiology and clinical interface. This volume.
Ciraulo, D. A., Sands, B. F., & Shader, R. I. (1988). Critical review of liability for benzodiazepine abuse among alcoholics. *Am J Psychiatry, 145,* 1501–1506.
Dupree, L. W., Broskowski, H., & Schonfeld, L. (1989). The gerontology alcohol project: A behavioral treatment program for elderly alcohol abusers. *The Gerontologist, 24,* 520–516.

Hale, W. E., May, E. E., Moore, M. T., et al. (1988). Meprobamate use in the elderly—A report from the Dunedin program. *J Am Geriatr Soc, 36,* 1003–1005.

LaGreca, A. J., Akers, R. L., & Dwyer, J. W. (1988). Life events and alcohol behavior among older adults. *The Gerontologist, 28,* 552–558.

Meyers, A., Hingson, R., Mucatel, M., et al. (1982). Social and psychological correlates of problem drinking in old age. *J Am Geriatr Soc, 30,* 452–456.

Osborne, E. (1979). The elderly alcoholic. *J Pract Nursing, 34,* 25–26.

Regier, D. A., Boyd, J. H., Burke, Jr, J. D., et al. (1988). One-month prevalence of mental disorders in the United States—based on five epidemiologic catchment area sites. *Arch Gen Psychiatry, 45,* 977–986.

Ross, H. E., Glaser, F. B., & Germanson, T. (1988). The prevalence of psychiatric disorders in patients with alcohol and other drug problems. *Arch Gen Psychiatry, 45,* 1023–1031.

U.S. Bureau of the Census (1987). Statistical abstract of the United States. Washington, D.C.: U.S. Government Printing Office.

Weiss, K. J., & Rosenberg, D. J. (1985). Prevalence of anxiety disorder among alcoholics. *J Clin Psychiatry, 46,* 3–5.

Wilsnack, R. W., & Cheloha, R. (1987). Women's roles and problem drinking across the lifespan. *Social Problems, 34,* 231–248.

Neurobiologic and Pharmacokinetic Consequences of Aging to the Development of Anxiety and Its Pharmacological Treatment

Anxiety in the Elderly: Neurobiological and Clinical Interface

8

Trey Sunderland, Brian A. Lawlor,
Rick A. Martinez, and Susan E. Molchan

It is unlikely that there exists a single neurobiological substrate for anxiety in the elderly. This chapter will review the literature of human anxiety research as it relates to the classical neurotransmitter systems. The neurotransmitter changes associated with the aging brain will then be reviewed as they contribute to the development of anxiety, or increase the predisposition to becoming anxious in old age. Because of the paucity of biological studies of anxiety in older subjects, studies of anxiety in younger subjects and studies of aging itself have been combined (Tables 8.1-8.5).

ADRENERGIC SYSTEM IN ANXIETY AND AGING

The involvement of the sympathetic nervous system in the "fight or flight" response has been recognized for decades (Cannon, 1929) and it is now generally accepted that the midbrain locus coeruleus, containing close to half the brain's norepinephrine neurons, is a crucial mediator of this response

(Aston-Jones & Bloom, 1981; Simson & Weiss, 1988). Consequently, clinical researchers have used various peripheral measures of adrenergic function to determine the degree of adrenergic dysregulation in anxious patients. Data from studies of anxious young adults do not always correspond to studies in the elderly. Villacres and colleagues (1987) found normal norepinephrine but increased epinephrine levels in young adult panic disorder patients at rest. This finding contrasts with the discovery of increased plasma norepinephrine and normal epinephrine in normal older men (Raskind et al., 1988). Halbreich and colleagues (1987) also reported that the norepinephrine metabolite, 3-methoxy-4-hydroxyphenylglycol (MHPG), increases with age (Table 8.1). Two groups reported decreased α-adrenergic binding on the platelets of young panic patients (Nesse et al., 1984; Uhde et al., 1985). In aging studies, α-adrenergic responsiveness has been shown to be either decreased or normal (Scarpace, 1986: Supiano et al., 1987). β-adrenergic sites have been studied in peripheral lymphocytes, and once again, a discrepancy was found between anxiety and aging studies. Although Brown and colleagues (1988) showed decreased numbers of β-adrenergic sites in younger adult panic disorder patients, several studies in the elderly revealed a normal number of β-adrenergic sites but a decreased affinity or responsiveness of these sites to normal stimulation (Vestal et al., 1979; Feldman et al., 1984; Heinsimer & Keflkowitz, 1985).

Using a challenge study model designed to test the functional sensitivity of certain adrenergic systems, investigators have administered specific agents such as the α_2-adrenergic agonist, clonidine, or the α_2-antagonist, yohimbine. In two studies of clonidine in young adult panic disorder patients, a blunted growth hormone response was found in patients as compared to controls (Uhde et al., 1986) and a greater decrease in blood pressure and peripheral MHPG was found in patients with panic disorder (Charney et al., 1986). In a study of young versus older controls, Raskind and colleagues (1988) reported that clonidine caused decreased cerebrospinal fluid (CSF) norepinephrine levels in younger but not older subjects, suggesting a possible decreased responsivity with age. In a subset of young panic disorder patients, yohimbine challenge was associated with increased anxiety, blood pressure, and peripheral cortisol and MHPG, but similar results were not found in patients with generalized anxiety disorder, obsessive-compulsive disorder, depression, or schizophrenia (Charney et al., 1987; Heninger & Charney, 1988). To date, no studies have been published on yohimbine challenges in the elderly.

Autopsy studies of elderly subjects have revealed a decreased number of neurons in the locus coeruleus (Vijayashankar & Brody, 1979) and decreased norepinephrine content in many brain areas (McGeer, 1978, 1981). In addition, monoamine oxidase (type B) levels are known to increase with age as well as with some dementing illnesses (Oreland & Fowler, 1982), and MHPG has also been noted to increase in selected brain areas with age (Gottfries et al., 1979). Recently, Raskind and colleagues (1989) demonstrated increased norepinephrine levels in the CSF of older men, as compared to younger controls. Taken together, these studies of adrenergic functioning (plasma catecholamines, α_2- and β-receptors, monoamine oxidase, and locus coeruleus neuropathology) suggest an age-related decrease in the noradrenergic function that may make older people more susceptible to anxiety.

SEROTONERGIC SYSTEM IN ANXIETY AND AGING

Studies of the serotonergic system in various anxiety disorders have produced mixed results (Table 8.2). Using challenge paradigms with either intravenous (iv) tryptophan or iv m-chlorophenylpiperazine (m-CPP), a serotonergically active metabolite of trazodone, one group found no abnormality in acute prolactin, growth hormone, or cortisol responses in young adult panic disorder patients (Charney & Heninger, 1986a; Charney et al., 1987). However, another group also studying young adults found that oral challenges with m-CPP increased behavioral and neuroendocrine responses in panic disorder patients (Kahn et al., 1988a, b). Studies of peripheral serotonin markers in young adults are also confusing as one

Table 8.1 Studies of the Adrenergic System in Anxiety Patients and Aging Subjects

Adrenergic system	Anxiety studies		Aging studies	
Peripheral measures				
Plasma	Increased EPI but normal NE at rest	Villacres et al, 1987	Increased NE at rest in older men	Raskind et al., 1989
			Increased MHPG at rest in men and women	Halbreich et al., 1987
Platelet	Decreased alpha-adrenergic sites in PD	Nesse et al., 1984 Uhde et al., 1985	Decreased or normal responsiveness of alpha-adrenergic site	Scarpace, 1986 Supiano et al., 1987
Lymphocyte	Decreased β-adrenergic sites in PD	Brown et al., 1988	Normal β-adrenergic number but decreased affinity and responsiveness	Vestal et al., 1979 Feldman et al., 1984 Heinsimer & Kefkowitz, 1985
Challenge Studies				
Clonidine	Decreased GH Response in PD & AGOR Increased Drop in BP and MHPG in PD	Uhde et al., 1986 Charney & Heninger, 1986b	Decreased CSF NE in young but not older controls	Raskind et al. 1989
Yohimbine	Increased Anxiety, BP, MHPG, and Cortisol	Charney et al., 1987	—	—

Central Measures

Cerebrospinal Fluid	—		Increased CSF NE in older men	Raskind et al, 1988
Brain	—		Decreased locus coeruleus neurons	Vijayashankar & Brody, 1979
			Decreased NE content in many brain areas	McGeer 1978, 1981
			Increased MHPG in some brain areas	Gottfries et al, 1979
			Increased MAO-B content in most brain areas	Oreland & Fowler, 1982

AGOR: agoraphobia; BP: blood pressure; CSF: cerebrospinal fluid; EPI: epinephrine; GH: growth hormone; MAO: monoamine oxidase; MHPG: 3-methoxy-4-hydroxy-phenylglycol; NE: norepinephrine; PD: panic disorder; PRL: prolactin.

Table 8.2 Studies of the Serotonergic System in Anxiety Patients and Aging Subjects

Serotonergic system	Anxiety studies		Aging studies	
Peripheral measures				
Platelet	Decreased [3]IMI binding in AGOR	Lewis et al, 1985	Decreased or normal [3]IMI binding	Langer et al, 1980 Lewis & McChesney, 1985
	No change in [3]IMI binding in GAD or PD ± AGOR	Schneider et al, 1987 Innis et al., 1987	No change or increase in MAO levels with age	Murphy et al., 1976 Bridge et al., 1985
Challenge studies				
Tryptophan (iv)	Normal PRL response in PD	Charney & Heninger, 1986a	Decreased PRL response in older women	Heninger et al., 1984
m-CPP (iv)	Normal PRL, GH, & cortisol response in PD	Charney et al., 1987	Decreased behavioral but not neuroendocrine sensitivity in older controls	Lawlor et al., 1989
m-CPP (po)	Increased behavioral and cortisol response in PD	Kahn et al., 1988a,b	—	—
Fenfluramine (po)	—	—	Decreased PRL response with age	McBride et al., 1986

Central measures				
Cerebrospinal Fluid	—		Increased CSF 5-HIAA	Gottfries et al, 1971 Post et al, 1984
Brain 5-HT	—		Decreased or no change in 5-HT in selected brain areas	Meek et al, 1977 Gottfries et al, 1979
Brain 5-HT Receptors	—		Decreased 5-HT1 receptors in biopsy material Increased 5-HT2 receptors in autopsy material	Middlemiss et al, 1986 Mann et al, 1985
Brain MAO	—		Increased MAO-B in brain tissue	Robinson et al, 1977 Oreland & Gottfries, 1986
PET Scan	Possible increase in metabolism of right parahippocampal region in PD	Reiman et al. 1986	Decreased 5-HT2 binding in certain brain areas	Wong et al, 1984

AGOR: agoraphobia; CSF: cerebrospinal fluid; GAD: generalized anxiety disorder; GH: growth hormone; iv: intravenous; MAO: monoamine oxidase; m-CPP: m-chlorophenylpiperazine; PET: positron emission tomography; PD: panic disorder; po: by mouth; PRL: prolactin; [3]IMI tritiated imipramine; 5-HT: serotonin; 5-HIAA: 5-hydroxyindoleacetic acid.

group reported decreased [³]IMI binding in patients with agoraphobia (Lewis et al., 1985) and others found normal [³]IMI binding in patients with generalized anxiety disorder or panic disorder with or without agoraphobia (Schneider et al., 1987; Innis et al., 1987). A recent study using PET scans (Reiman et al., 1986) showed a possible increase in glucose metabolism in the right parahippocampal region of young adult panic disorder patients.

Studies of the serotonin functioning in the elderly show somewhat more consistent results. Challenge studies have revealed decreased behavioral or neuroendocrine responses to iv m-CPP and tryptophan, respectively (Heninger et al., 1984; Lawlor et al., 1989b). Peripheral measures of serotonin markers have been either normal or somewhat decreased (Murphy et al., 1976; Langer et al., 1980; Lewis & McChesney, 1985). Studies of central serotonin function in the elderly also revealed decreased or normal serotonin (5-HT) levels in various brain areas (Meek et al., 1977; Gottfries et al., 1979) as well as increased CSF 5-hydroxyindoleacetic acid levels (Gottfries et al., 1971; Post et al., 1984). 5-HT$_1$ receptor levels have been shown to be decreased in the elderly (Middlemiss et al., 1986), but conflicting results have been reported for 5-HT$_2$: increased 5-HT$_2$ receptors at autopsy (Mann et al., 1985) but decreased using PET scan serotonergic ligands (Wong et al., 1984).

CHOLINERGIC SYSTEM IN ANXIETY AND AGING

Few cholinergic studies have been published in the area of anxiety research (Table 8.3). Currently, the only two studies that relate to the area of anxiety research in the cholinergic system are studies on sleep. One study reveals normal rapid eye movement (REM) latency in patients with panic disorder and generalized anxiety disorder (Mellman et al., 1989), and the other demonstrates a worsening of behavior symptoms in panic disorder patients following sleep deprivation (Roy-Byrne et al., 1986a). Many aging studies, however, show changes in the cholinergic system. Studies of sleep in the elderly report

Table 8.3 Studies of the Cholinergic System in Anxiety Patients and Aging Subjects

Cholinergic system	Anxiety studies		Aging studies	
Sleep measures				
Sleep Architecture	Normal REM latency in PD & GAD	Mellman et al., 1989	Increased wakefulness, decreased SWS, and decreased REM latency with increasing age	Reynolds & Kupfer, 1987
Sleep Deprivation	Worsening of symptoms with sleep deprivation in PD	Roy-Byrne et al., 1986a	—	—
Challenge studies				
Scopolamine (iv)	—	—	Increased behavioral and cognitive sensitivity with age	Drachman, 1977; Sunderland et al., 1987
ACh Agonists	—	—	—	—
Brain Measures				
ACh Neurons	—	—	Decreased with age	Bowen, 1984; McGeer et al., 1984
CAT Levels	—	—	Decreased or normal	Bartus et al., 1982; Bowen, 1984
Receptors	—	—	Decreased, normal, or increased QNB binding; Decreased nicotinic sites with age	Yamamura, 1981; Flynn & Mash, 1986; Perry et al., 1987

ACh: acetylcholine; CAT: choline acetyltransferrase; GAD: generalized anxiety disorder; iv: intravenous; PD: panic disorder; PRL: prolactin; QNB: quinuclidinyl benzilate; REM: rapid eye movement (sleep); SWS: slow wave sleep.

decreased slow wave sleep, REM latency, and total wakeful-
ness with increasing age (Lawlor et al., 1989a). Furthermore,
the elderly have increased cognitive and behavioral sensitivity
to parenteral challenge with anticholinergic agents such as
scopolamine (Drachman, 1977; Sunderland et al., 1987). Centrally, cholinergic neurons and the synthetic enzyme, choline
acetyltransferase, are known to decrease with age (Bartus et
al., 1982; McGeer et al., 1984). It is more difficult, however, to
determine which receptor subtypes change with age. Studies
attempting to assess muscarinic binding with radiolabeled quinuclidinyl benzilate (QNB) have revealed increased, decreased,
or normal levels in the elderly (for review, see Yamumura,
1981). Other studies have shown nicotine binding to be consistently decreased with age (Flynn & Mash, 1986; Perry et al.,
1987).

GABAERGIC SYSTEM IN ANXIETY AND AGING

It is estimated that γ-aminobutyric acid (GABA), the major
centrally active inhibitory neurotransmitter in the central nervous system (CNS), is present in up to 30% of brain synapses
(Chase et al., 1976; Enna & Gallagher, 1983). As GABA and
benzodiazepine receptors are thought to be intricately connected around the chloride channel (Teicher, 1988), it is not
surprising that GABA neurotransmission is also closely involved in the biology of anxiety.

Benzodiazepines, the major class of antianxiety agents in use
today, are thought to work by enhancing the effects of GABA
on the transport of chloride across neuronal membranes (Paul
et al., 1986). Without intrinsic GABA transmission, the anti-
anxiety action of benzodiazepines is markedly diminished.
Thus, drugs, normal aging, or illness which alter GABA binding
may also affect the therapeutic potential of benzodiazepines.

As humans age, central GABA levels appear to decrease or
remain normal (McGeer & McGeer, 1976; Allen et al., 1983;
Bareggi et al., 1985); levels of the synthetic enzyme, glutamic
acid decarboxylase, also decrease (McGeer, 1981). With age,

GABA receptor levels also remain normal or are somewhat reduced (Allen et al., 1983; Komiskey, 1988) (Table 8.4). These findings are especially interesting because results from animal studies suggest that "stressors" are associated with decreased GABA receptor binding, specifically the $GABA_A$ receptor subtype.

Age-related changes in the GABAergic system may be responsible for the changes in clinical symptoms of the elderly and their increased sensitivity to drug treatment. For instance, studies in animals indicate that both GABA and benzodiazepine binding varies across time of day and that these differences are ag-related (Niles et al., 1988). These results suggest possible circadian variability in drug responsiveness across the age spectrum. Other studies suggest unequal changes in GABA and benzodiazepine receptors with age such that the ratio or function of these interconnected receptors differs in older subjects. As with the well-documented pharmacokinetic changes that alter exogenously administered drug effects (Greenblatt et al., 1982), all of these changes in the central GABA-benzodiazepine system point towards age-related variability in the expression and treatment of anxiety. If the various subtypes of anxiety disorders can, as suggested in a recent hypothesis (Gorman et al., 1989), be differentiated neuroanatomically, then more specific clinical, neuroimaging, and pharmacological studies with elderly patients as compared to younger patients may be of significant value in geriatric anxiety research.

NEUROENDOCRINE MARKERS
IN ANXIETY AND AGING STUDIES

As hormonal responses cannot always be easily attributed to a specific neurotransmitter system, we have grouped a number of neuroendocrine tests in our review of anxiety and aging studies (Table 8.5). Unlike depressed patients, young anxious patients do not have normal dexamethasone suppression (Bueno et al., 1984; Grunhaus et al., 1987) or any change in

Table 8.4 Studies of the GABAergic System in Anxiety Patients and Aging Subjects

GABAergic system	Anxiety studies		Aging studies	
Peripheral measures	—		No relationship between age and endogenous diazepam binding inhibitor	Barbaccia et al., 1986
Challenge studies	Increased anxiety following "inverse agonists" (i.e., β-CCE or FG-7142)	Dorow et al., 1983 Paul et al., 1986	—	—
	Decreased animal stress response following benzodiazepine antagonist (i.e., RO-15-1788)	Biggio, 1983	—	—
Central Measures GABA Neurons	—		Decreased or normal in selected brain areas	McGeer & McGeer, 1976 Spokes, 1979 Allen et al., 1983
GABA Levels	—		Decreased in frontal cortex and CSF	Rossor et al., 1984 Bareggi et al., 1985
GABA Receptors	Decreased GABA-A receptors following inescapable shock in animals	Biggio, 1983	Decreased or normal	Allen et al., 1983 Komiskey et al., 1988
Glutamic Acid Decarboxylase (GAD)	—		Decreased in thalamus	McGeer, 1981

β-CCE: β-carboline 3-carboxylate ethyl ester; CSF: cerebrospinal fluid; GABA: gamma-aminobutyric acid.

Table 8.5 Studies of Neuroendocrine Biological Markers in Anxious Patients and Aging Subjects

Biological Markers	Anxiety studies		Aging studies	
Neuroendocrine Markers				
Dexamethasone	Mostly normal in PD except when depression concurrent	Bueno et al., 1984 Grunhaus et al., 1987	No changes with age in normals	Tourigny-Rivard et al., 1981
Cortisol	No change in mean urinary free cortisol in PD, GAD, or social phobia	Rosenbaum et al., 1983 Stein & Uhde, 1988	Increased plasma cortisol with age	Davis et al., 1984
Growth Hormone	Blunted GH response to clonidine	Uhde et al., 1986	Decreased 24-h GH secretion	Zadik et al., 1985
			Blunted GH response to multiple challenge agents (i.e., clonidine, amphetamine, GHRF)	Veith & Raskind, 1988
			Decreased GH producing cells with age	Sun et al., 1984
Prolactin	Normal PRL response to m-CPP in PD	Charney et al., 1987	Normal PRL response to m-CPP	Lawlor et al., 1989
	Decreased PRL response to fenfluramine	McBride et al., 1986		
TSH	Abnormal (increased & decreased) TSH responses in subset of PD	Roy-Bryne et al., 1986b	Blunted TSH response to TRH in older men	Snyder & Utiger, 1972

DST: dexamethasone; GAD: generalized anxiety disorder; GH: growth hormone; GHRF: growth hormone releasing factor; m-CPP: m-chlorophenylpiperazine; PD: panic disorder; PRL: prolactin; TRH: thryotropin-releasing hormone; TSH: thyrotropin-stimulating hormone.

urinary-free cortisol, as compared to normal controls (Rosenbaum et al., 1983; Stein & Uhde, 1988). As noted previously,
anxiety patients have a blunted growth hormone response to
clonidine (Uhde et al., 1986) and a normal prolactin response to
m-CPP (Charney et al., 1987). Interestingly, the thyroid-
stimulating hormone (TSH) response to thyrotropin-releasing
hormone (TRH) has been shown to be either increased, decreased, or normal in subsets of panic disorder patients (Roy-
Byrne et al., 1986b; Stein & Uhde, 1988).

Studies of neuroendocrine function in the elderly reveal
somewhat different results. While plasma cortisol increases
with age (Davis et al., 1984), the response to dexamethasone
remains normal in older controls (Tourigny-Rivard et al., 1981).
In response to fenfluramine or clonidine, however, older subjects have a definite blunting of growth hormone and prolactin
(McBride et al., 1986; Veith and Raskind, 1988). However, these
results cannot be compared to results in younger subjects since
the number of cells producing growth hormones decreases
with age (Sun et al., 1984) and growth hormone secretion is
therefore lower in the elderly (Zadik et al., 1985). Contrary to
the findings of normal cortisol levels in older men following
dexamethasone, the same group shows a blunted TSH response when challenged with exogenous TRH (Snyder &
Utiger, 1972).

THE AGING BRAIN: BIOLOGICAL OVERLAP
BETWEEN ANXIETY AND AGING

One complication of any psychiatric study of the elderly is
the existence of at least two pathological conditions—the identified psychiatric difficulty (i.e., anxiety) and aging itself. Because the underlying brain substrate varies considerably with
increasing age, it is difficult to compare anxiety syndromes
from patients in different age groups. As seen in Table 8.6, there
is some biological similarity between the aging process and
anxiety. However, this overlap is limited and even misleading at

Table 8.6 Summary of Important Biological Markers in Studies of Anxious Patients and Aging Subjects

Summary	Anxiety disorders	Normal aging
Adrenergic functioning		
Brain content	—	Decrease
CSF levels	—	Increase
Platelet alpha sites/response	Decrease/?	?/Decrease or Normal
Lymphocyte beta sites/response	Decrease/—	—/Decrease
Plasma EPI/NE	Increase/Normal	Normal/Increase
Yohimbine response	Increase	—
Serotonin functioning		
Brain -5-HT content	—	Decrease or Normal
-MAO-B	—	Increase
-Receptors	—	Decrease
-Metabolism	Increase	Decrease
CSF 5-HIAA	—	Increase
Platelet [3]IMI	Decrease or Normal	Decrease or Normal
Challenge-Endocrine	Normal	Normal or Decrease
-Behavioral	Normal	Decrease
Cholinergic functioning		
Brain -ACh Neurons	—	Normal or Decrease
-CAT	—	Normal or Decrease
-Receptors	—	Normal or Decrease
Sleep Measures	Normal	Decrease
SCOP Challenge	—	Increase
Brain imaging		
rCBF	Increase	Normal
PET -glucose	Increase	Decrease
-5-HT2 binding	—	Decrease
Neuroendocrine Measures		
Cortisol (BL/DST)	Normal/Normal	Increase/Normal
Growth hormone (BL/CLON)	Normal/Decrease	Decrease/Decrease
Prolactin (BL/m-CPP)	Normal/Normal	Normal/Normal
TSH (BL/TRH)	?/Decrease	Normal/Decrease (men)

ACh: acetylcholine; BL: baseline; CAT: choline acetyltransferase; CLON: clonidine, CSF: cerebrospinal fluid; DST: dexamethasone; EPI: epinephrine; [3]IMI: tritiated imipramine; MAO: monoamine oxidase; m-CPP: m-chlorophenylpiperazine; NE: norepinephrine; PET: positron emission tomography; rCBF: regional cerebral blood flow; TRH: thyrotropin-releasing hormone; SCOP: scopolamine; 5-HT: serotonin; 5-HIAA: 5-hydroxyindoleacetic acid.

times. For instance, although adrenergic abnormalities exist in both anxiety and aging, plasma epinephrine is increased in young adults with anxiety disorders, and plasma norepinephrine is increased in normal aging. Similarly, the number of lymphocyte β-receptor sites are known to decrease in younger patients with anxiety disorders while it is the response of β-receptors that decreases in normal aging. Clear-cut differences also exist between the biology of aging and the anxiety of young adults. In younger patients with anxiety, glucose utilization and blood flow may increase, at least regionally, whereas older controls have decreased or normal values. In addition, serotonin function decreases across a host of measures in normal aging, while some serotonergic function increases and other functions decrease in anxiety disorders. Thus, unlike depression, in which the aging process does partially imitate the biology of depression (Veith & Raskind, 1988), there is relatively little overlap between normal aging and the moving diagnostic target of anxiety disorders.

FUTURE DIRECTIONS IN BIOLOGICAL ANXIETY RESEARCH WITH THE ELDERLY

When standing in the middle of unchartered territory, it is easy to suggest future directions. Such is the case for biological research concerning anxiety disorders in the elderly. So little is known about the phenomenology or biology of anxiety in older subjects, that almost any carefully done study will increase the knowledge in this field. Nonetheless, a few priorities are worth outlining. Above all, careful attention should be paid to the diagnostic criteria used in future epidemiological and pharmacological studies. Given the confusion in psychiatric nomenclature over the last two decades, this is no simple matter, especially since the geriatric population frequently suffers from numerous coexistent medical problems that can mimic or initiate anxiety symptoms.

Ideally, researchers should be able to diagnose homogeneous populations using universally accepted criteria. Without such specific clinical criteria, however, the response of patients to pharmacological challenge or chronic drug treatment itself may provide biological criteria for further classification of elderly anxious patients. These challenge approaches could include relatively selective adrenergic agents such as yohimbine and clonidine, serotonergic agents such as m-CPP, alaproclate, and metergoline, or cholinergic drugs such as nicotine, arecoline, scopolamine, and physostigmine. Furthermore, the GABA system has not yet been evaluated in the elderly, and carefully controlled challenge paradigms with GABA antagonists, inverse agonists, benzodiazepines, or even alcohol would greatly increase our knowledge in this area.

The emerging field of brain imaging has created many opportunities for future research in the elderly. PET studies with fluorodeoxyglucose have furthered the progress of metabolic brain mapping (Kuhl et al., 1984; Dastur, 1985; Reiman, 1988). in the future, exciting possibilities involve the use of radiolabeled PET and SPECT ligands. Specifically targeted at individual brain peptide and neurotransmitter systems, these ligands will enable researchers to compare various psychiatric conditions and to perform longitudinal follow-up of drug-induced state changes.

Thus, even if current clinical diagnostic criteria do not allow researchers to discriminate and subtype anxiety populations in the elderly, it is possible that future drug, neuroendocrine, and brain imaging studies will provide biological markers for this purpose. At the very least, these studies will help us obtain important biological information in what is now mostly an unexplored area of geriatric psychiatry.

COMMENTARY

1. The GABA system may not change with age. There is no change in the number of BZ-GABA receptors although there may be a change in the sensitivity of these receptors.

2. It is likely that anxiety is related to a number of neurotransmitter systems. Anxiety in the elderly and treatment of anxiety in the elderly may therefore depend on the balance and function among these neurotransmitter systems.

REFERENCES

Allen, S. L., Benton, J. S., Goodhardt, M. I., Haan, E. A., Sims, N. R., Smith, C. C. T., Spillane, J. A., Bowen, D. M., & Davison, A. N. (1983). Biochemical evidence of selective nerve cell changes in the normal aging human and rat brain. *J Neurochem 41*, 256–265.

Aston-Jones, G., & Bloom, E. E. (1981). Norepinephrine-containing locus coeruleus neurons in behaving rats exhibit pronounced response to non-noxious environmental stimuli. *J Neurosci, 1*, 887–900.

Barbaccia, M. L., Costa, E., Ferrero, P., Guidotti, A., Roy, A. Sunderland, T. Pickar, D., Paul, S. M., & Goodwin, F. K. (1986). Diazepam-binding inhibitor. A brain neuropeptide present in human spinal fluid: Studies in depression, schizophrenia, and Alzheimer's disease. *Arch Gen Psychiatry, 43*, 1143–1147.

Bareggi, S. R., Franceschi, M., & Smirne, S. (1985). Neurochemical findings in cerebrospinal fluid in Alzheimer's disease. In C. G. Gottfries (Ed.), *Normal aging, Alzheimer's disease, and senile dementia: Aspects on etiology, pathogenesis, diagnosis, and treatment* (pp. 203–212). Brussels: Editions de l'Universite de Bruxelles.

Bartus, R. T., Dean, R. L., Beer, B., & Lippa, A. S. (1982). The cholinergic hypothesis of geriatric memory dysfunction. *Science, 217*, 408–417.

Biggio, G. (1983). The action of stress, beta-carbolines, diazepam, and RO15-1788 on GABA receptors in the rat brain. In G. Biggio & E. Costa (Eds.), *Advances in biochemical psychopharmacology* (pp. 105–119). *Vol. 38*. New York: Raven Press.

Bowen, D. M. (1984). Cellular aging: Selective vulnerability of cholinergic neurones in human brain. In H. W. Sauer (Ed.), *Monographs in developmental biology. Vol. 17*. (pp. 42–59). Basel: S. Karger.

Bridge, T. P., Soldo, B. I., Phelps, B. H., Wise, C. D., Francak, M. J., &

Wyatt, R. J. (1985). Platelet monoamine oxidase activity: Demographic characteristics contribute to enzyme activity variability. *J Gerontol, 40,* 23–28.

Brown, S-L., Charney, D. S., Woods, S. W., Heninger, G. R., & Tallman, J. (1988). Lymphocyte β-adrenergic receptor binding in panic disorder. *Psychopharmacology, 94,* 24–28.

Bueno, J. A., Sabanes, F., Gascon, J., Gasto, C., & Salamero, M. (1984). Dexamethasone suppression test in patients with panic disorder and secondary depression. *Arch Gen Psychiatry, 41,* 723–724.

Cannon, W. B. (1929). *Bodily changes in pain, hunger, fear, and rage: An account of recent researches into the function of emotional excitement.* New York: D. Appleton and Company.

Charney, D. S., & Heninger, G. R. (1986a). Serotonin function in panic disorders: The effect of intravenous tryptophan in healthy subjects and patients with panic disorder before and during alprazolam treatment. *Arch Gen Psychiatry, 43,* 1059–1065.

Charney, D. S., & Heninger, G. R. (1986b). Abnormal regulation of noradrenergic function in panic disorders: Effects of clonidine in healthy subjects and patients with agoraphobia and panic disorder. *Arch Gen Psychiatry, 43,* 1042–1054.

Charney, D. S., Woods, S. W., Goodman, W. K., & Heninger, G. R. (1987). Serotonin function in anxiety: II. Effects of the serotonin agonist m-CPP in panic disorder patients and healthy subjects. *Psychopharmacology, 92,* 14–24.

Charney, D. S., Woods, S. W., Goodman, W. K., Heninger, G. R. (1987). Neurobiological mechanisms of panic anxiety: Biochemical and behavioral correlates of yohimbine-induced panic attacks. *Am J Psychiatry, 144,* 1030–1036.

Chase, T. N., Roberts, E., Tower, D. B. (1976). *GABA in nervous system function.* New York: Raven Press.

Dastur, D. K. (1985). Cerebral blood flow and metabolism in normal human aging, pathological aging, and senile dementia. *J Cereb Blood Flow Metab, 5,* 1–9.

Davis, K. L., Davis, B. M., Mathe, A. A., Mohs, R. C., Rothpearl, A. B., Levy, M. I., Gorman, L. K., & Berger, P. (1984). Age and the dexamethasone suppression test in depression. *Am J Psychiatry, 141,* 872–874.

Dorow, R. Horowski, R., Paschelke, G., & Amin, M. (1983). Severe anxiety induced by FG 7142, a beta-carboline ligand for benzodiazepine receptors. *Lancet, 2,* 98–99.

Drachman, D. A. (1977). Memory and cognitive function in man: Does the cholinergic system have a specific role? *Neurology, 27,* 783–790.

Enna, S.J., & Gallagher, J. P. (1983). Biochemical and electrophysiological characteristics of mammalian GABA receptors. *Int Rev Neurobiol, 24,* 181–212.

Feldman, R. D., Limbird, L. E., Nadeau, J., Robertson, D., & Wood, A. J. J. (1984). Alterations in leukocyte β-receptor affinity with aging. *N Eng J Med, 310,* 815–819.

Flynn, D. D., & Mash, D. C. (1986). Characterization of L-[³H]nicotine binding in human cerebral cortex: Comparison between Alzheimer's disease and the normal. *J Neurochem, 47,* 1948–1954.

Gorman, J. M., Liebowitz, M. R., Fyer, A. J., & Stein, J. (1989). A neuroanatomical hypothesis for panic disorder. *Am J Psychiatry, 146,* 148–161.

Gottfries, C. G., Adolfsson, R., Oreland, L., Roos, B. E., & Winblad, B. (1979). Monoamines and their metabolites and monoamine oxidase activity related to age and to some dementia disorders. In J. Crooks & I. H. Stevenson (Eds.), *Drugs and the elderly* (pp. 189–197). Baltimore: University of Park Press.

Gottfries, C. G., Gottfries, I., Johansson, B., Olsson, R., Persson, T., Roos, B-E., & Sjostrom, R. (1971). Acid monoamine metabolites in human cerebrospinal fluid and their relations to age and sex. *Neuropharmacology, 10,* 665–672.

Greenblatt, D. J., Sellers, E. M., & Shader, R. I. (1982). Drug disposition in old age. *N Eng J Med, 306,* 1081–1088.

Grunhaus, L., Flegel, P., Haskett, R. F., & Greden, J. F. (1987). Serial dexamethasone suppression tests in simultaneous panic and depressive disorders. *Biol Psychiatry, 22,* 332–338.

Halbreich, U., Sharpless, N., Asnis, G. M., Endicott, J., Goldstein, S., Vital-Herne, J., Eisenberg, J., Zander, K., Kang, B-J., Shindledecker, R., & Yeh, C-M. (1987). Afternoon continuous plasma levels of 3-methoxy-4-hydroxyphenylglycol and age. *Arch Gen Psychiatry, 44,* 804–812.

Heinsimer, J. A., & Kefkowitz, R. J. (1985). The impact of aging on adrenergic receptor function: Clinical and biochemical aspects. *J Am Geriatr Soc, 33,* 184–188.

Heninger, G. R., & Charney, D. S. (1988). Monoamine receptor systems and anxiety disorders. *Psychiatr Clin North Am, 11,* 309–326.

Heninger, G. R., Charney, D. S., & Sternberg, S. E. (1984). Serotonergic function in depression: Prolactin response to intravenous tryptophan in depressed patients and healthy subjects. *Arch Gen Psychiatry, 41*, 398–402.

Innis, R. B., Charney, D. S., & Heninger, G. R. (1987). Differential ³H-imipramine platelet binding in patients with panic disorder and depression. *Psychiatry Res, 21*, 33–41.

Jefferson, J. W. (1988). Biologic systems and their relationship to anxiety. *Psychiatr Clin North Am, 11*, 463–472.

Kahn, R. S., Asnis, G. M., Wetzler, S. & Van Praag, H. M. (1988a). Neuroendocrine evidence for serotonin receptor hypersensitivity in panic disorder. *Psychopharmacology, 96*, 360–364.

Kahn, R. S., Wetzler, S., Van Praag, H. M., Asnis, G. M., Strauman, T. (1988b). Behavioral indications for serotonin receptor hypersensitivity in panic disorder. *Psychiatry Res, 25*, 101–104.

Komiskey, H. L., Raemont, L. M., & Mundinger, K. L. (1988). Aging: Modulation of GABA$_A$ binding sites by ethanol and diazepam. *Brain Res, 458*, 37–44.

Kuhl, D. E., Metter, E. J., Riege, W. H., & Hawkins, R. A. (1984). The effect of normal aging on patterns of local cerebral glucose utilization. *Ann Neurol*, Suppl. 15, S133–S137.

Langer, S. Z., Briley, M. S., Raisman, R. Henry, J. F., & Morselli, P. L. (1980). Specific ³H-imipramine binding in human platelets. *Arch Pharmacol, 313*, 189–194.

Lawlor, B. A., Newhouse, P. A., Balkin, T. J., Molchan, S. E., Mellow, A. M., Murphy, D. L., & Sunderland, T. (1989a). A preliminary study of the effects of the serotonin agonist, m-chlorophenylpiperazine (m-CPP), on sleep architecture and behavior in healthy volunteers. *Biol Psychiatry* (Submitted).

Lawlor, B. A., Sunderland, T. Hill, J. L., Mellow, A. M., Molchan, S. E., Mueller, E. A., Jacobsen, E. M., & Murphy, D. L. (1989b). Evidence for a decline with age in behavioral responsivity to the serotonin agonist, m-chlorophenylpiperazine, in healthy human subjects. *Psychiatry Res* (in press).

Lewis, D. A., & McChesney, C. (1985). Tritiated imipramine binding distinguishes among subtypes of depression. *Arch Gen Psychiatry, 42*, 485–488.

Lewis, D. A., Noyes, R., Coryell, W., & Clancy, J. (1985). Tritiated imipramine binding to platelets is decreased in patients with agoraphobia. *Psychiatry Res, 16*, 1–9.

Mann, J. J., Petito, C., Stanley, M., McBride, P. A., Chin J., & Philgene, A. (1985). Amine receptor binding and monoamine oxidase activity in postmortem human brain tissue: Effect of age, gender, and postmortem delay. In G. D. Burrows, T. R. Norman, & L. Dennerstein (Eds.), *Clinical and pharmacological studies in psychiatric disorders* (pp. 37–39). London: John Wiley and Co.

McBride, P. A., Kream, J., Anderson, G., Stanly, M., & Mann, J. J. (1986). Effect of age upon measures of central and peripheral serotonergic function in human subjects. *Society for Neuroscience Abstracts* 1313 (abstract).

McGeer, E. G. (1981). Neurotransmitter systems in aging and senile dementia. *Prog Neuropsychopharmacol, 5,* 435–445.

McGeer, E., & McGeer, P. L. (1976). Neurotransmitter metabolism in the aging brain. In R. D. Terry & S. Gershon (Eds.), *Neurobiology of aging. Aging, Vol. 3.* (pp. 389–403). New York: Raven Press, pp. 389–403.

McGeer, P. L., McGeer, E. G., Suzuki, J., Dolman, C. E., & Nagai, T. (1984). Aging, Alzheimer's disease, and the cholinergic system of the basal forebrain. *Neurology, 34,* 741–745.

Meek, J. L., Bertilsson, L., Cheney, D. L., Zsilla, G., & Costa, E. (1977). Aging-induced changes in acetylcholine and serotonin content of discrete brain nuclei. *J Gerontol, 32,* 129–131.

Mellman, T. A., & Uhde, T. W. (1989). Sleep in panic and generalized anxiety disorders. In J. C. Ballenger (Ed.), *Neurobiological aspects of panic disorder.* New York: Alan R. Liss (in press).

Middlemiss, D. N., Palmer, A. M., Edel, N., & Bowen, D. M. (1986). Binding of the novel serotonin agonist 8-hydroxy-2-(di-n-propylamino) tetralin in normal and Alzheimer brain. *J Neurochem, 46,* 993–996.

Niles, L. P., Pulido, O. M., & Pickering, D. S. (1988). Age-related changes in GABA and benzodiazepine receptor binding in rat brain are influenced by sampling time. *Prog Neuropsychopharmacol Biol Psychiatry, 12,* 337–344.

Oreland, L., & Fowler, C. (1982). Brain and platelet monoamine oxidase activities in relation to central monoaminergic activity in mice and man. In K. Kamijo, E. Usdin & T. Nagatsu (Eds.), *Monoamine Oxidase: Basic and clinical frontiers.* (pp. 312–320). Amsterdam: Excerpta Medria.

Oreland, L., & Gottfries, C-G. (1986). Brain and brain monoamine oxidase in aging and in dementia of Alzheimer's type. *Prog Neuropsychopharmacol Biol Psychiatry, 10,* 533–540.

Paul, S. M., Crawley, J. N., & Skolnick, P. (1986). The neurobiology of anxiety: The role of the GABA/benzodiazepine receptor complex. In P. A. Berger, & K. H. Brodie (Eds.), *American hand-*

book of psychiatry. Vol. 8. (pp. 581–596). New York: Basic Books.

Perry, E. K., Perry, R. H., Smith, C. J., Dick, D. J., Candy, I. M., Edwardson, J. A., Fairbairn, A., & Blessed, G. (1987). Nicotinic receptor abnormalities in Alzheimer's and Parkinson's diseases. *J Neurol Neurosurg Psychiatry, 50,* 806–809.

Post, R. M., Ballenger, J. C., & Goodwin, F. K. (1984). Cerebrospinal fluid studies of neurotransmitter function in manic and depressive illness. In R. M. Post & J. C. Ballenger (Eds.), *Neurobiology of mood disorders.* (pp. 685–717). Baltimore: Williams and Wilkins.

Raskind, M. A., Peskind, E. R., Veith, R. C., Beard, J. C., Gumbrecht, G., & Halter, J. B. (1988). Increased plasma and cerebrospinal fluid norepinephrine in older men: Differential suppression by clonidine. *J Clin Endocrinol Metab, 66,* 438–443.

Reiman, E. M. (1988). The quest to establish the neural substrates of anxiety. *Psychiatr Clin North Am, 11,* 295–307.

Reiman, E. M., Raichle, M. E., Robins, E., Butler, F. K., Herscovitch, P., & Perlmutter, J. (1986). The application of positron emission tomography to the study of panic disorder. *Am J Psychiatry, 143,* 469–477.

Reynolds, C. F., & Kupfer, D. J. (1987). Sleep research in affective illness: State of the art circa 1987. *Sleep, 10,* 199–215.

Robinson, D. S., Sourkes, T. L., Nies, A., Harris, L.S., Spector, S., Bartlett, D.L. & Kaye, I. S. (1977). Monoamine metabolism in human brain. *Arch Gen Psychiatry, 34,* 89–92.

Rosenbaum, A. H., Schatzberg, A. F., Jost, F. A., Cross, P. D., Wells, L. A., Jiang, N. S., & Maruta, T., (1983). Urinary free cortisol levels in anxiety. *Psychosomatics, 24,* 835–837.

Rossor, M. N., Iversen, L. L., Reynolds, G. P., Mountjoy, C. Q., & Roth, M. (1984). Neurochemical characteristics of early and late onset types of Alzheimer's disease. *Br Med J, 288,* 961–964.

Roy-Byrne, P. P., Uhde, T. W., & Post, R. M. (1986a). Effects of one night's sleep deprivation on mood and behavior in panic disorder: Comparison with depressed patients and normal controls. *Arch Gen Psychiatry, 43,* 895–899.

Roy-Byrne, P. P., Uhde, T. W., Rubinow, D. R., & Post, R. M. (1986b). Reduced TSH and prolactin responses to TRH in patients with panic disorder. *Am J Psychiatry, 143,* 503–507.

Scarpace, P. J. (1986). Decreased α-adrenergic responsiveness during senescence. *Fed Proc, 45,* 51–54.

Schneider, L. S., Munjack, D., Severson, J. A., & Palmer, R. (1987): Platelet [³H]imipramine binding in generalized anxiety disorder, panic disorder, and agoraphobia with panic attacks. *Biol Psychiatry, 22,* 59–66.

Simson, P. E., & Weiss, J. M. (1988). Altered activity of locus coeruleus in an animal model of depression. *Neuropsychopharmacology, 1,* 287–295.

Snyder, P. J., & Utiger, R. D. (1972). Response to thyrotropin releasing hormone (TRH) in normal man. *J Clin Endocrinol Metab, 34,* 380–385.

Spokes, E. G. (1979). An analysis of factors influencing measurements of dopamine, noradrenaline, glutamate decarboxylase and choline acetylase in human postmortem brain tissue. *Brain, 102,* 333–346.

Stein, M. B., & Uhde, T. W. (1988). Panic disorder and major depression: A tale of two syndromes. *Psychiatr Clin North Am, 11,* 441–461.

Sun, Y. K., Xi, Y. P., Fenoglio, C. M., Pushparaj, N., O'Toole, K. M., Kledizik, G. S., Nette, E. G., & King, D. W. (1984). The effect of age on the number of pituitary cells immunoreactive to growth hormone and prolactin. *Hum Pathol, 15,* 169–180.

Sunderland, T., Tariot, P. N., Cohen, R. M., Weingartner, H., Mueller, E. A., & Murphy, D. L. (1987). Anticholinergic sensitivity in patients with dementia of the Alzheimer type and age-matched controls: A dose-response study. *Arch Gen Psychiatry, 44,* 418–426.

Supiano, M. A., Linares, O. A., Halter, J. B., Reno, K. M., & Rosen, S. G. (1987). Functional uncoupling of the platelet α_2-adrenergic receptor-adenylate cyclase complex in the elderly. *Clin Endocrinol Metab, 64,* 1160–1164.

Teicher, M. H. (1988). Biology of Anxiety. *Med Clin North Am, 72,* 791–814.

Tourigny-Rivard, M. F., Raskind, M., & Rivard, D. (1981). The dexamethasone suppression test in an elderly population. *Biol Psychiatry, 16,* 1177–1184.

Uhde, T. W., Boulenger, J-P., Roy-Byrne, P. P., Geraci, M. F., Vittone, B. J., Post, R. M. (1985). Longitudinal course of panic disorder: Clinical and biological considerations. *Prog Neuropsychopharmacol Biol Psychiatry, 9,* 39–51.

Uhde, T. W., Vittone, B. J., Siever, L. J., Kaye, W. H., & Post, R. M. (1986). Blunted growth hormone response to clonidine in panic disorder patients. *Biol Psychiatry, 21,* 1081–1085.

Veith, R. C., & Raskind, M. A. (1988). The neurobiology of aging: Does it predispose to depression? *Neurobiol Aging, 9*, 101–117.

Vestal, R. E., Wood, A. J. J., Shand, D. G. (1979). Reduced β-adrenoceptor sensitivity in the elderly. *Clin Pharmacol Ther, 26*, 181–186.

Vijayashankar, N., & Brody, H. (1979). A quantitative study of the pigmented neurons in the nuclei locus coeruleus and subcoeruleus in man as related to aging. *J Neuropathol Exp Neurol, 38*, 490–497.

Villacres, E. C., Hollifield, M., Katon, W. J., Wilkinson, C. W., & Veith, R. C. (1987). Sympathetic nervous system activity in panic disorder. *Psychiatry Res, 21*, 313–321.

Wong, D. F., Wagner, H. N., Dannals, R. F., Links, J. M., Frost, J. J., Ravert, H. T., Wilson, A. A., Rosenbaum, A. E., Gjedde, A., Douglass, K. H., Pentronis, J. D., Folstein, M. F., Toung, J. K. T., Burns, H. D., & Kuhar, J. J. (1984). Effects of age on dopamine and serotonin receptors measured by positron tomography in the living brain. *Science, 226*, 1393–1396.

Yamamura, H. I. (1981): Neurotransmitter receptor alterations in age-related disorders. In S. J. Enna, T. Samorajski, B. Beer (Eds.), *Brain neurotransmitters and receptors in aging and age-related disorders. Vol. 17.* (pp. 143–147). New York: Raven Press.

Zadik, Z., Chalew, S. A., McCarter, R. J., Meistats, M., & Kowarski, A. A. (1985). The influence of age on the 24-hour integrated concentration of growth hormone in normal individuals. *J Clin Endocrinol, 60*, 513–516.

Benzodiazepines in the Elderly: Pharmacokinetics and Drug Sensitivity

9

David J. Greenblatt and Richard I. Shader

Clinical experience and epidemiologic data suggest that elderly individuals are more sensitive to the central depressant effects of benzodiazepines. The Boston Collaborative Drug Surveillance Program evaluated factors influencing the frequency of adverse reactions to benzodiazepine derivatives occurring in hospitalized medical patients. Extensive data on the antianxiety agents chlordiazepoxide and diazepam, and on the hypnotic agents flurazepam and nitrazepam, demonstrated an increased frequency of unwanted central nervous system depression (evidenced mainly as drowsiness, confusion, ataxia, etc.) increased with increasing daily dosage (BCDSP, 1973; Greenblatt et al., 1977; Greenblatt & Allen, 1978). However, adverse reactions also increased in frequency with greater patient age, even after accounting for daily dosage. The studies of flurazepam and nitrazepam are of particular interest, in that the increased frequency of adverse reactions among the elderly was evident mainly at the highest daily doses; at low or

Supported in part by Grants MH-34223, AG-00106, and DA-05258 from the Department of Health and Human Services.

moderate doses, the difference between young and elderly individuals was not nearly as pronounced.

PHARMACOKINETIC COMPONENT

Alterations in drug distinction, elimination, and clearance have been the subject of numerous original research articles and reviews (Greenblatt et al., 1982b, 1986b; Schmucker, 1985; Vestal, 1982). Like many other classes of drugs, age may alter the pharmacokinetics of benzodiazepine derivatives. Although results are not uniformly consistent from study to study, several general conclusions can be stated. For benzodiazepine derivatives biotransformed by hepatic microsomal oxidative reactions (in particular, aliphatic hydroxylation or N-demethylation), old age is associated with reduced metabolic clearance (Table 9.1). In many studies, the age-related decrement in clearance has been more evident in men than in women. For benzodiazepines metabolized by glucuronide conjugation or by nitroreduction, minimal if any age-related changes in clearance are evident. The effect of age on hepatic metabolizing capacity for benzodiazepine derivatives is similar to that reported for many other classes of drugs (Greenblatt et al., 1982b, 1986b).

Table 9.1 Benzodiazepine Derivatives Whose Clearance May Be Impaired in Healthy Elderly Humans

chlordiazepoxide
diazepam
desmethyldiazepam
desalkylflurazepam
midazolam
triazolam
alprazolam
brotizolam

The consequences of altered benzodiazepine clearance depends on whether one refers to a single dose as opposed to a multiple dose treatment situation (Greenblatt & Koch-Weser, 1975; Greenblatt & Shader, 1985). In the case of single dose drug administration, the consequences in turn depend on whether the particular benzodiazepine is a "high clearance" or a "low clearance" compound (Wilkinson, 1987; Pond & Tozer, 1984). Most oxidized benzodiazepines (chlordiazepoxide, diazepam, desmethyldiazepam, alprazolam) have a hepatic clearance value considerably less than hepatic blood flow. As such, presystemic extraction is minimal, and absolute bioavailability after oral administration is close to 100%. Age-related alterations in hepatic clearance are evidenced mainly as a prolongation in half-life rather than increased peak serum or plasma concentrations (Figure 9.1). Assuming that the same plasma concentration-effect relationship holds in both young and elderly, one could anticipate that the maximum intensity of action of such a drug would not be altered in the elderly, but a prolonged duration of action might be possible. For "high extraction" compounds (such as triazolam and midazolam), reduced clearance in the elderly might lead to higher peak plasma concentrations, as well as possible prolongation of elimination half-life (Figure 9.2). As such, both the maximum intensity of action, as well as the duration of clinical action, might theoretically be prolonged in elderly as opposed to young individuals. We should emphasize, however, that altered pharmacokinetics have not been proven to be the cause of enhanced intensity and/or duration of benzodiazepine action that may occur following single doses in elderly persons.

During chronic administration, the principal concern is the extent of drug accumulation, quantitated as the steady-state serum or plasma drug concentration. Steady-state concentration is directly proportional to the dosing rate, and inversely proportional to clearance; accordingly, reduced clearance in the elderly implies increased accumulation as any given dosing rate. Increased accumulation, as a direct consequence of reduced clearance, has been reported in elderly male subjects during chronic administration of flurazepam (a precursor of

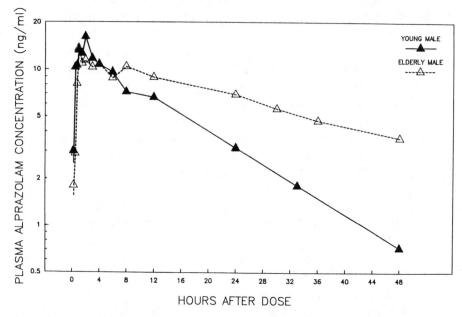

Figure 9.1 Plasma alprazolam concentrations following a single 1.0 mg oral dose in representative young and elderly volunteers. Clearance is reduced in the elderly subject. This is evident as a prolongation of elimination half-life, with no important change in peak plasma concentration.

the metabolite desaklylflurazepam) (Greenblatt et al., 1981), and of clobazam (Greenblatt et al., 1983). One could speculate that increased steady-state plasma concentrations in elderly persons might enhance the likelihood of toxicity, but again this has not been clearly documented.

Review articles and secondary sources commonly suggest that altered gastrointestinal physiology and function among elderly individuals may lead to a delay in the rate of drug absorption, and/or a reduction in the extent of drug absorption (Richey & Bender, 1977; Bender, 1968). These statements are not well substantiated by scientific evidence. Although the rate of gastric emptying may be somewhat delayed in the elderly (Evans et al.,

1981; Moore et al., 1983; Horowitz et al., 1984), absolute bioavailability studies have failed to demonstrate an age-related alteration either in the rate or extent of absorption of the benzodiazepines diazepam (Divoll et al., 1983), chlordiazepoxide (Greenblatt et al., 1989a), or lorazepam (Greenblatt et al., 1979). Likewise, age does not significantly influence the rate or extent of absorption of the analgesics aspirin (as a precursor of salicyclic acid) (Greenblatt et al., 1986a), acetaminophen (Divoll et al., 1982), or antipyrine (Greenblatt et al., 1988), nor of the antidepressant agent trazodone (Greenblatt et al., 1987).

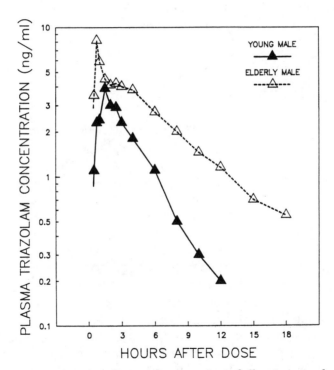

Figure 9.2 Plasma triazolam concentrations following single 0.5 mg oral dose in representative young and elderly volunteers. Clearance is reduced in the elderly subject. This is evident as a prolongation of half-life, as well as increased peak plasma concentrations.

A second important piece of misinformation quoted in some review articles relates to the interpretation of age-related alterations in drug protein binding. It is correct to state that plasma albumin concentrations tend to decline with age. Since benzodiazepines (as well as many other drugs) are bound to serum albumin to varying degrees, reduced concentrations of the binding protein may lead to an increased free fraction of drug in serum or plasma (Greenblatt et al., 1980, 1986b). The incorrect conclusion, however, is that this leads to a higher free drug concentration in serum or plasma, and therefore enhanced pharmacologic activity (Thompson et al., 1983). In fact, a change in free fraction does not lead to a change in free concentration at steady state, and therefore does not by itself change pharmacologic activity. This seemingly counterintuitive fact is discussed in detail elsewhere (Greenblatt et al., 1982a, 1986b).

THE PHARMACODYNAMIC COMPONENT

The pharmacodynamic "sensitivity" to benzodiazepines may be enhanced in elderly persons, regardless of an age-related change in pharmacokinetics. Pharmacodynamic sensitivity generally refers to the intensity of drug response at any specific plasma concentration, brain concentration, or receptor occupancy. Enhanced "sensitivity" implies increased intensity of drug action despite similar plasma or brain concentrations. An increase in "net" response to a benzodiazepine in an elderly person clearly may involve both a pharmacokinetic component (leading to higher receptor site concentrations) as well as a pharmacodynamic component (enhanced response at any given receptor site concentration).

Altered pharmacokinetics in the elderly may be studied without regard to pharmacodynamics. That is, one may study age-related alterations in drug distribution and clearance without a simultaneous attempt to measure drug response. The reverse, however, is not true—a real change in drug "sensitivity" cannot be validated without excluding or accounting for any age-related changes in plasma levels or pharmacokinetics.

Studies of altered benzodiazepine sensitivity in the elderly present important methodologic complexities, particularly in human studies. Young and elderly populations must be studied simultaneously to assure the availability of appropriate comparisons; since elderly men and elderly women are not necessarily pharmacokinetically comparable, each study must involve young and elderly populations of both men and women. Emotional and medical illness may potentially alter benzodiazepine sensitivity, and such diseases must be carefully excluded to assure that age itself, as opposed to age combined with disease, is the subject of study. Likewise, coadministration or abuse of other drugs which could alter kinetics and drug sensitivity must also be excluded. Measures of pharmacodynamic outcome must be carefully selected. Outcome measures must be chosen from a group of largely subjective variables which are potentially responsive to the study setting, practice effects, or other nonspecific influences; such measures must be ratings of anxiolytic or sedative effects, performance on a variety of psychological, motor, or intellectual tests, or the capacity for information acquisition and recall. More objective measures of response are being increasingly utilized; these include saccadic eye movement velocity, tremor, postural sway, or the electroencephalogram (Hommer et al., 1986; Greenblatt et al., 1989b). Regardless of the approach to quantitation, investigators must contend with the problem of appropriate interpretation of drug-related changes, (relative to those associated with placebo) in young and elderly groups whose baseline performance characteristics may differ substantially (Figure 9.3).

A number of clinical studies have involved the "naturalistic" setting of intravenous diazepam administration for the purpose of producing sedation prior to endoscopy. These studies demonstrate that a lower total dose, as well as a lower plasma concentration, is required to produce a given degree of sedation in elderly as opposed to young individuals (Reidenberg

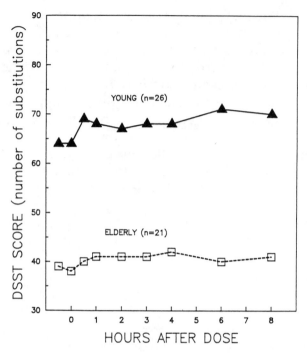

Figure 9.3 Scores on the Digit-Symbol Substitution Test (DSST) in a group of healthy young and elderly volunteers who took different parallel versions of the test, at multiple times before and after a single oral dose of placebo. Each point is the mean for all subjects at the corresponding time. Note that there was minimal change in performance over time in either group in response to placebo. However the significantly different intrinsic performance characteristics between groups could complicate the interpretation and comparison of changes occurring in reponse to active drug.

et al., 1978; Cook et al., 1984; Giles et al., 1978). The results are consistent with increased benzodiazepine "sensitivity" in the elderly; however, the results of these naturalistic studies are complicated by the heterogeneous nature of the study population. The response to diazepam is strongly influenced by such factors as previous use of benzodiazepines, other sedatives, or alcohol. A second type of study utilizes single "test" doses of benzodiazepines in healthy young and elderly volunteers, followed by multiple measurements of plasma concentration and pharmacodynamic effect. Not all studies of this type have involved adequate comparisons with young populations. Those studies that are well controlled and reasonably definitive demonstrate enhanced benzodiazepine sensitivity in elderly subjects that is either not explained, or only partially explained, by alterations in pharmacokinetics (Castleden et al., 1977; Swift et al., 1985a, 1985b; Pomara et al., 1984, 1985). Again, interpretation of these clinical results is complicated because of intrinsic baseline differences between young and elderly, either prior to dosage, or in response to placebo, such that appropriate approach to statistical analysis of drug associated changes is not entirely clear. Moreover, age-related differences in drug response may be quantitatively different, depending on the particular pharmacodynamic outcome. Finally, in both young and elderly groups there is evidence of "acute tolerance," in which drug-associated impairments return to baseline well before plasma concentrations have fallen to zero.

MECHANISM OF ALTERED SENSITIVITY

Experimental studies have attempted to elucidate the mechanism of altered benzodiazepine sensitivity in aging organisms. Animal studies have largely confirmed the clinical observation. CNS depression in aging animals (usually rodents) increases with the age of the animal despite similar doses and/or brain concentrations of the particular benzodiazepine. However, a number of in vitro studies of benzodiazepine receptors in the brain of aged as opposed to young animals consistently show minimal or no age-related change in the total number of active binding sites, or in the specific receptor affinity (Reeves & Schweizer, 1983; Pedigo et al., 1981; Meyers & Komiskey, 1985; Heusner & Bosmann, 1981; Komiskey & MacFarlan, 1983; Tsang et al., 1982; Miller et al., 1989). Our in vivo studies have likewise demonstrated a trend toward reduced benzodiazepine receptor affinity in aging as opposed to young animals. Thus,

findings available to date suggest that enhanced benzodiazepine sensitivity in the elderly is likely attributable to the coupling between receptor occupancy and subsequent cellular
function rather than to a change in receptor affinity or number
(Miller et al., 1989).

CONCLUSION

Understanding of the nature and mechanism of altered benzodiazepine response in the elderly should help clinicians anticipate
and cope with the problem, as well as facilitate the search for
drugs or drug classes with greater specificity of action. Limitations of our currently available research tools must be recognized. The applicability of experimental studies to the human
situation cannot be assumed unless specifically validated. Likewise human studies involving "contrived" laboratory tests of
physiologic measures do not necessarily apply to "real life" situations. Furthermore, the clinical problem of drug response in the
elderly frequently intersects with other factors that may influence drug kinetics and response, such as emotional and physical
disease, use or abuse of other prescription or over-the-counter
medications, over- or undernutrition, and other unknown genetic or environmental factors. Nonetheless, the available research tools are becoming more sophisticated, and substantive
contributions to the scientific and clinical discipline of pharma-
cogeriatrics are being made with increasing frequency.

COMMENTARY

1. Alcohol doesn't have significant influence on pharmacokinetics
although it has a clear influence on pharmacodynamics of benzodiazepines.
2. Benzodiazepines bind to albumin. As the binding protein decreases with age the fractional extent of binding increases. Thus, of
the total amount of benzodiazepine, there will be a higher fractional
amount that is unbound. However, the higher unbound fraction also

means a higher unbound concentration. When there is an increase in free fraction, there is a decrease in total concentration so that the free concentration doesn't change. The excess free concentrations metabolize and are distributed.

3. Theoretically, if you acutely displace a benzodiazepine from its binding site with a drug such as coumarin, you may get a temporary increase in effect of the benzodiazepine followed by rapid equilibrium. This is probably clinically insignificant.

4. The metabolic rate of benzodiazepines and other drugs may vary widely in nursing home populations. This is most likely due to day to day perturbations in diet and use of other drugs. When diet and other drugs are controlled, metabolism tends to stay the same.

5. Age related changes in hepatic blood flow play a minor role in drug metabolism, even for high extraction drugs. Usually one thinks that the pharmacokinetics of short half life benzodiazepines are unaffected by age. But these present data show that triazolam kinetics are affected by age. This is because the age affect is dependent on the metabolic pathway of the particular drug being studied and not dependent on its half life. Up until six years ago, the only short half life drugs available for use and study were oxazepam lorazepam and temazepam which all happen to be conjugated and thus were unaffected by age. Now we have triazolam and alprazolam which are both oxidized and their steady state levels are influenced by age even though they have a short half life.

6. There is a controversy whether the anterograde amnesia from triazolam is worse than for other benzodiazepines. This anterograde amnesia may be dose dependent rather than correlated with a specific drug.

7. All benzodiazepines are the same at the receptor site for alprazolam. At low brain concentrations, alprazolam produces hyperactivity and receptor up regulation. The doses in humans that produces this up regulation is approximately one milligram per day. This raises the question of whether or not this up regulation is related to the difficulty that some patients have in giving up the last milligram of alprazolam.

ACKNOWLEDGMENTS

We are grateful for the assistance of Lawrence G. Miller, Jamie G. Barnhill, Joseph M. Scavone, Jerold S. Harmatz, H. Friedman, and Hermann R. Ochs.

REFERENCES

Bender, A. D. (1968). Effects of age on intestinal absorption. Implications for drug absorption in the elderly. *J Amer Geriatr Soc, 16,* 1331–1339.

Boston Collaborative Drug Surveillance Program (1973). Clinical depression of the central nervous system due to diazepam and chlordiazepoxide in relation to cigarette smoking and age. *N Engl J Med, 288,* 277–280.

Castleden, C. M., George, C. F., Marcer, D., & Hallett, C. (1977). Increased sensitivity to nitrazepam in old age. *Brit Med J, 1,* 10–12.

Cook, P. J., Flanagan, R., James, I. M. (1984). Diazepam tolerance: Effect of age, regular sedation, and alcohol. *Brit Med J, 289,* 351–353.

Divoll, M., Ameer, B., Abernethy, D. R., & Greenblatt, D. J. (1982). Age does not alter acetaminophen absorption. *J Amer Ger Soc, 30,* 240–244.

Divoll, M., Greenblatt, D. I., Ochs, H. R., & Shader, R. I. (1983). Absolute bioavailability of oral and intramuscular diazepam: Effect of age and sex. *Anesthes Analges, 62,* 1–8.

Evans, M. A., Triggs, E. J., Cheung, M., Broe, G. A., & Creasey, H. (1981). Gastric emptying rate in the elderly: Implications for drug therapy. *J Amer Ger Soc, 29,* 201–205.

Giles, H. G., MacLeod, S. M., Wright, J. R., & Sellers, E. M. Influence of age and previous use on diazepam dosage required for endoscopy. *Can Med Assoc J, 118,* 513–514.

Greenblatt, D. J., Abernethy, D. R., Boxenbaum, H. G., Matlis, R., Ochs, H. R., Harmatz, J. S., Shader, R. I. (1986a). Influence of age, gender, and obsesity on salicylates kinetics following single doses of aspirin. *Arth Rheum, 29,* 971–980.

Greenblatt, D. J., Abernethy, D. R., & Shader, R. I. (1986). Pharmacokinetic aspects of drug therapy in the elderly. *Ther Drug Mon, 8,* 249–255.

Greenblatt, D. J., & Allen, M. D. (1978). Toxicity of nitrazepam in the elderly: A report from the Boston Collaborative Drug Surveillance Program. *Brit J Clin Pharmacol, 5,* 407–413.

Greenblatt, D. J., Allen, M. D., Harmatz, J. S., & Shader, R. I. (1980). Diazepam disposition determinants *Clin Pharmacol Ther, 27,* 301–312.

Greenblatt, D. J., Allen, M. D., Locniskar, A., Harmatz, J. S., & Shader,

R. I. (1979). Lorazepam kinetics in the elderly. *Clin Pharmacol Ther, 26,* 103–113.

Greenblatt, D. J., Allen, M. D., & Shader, R. I. (1977). Toxicity of high-dose flurazepam in the elderly. *Clin Pharmacol Ther, 21,* 355–361.

Greenblatt, D. J., Divoll, M. K., Abernethy, D. R., Ochs, H. R., Harmatz, J. S., & Shader, R. I. (in press, 1989a). Age and gender effects on chlordiazepoxide kinetics: Relation to antipyrine disposition. *Pharmacology.*

Greenblatt, D. J., Divoll, M. K., Harmatz, J. S., & Shaker, R. I. (1988). Antipyrine absorption and disposition in the elderly. *Pharmacology, 36,* 125–133.

Greenblatt, D. J., Divoll, M., Harmatz, J. S., MacLaughlin, D. S., & Shader, R. I. (1981). Kinetics and clinical effects of flurazepam in young and elderly noninsomniacs. *Clin Pharmacol Ther, 30,* 475–486.

Greenblatt, D. J., Divoll, M., Puri, S. K., Ho, I., Zinny, M. A. & Shader, R. I. (1983). Reduced single-dose clearance of clobazam in elderly men predicts increased multiple-dose accumulation. *Clin Pharmacokin, 8,* 83–94.

Greenblatt, D. J., Ehrenberg, B. L., Gunderman, J., Locniskar, A., Scavone, J. M., Harmatz, J. S., & Shader, R. I. (in press, 1989b). Pharmacokinetic and EEG study of intravenous diazepam, midazolam, and placebo. *Clin Pharmacol Ther.*

Greenblatt, D. J., Friedman, H., Burstein, E. S., Scavone, J. M., Blyden, G. T., Ochs, H. R., Miller, L. G., Harmatz, J. S., & Shader, R. I. Trazodone kinetics: Effect of age, gender, and obesity. *Clin Pharmacol Ther, 42,* 193–200.

Greenblatt, D. J., & Koch-Weser, J. (1975). Clinical pharmacokinetics. *N Engl J Med, 293,* 702–705, 964–970.

Greenblatt, D. J., Sellers, E. M., & Koch-Weser, J. (1982a). Importance of protein binding for the interpretation of serum or plasma drug concentrations. *J Clin Pharmacol, 22,* 259–263.

Greenblatt, D. J., Sellers, E. M., & Shader, R. I. (1926). Drug disposition in old age. *N Engl J Med, 306,* 1081–1088.

Greenblatt, D. J., & Shader, R. I., (1985). *Pharmacokinetics in clinical practice.* Philadelphia: W. B. Saunders.

Hommer, D. W., Matsuo, V., Wolkowitz, O., Chrousos, G., Greenblatt, D. J., Weingartner, H., & Paul, S. M. (1986). Benzodiazepine sensitivity in normal human subjects. *Arch Gen Psychiatry, 43,* 542–551.

Heusner, J. E., & Bostmann, H. B., (1981). GABA stimulation of ^{3}H-diazepam binding in aged mice. *Life Sci, 29*, 971–974.

Horowitz, M., Maddern, G. J., Chatterton, B. E., Collins, R. J., Harding, P. E., & Shearman, D. J. C. (1984). Changes in gastric emptying rates with age. *Clin Sci, 67*, 213–218.

Komiskey, H. L., & MacFarlan, M. F. (1983). Aging: Effect on neuronal and non-neuronal benzodiazepine binding sites. *Neurochem Res, 8*, 1135–1141.

Meyers, M. B., & Komiskey, H. L. (1985). Aging: Effect on the interaction of ethanol and pentobarbital with the benzodiazepine-GABA receptor-ionophore complex. *Brain Res, 343*, 262–267.

Miller, L. G., Greenblatt, D. J., Roy, R. B., & Shader, R. I. (1989). Alterations in $GABA_A$ receptor function in aged mice (abstract). *Clin Pharmacol Ther*, 45:135.

Moore, J. G., Tweedy, C., Christian, P. E., & Datz, F. L. (1983). Effect of age on gastric emptying of liquid solid meals in man. *Dig Dis Sci, 28*, 340–344.

Pedigo, N. W., Schoemaker, H., Morelli, M., McDougal, J. N., Malick, J. B., Burks, T. F., & Yamamura, H. I. (1981). Benzodiazepine receptor binding in young, mature and senescent rat brain and kidney. *Neurobiol Aging, 2*, 83–88.

Pomara, N., Stanley, B., Block, R., Berchou, R. C., Stanley, M., Greenblatt, D. J., Newton, R. E., & Gershon, S. (1985). Increased sensitivity of the elderly to the central depressant effects of diazepam. *J Clin Psychiatry, 46*, 185–187.

Pomara, N., Stanley, B., Block, R., Guido, J., Russ, D., Berchou, R., Stanley, M., Greenblatt, D. J., Newton, R. E., & Gershon, S. (1984). Adverse effects of single therapeutic doses of diazepam on performance in normal geriatric subjects: Relationship to plasma concentrations. *Psychopharmacology, 84*, 342–346.

Pond, S. M., & Tozer, T. N. (1984). First-pass elimination: Basic concepts and clinical consequences. *Clin Pharmacokin, 9*, 1–25.

Reeves, P. M., & Schweizer, M. P. (1983). Aging, diazepam exposure and benzodiazepine receptors in rat cortex. *Brain Res, 270*, 376–379.

Reidenberg, M. M., Levy, M., Warner, H., Coutinho, C. B., Schwartz, M. A., Yu, G., & Cheripko, J. (1978). Relationship between diazepam dose, plasma level, age, and central nervous system depression. *Clin Pharmacol Ther, 23*, 371–374.

Richey, D. P., & Bender, A. D. (1977). Pharmacokinetic consequences of aging. *Ann Rev Pharmacol Toxicol, 17*, 49–65.

Schmucker, D. L. (1985). Aging and drug disposition: An update. *Pharmacol Rev, 37,* 133–148.

Swift, C. G., Ewen, J. M., Clarke, P., & Stevenson, I. H. (1985a). Responsiveness to oral diazepam in the elderly: Relationship to total and free plasma concentrations. *Br J Clin Pharmacol, 20,* 111–118.

Swift, C. G., Swift, M. R., Ankier, S. I., Pidgen, A., & Robinson, J. (1985b). Single dose pharmacokinetics and pharmacodynamics of oral loprazolam in the elderly. *Br J Clin Pharmacol, 20,* 119–128.

Tsang, C. C., Speeg, K. V., & Wilkinson, G. R. (1982). Aging and benzodiazepine binding in the rat cerebral cortex. *Life Sci, 30,* 343–346.

Thompson, T. L., Moran, M. G., & Nies, A. S. (1983). Psychotropic drug use in the elderly. *N Engl J Med, 308,* 134–138, 194–199.

Vestal, R. E. (1982). Pharmacology and aging. *J Amer Ger Soc, 30,* 191–200.

Wilkinson, G. R. (1985). Clearance approaches in pharmacology. *Pharmacol Rev, 39,* 1–47.

Treatment of the Anxious Elderly Patient

IV

Pharmacologic Treatment of the Anxious Elderly Patient

10

Carl Salzman

Benzodiazepines are widely used drugs for the treatment of a variety of symptoms in older patients (Beers et al., 1988; Fancourt & Castleden, 1986; Nakra & Grossberg, 1986; Pinsker & Suljaga-Petchel, 1984; Salzman, 1988; Thompson et al., 1983; Tobias et al., 1988; Turnbull & Turnbull, 1985; Wilson, 1982). Studies indicate that benzodiazepine use among older patients ranges from 17% to nearly 50% (Table 10.1). Benzodiazepines are prescribed to older patients primarily for tension or as part of the treatment of a medical illness (Table 10.2). More than half of older patients who take benzodiazepines consider them to be helpful. The model long term benzodiazepine user is an older patient who suffers from medical illness, may be depressed as well as anxious, and makes frequent visits to physicians (Mellinger et al., 1984). According to one study, fifty percent of such patients take benzodiazepines regularly for many years, and take the same dose as originally prescribed and do not complain of frequent or troublesome side effects. 70% of older outpatients surveyed, however, take benzodiazepines only occasionally for symptomatic release although the vast majority of such older patients keep benzodiazepines available at home for such occasional use (Pinsker & Suljaga-Petchel, 1984).

Table 10.1 Use of Anxiolytics by Elderly

Data on elderly Benzodiazepine use	Date	Reference
40–50% of nursing home patients; 17% of outpatients	1986	Allen
36.5% elderly general practice patients	1988	Beers
33% of general hospital patients	1975	Salzman
24% of intermediate-care facility residents	1988	Lyndon
18.0% elderly living in community	1973	Parry

For many years, the psychiatric literature has offered recommendations for the use of benzodiazepines for the treatment of anxiety in the elderly. Most of these recommendations have been derived from clinical experience, especially with younger patients, extrapolation from research studies of younger patients, or from studies of nonsymptomatic elderly volunteers (Ayd, 1957, 1960; Beber, 1971; Crook, 1982; Dawson-Butterworth, 1970; Deberdt, 1977; DeLemos et al., 1965; Epstein, 1978; Exton-Smith, 1962, 1963; Goldstein, 1967; Halliday & Mihlay, 1966; Jones, 1962; Kirven & Montero, 1973; Lehmann & Ban, 1988; Merlis & Koepke, 1975; Salzman & Shader, 1974; Sanders, 1965; Tewfik et al., 1970; Welborn, 1961; Winkelman, 1971); only a relatively few research studies have been conducted in anxious elderly patients (Lehmann & Ban, 1969; Merlis &

Table 10.2 Benzodiazepines in Outpatients (Pinsker, 1984)

70% only use BZ prn
84% keep BZ at home
40–60% consider BZ helpful
50% still taking original dose
50% obtained prescription > 5 years earlier
only 12% had side effects
        Main Indications
        Tension
        Medical Problems

Koepke, 1975). This chapter will critically review part research studies as well as current recommendations for the use of benzodiazepines in older patients.

RESEARCH STUDIES

Despite the more than 25 year availability of benzodiaze-pines for the treatment of anxious elderly patients, there are relatively few research studies conducted that examine the therapeutic effect of these drugs for this specific population. A summary of these studies available in the English language literature are presented in Table 10.3. For benzodiazepines, there are only 19 studies comprising a total of approximately 1100 patients, although there are numerous studies of benzo-diazepine effects in mixed age populations many of which include some older patients. Studies of drugs specifically la-beled as antianxiety agents and given only for anxiety, to el-derly patients are shown in Tables 10.4a–d and 10.5. Many of these research studies are seriously flawed and would not meet contemporary criteria for research design and methodology if conducted today, so that the clinical usefulness of therapeutic recommendations that are based on these studies must be questioned. For example, outcome criteria varied from study to study as did duration of benzodiazepine treatment. Concom-itant drug treatment usually was not controlled, nor were sub-jects matched or stratified according to the presence or ab-sence of medical/psychiatric illness. The actual antianxiety effect of drugs when given to older patients was rarely de-

Table 10.3 Research Studies of Drugs Used to Treat Anxious Elderly Patients

Total # of Studies	19
Total # of Patients (approx)	1100
# of PBO Controlled Studies	6
# of Comparable Studies	7

Table 10.4a Benzodiazepine Studies in the Elderly: CHLORDIAZEPOXIDE

Author	N	Age	Drugs & dose	Duration of RX	Dependent variables	Results
Jones 1962	25	59–92	30–40 mg		Case hx	4 case hx of elderly presented excellent reduction of serious agitation; anxiety not mentioned
Goldstein 1967	43	66–95	CDX 20–45 vs tybamate 1000–4000	6 wks	Clyde Mood Scale	CDX better for anxiety; more sedating
Stotsky 1972	63		20 mg CDX vs 60 mg butisol	14 days		Both drugs effective, CDX less efficacious
Beber 1971	63 inpts	68–90	CDX 40 vs perphenazine/ amitriptyline 2/10	8 wks crossover	Global Ratings	Both drugs effective; higher side effects with CDX 74% 45% dizzy; 25% light-headed; 31% excited

Table 10.4b DIAZEPAM

Author	N	Age	Drugs & dose	Duration of RX	Dependent variables	Results
Lynch 1981	35	60–81	10 mg oral vs 10 mg suppository	7 nights	Modified HAM-A; Interview	Both DZ preparations very effective; no differences between preparations. No differences in blood levels. Slightly more sedation with suppository.
Kirven 1973	56	"geriatric"	DZ 9 thioridazine 38.9	4 wks	HAM-A Nosie	Thioridazine better for control of behavior sx of "senility." DZ better for insomnia, depressed mood, agitation, and prevention of cognitive function.
DeLemos 1965	50	organic brain syndrome	DZ 7.5 vs PBO	8 wks	Nurses' Ratings	Better than PBO for anxiety and hyperactivity.
Covington 1975	40	"senile"	DZ $\bar{x}$ 7.2 thioridazine $\bar{x}$ 32.9	4 wks	HAM-A Noise	DZ not as good for organic symptoms but better for those who are "tense" without being agitated and confused.
Chesrow 1962	58	41–88 mixed dx	DZ 3 mg vs DZ 6 mg	6 mths	Clinical Evaluation	16/24 patients with "anxiety" reaction. DZ produced marked improvement; moderate improvement.

Table 10.4c LORAZEPAM

Author	N	Age	Drugs & dose	Duration of RX	Dependent variables	Results
Ancill 1987	20 inpts	67–91 $\bar{x}$ 78	LZ 3.8/day	18 wks	Clinical Assessment of chart	Retrospective review of side effects—over sedation 19/20 amnestic syndroms 18/20 confusion 14/20 ataxia 10/20 depression 8/20

Table 10.4d OXAZEPAM

Author	N	Age	Drugs & dose	Duration of RX	Dependent variables	Results
Chesrow 1965	148 Hospitalized Organic	"geriatric"	OX 20–50 vs CDX 10–50 vs PBO	26 wks	Global Rating	OX CDX for global improvement; both better than PBO
Koepke 1982	220 outpts	67.5	OX 30 vs PBO	4 wks	TMAS; HAM-A Hopkins Checklist Global	OX significantly greater decrease in anxiety, tension; very few side effects
Sanders 1965	96 inpts	79	OX 20–90 vs PBO	8 wks	Physicians Nurses Global	OX significantly superior to PBO, with mild to moderate drowsiness
Tewfik 1970	42 inpts	73	OX 30 mg vs haloperidol, thioridazine tybamate, chlorpromazine PBO	36 wks	Nurses' Global Ratings	All effective in controlling behavior
Halliday 1966	inpts ("schiz. & organic")	"aged"	OX 40–60 PBO	14 wks	BPRS Global	Patients who had previous medication (not specified) showed "significant improvement with OX

Table 10.5 Buspirone

Author	N	Age	Drugs & dose	Duration of RX	Dependent variables	Results
Levine 1989	41	80+	15 mg	4 wks	HAM-A Global	80% of octogenarians improved; mild and infrequent side effects.
Napoliello 1986	677 outpts	60–66	20 mg	28 days	HAM-A	Effective antianxiety; 10% worsened predominant side effects: dizziness, headache, sleep disturbance, GI upset.
Singh 1988	12	66–75	5–30	4 wks	HAM-A POMS Lipman & Rickels	Average therapeutic dose 20 mg (dose finding study). No muscle relaxant properties. Marked improvement in anxiety, loss of tension.
Robinson 1988	605	$\bar{x}$ 70.8	15 mg	4 wks	HAM-A Physician Global	Up to 65% reduction in HAM-A by 4 wks 41% experienced side effects; mainly dizziness, GI upset, sleeplessness, headache, and vomiting.

scribed in detail and often was based on a single global rating. Many studies included younger patients and rarely made a distinction between drug effect in the old patients verses younger patients. The most serious methodological flaw in nearly all of these studies, however, was the inappropriate diagnosis of the patients included in the research sample. There were four specific categories of diagnostic confusion (Table 10.6):

1. In nearly all of the studies, benzodiazepine anti-anxiety agents were given to elderly patients in hospitals or in nursing homes for the treatment of behavioral disruption, agitation, and restlessness secondary to organic mental disturbance (i.e., dementia or psychosis). The term "anxiety" in these studies, therefore, was used to denote an objective state of restlessness, rather than to describe the more typical subjective affective state of anxiety as experienced in younger adults.

2. Unlike typical anxious outpatients, many elderly research study subjects were verbally unable to describe their anxiety symptoms, or were not asked to do so. There has been only one outpatient study of anxious but healthy elderly patients who were able to report changes in their subjective experience of anxiety (Koepke et al., 1982).

3. In a similar fashion, most studies did not discriminate between acute onset of anxiety versus chronic ongoing anxiety, and, in no study was there a discussion of the etiology of the anxiety, time of its onset, or its duration. Thus, there was no distinction between anxiety as a reaction to a recent acute stress, versus anxiety that was part of an ongoing and long standing psychiatric disturbance.

4. Lastly, there was no consideration of anxiety as either a primary disorder, or as a secondary phenomenon related to ongoing physical illness. Given the high frequency of organic mental impairment and

Table 10.6 Methodologic Flaws in Anxiolytic Research

Diagnostic Confusion in Research Studies

Agitation vs Anxiety
Inpatient vs Outpatient
Acute vs Chronic Symptoms
Primary vs Secondary Symptoms

physical illness in these patients, one might assume that "anxiety" as a target symptom may have been actually either part of another disturbance or a secondary byproduct of it in some older patients.

Some of the recent clinical recommendations are summarized in Table 10.7.

In summary, there has been a lack of controlled research studies of medications used to treat anxiety in the elderly. The concept of anxiety itself has been poorly defined, varied from study to study, and in virtually all cases would not correspond to the concept of anxiety either as defined either by contemporary research or clinical diagnostic criteria. In many of the studies, anxiety was actually behavioral agitation rather than an inner subjective state of apprehension and dread.

It seems apparent, therefore, that recommendations regarding the clinical use of anti-anxiety drugs in elderly patients, should not be based on these few, inadequate studies. Indeed, most of the numerous recommendations regarding benzodiazepine prescription to elderly outpatients, rarely cite these studies as support for therapeutic use recommendations.

On what bases have the clinical recommendations for anxiolytic use been derived? Guidelines for benzodiazepine prescription to older patients have been derived from three other sources: 1. Studies of anxiolytics in young adult patients; 2. Studies of pharmacokinetic parameters of anxiolytics in the elderly; 3. Studies of anxiolytic toxicity in the elderly.

As with many recommendations for the use of psychotropic drugs in older patients, the primary source of clinical benzodiazepine use is derived from experience with younger adult patients. Since the introduction of benzodiazepines into medicine, it has been assumed that older patients respond similarly to younger adults, although to lower doses. Older patients are more sensitive to benzodiazepines (Carskadon et al., 1982; Cutler & Narang, 1984; Fancourt & Castleden, 1986; Salzman, 1989a) but there is no qualitative difference in therapeutic effect between older and younger adult patients. Certain side effects (see below) are more common in the elderly (Ray et al., 1987; Spiers et al., 1986).

Table 10.7 Recent Clinical Suggestions for Using Antianxiety Agents in the Elderly

Allen 1986	Use low dose; short half-life benzodiazepines may produce memory loss, confusion, ataxia, sedation
Cutler 1984	Reduce benzodiazepine dose by 50–75% of recommended dose for young and middle-aged adults
Fancourt 1986	Limit benzodiazepine use to 4 weeks
Hershey 1988	Recommends lorazepam and alprazolam as 1st choice; oxazepam 2nd. Tolerance may develop to alprazolam
Jenike 1983	Use lower starting dose of benzodiazepines
Kanowski 1985	Short-term benzodiazepine use only; may cause dependency and impair alertness, coordination
Larson 1987	Cognitive impairment especially likely with long half-life benzodiazepines
Nakra 1986	Only short-term anti-anxiety use; elderly liable to prolong drug use; use dose $1/3$–$1/2$ of younger adult dose
Petrie 1983	Short half-life benzodiazepines are preferred
Sallis 1982	Hazards of anxiolytic drugs outweigh small therapeutic benefit and do not justify their routine use in elderly
Salzman 1989a,c	Concern expressed regarding overuse of benzodiazepines and cognitive toxicity in elderly
Shader 1982	Risk of anxiolytic use increased because of physical illness and polypharmacy; must balance potential risk vs potential therapeutic effect
Thompson 1983	Need for reduced doses of benzodiazepines, also use increased dose intervals for long half-life benzodiazepines; do not use with depression; benzodiazepines may worsen symptoms of mild or subclinical dementia
Tobias 1988	Short half-life benzodiazepines preferred
Turnbull 1986	Short half-life benzodiazepines preferred

Extensive studies of pharmacokinetics of benzodiazepines in the elderly have provided a second major source of prescribing information for clinicians. These studies have indicated that older patients differ from younger adults in pharmacologic disposition of benzodiazepines. In the elderly, the metabolism of long half-life benzodiazepines is impaired with age leading to prolonged elimination half-life. However, the normal aging process has no significant impact on short half-life benzodiazepine pharmacokinetics (Bareggi et al., 1986; Greenblatt et al., 1978, 1981; Kraus et al., 1978; Roberts et al., 1978).

The third major source of prescribing guidelines for the elderly comes indirectly from studies of anxiolytic toxicity in the elderly. Impairment in three categories of functioning is common when therapeutic doses of benzodiazepines are given to older patients, either acutely, or on a chronic maintenance basis. These three categories of impairment are: 1. decreased arousal (sedation) (Ancill et al., 1987); 2. reduced psychomotor speed and accuracy (Salzman, 1989c) and 3. impaired attention and short term recall (Larson et al., 1987; Pomara et al., 1984, 1985).

In summary, anxiolytic treatment of elderly patients is not based on research studies of specific drug effect in this patient population. Rather, prescribing recommendations have gradually accumulated from sources other inducing anecdotal and clinically based experience and studies of pharmacokinetics and toxicity in the elderly. Together, these studies indicate that although benzodiazepines are effective in older anxious patients, they may have a prolonged effect and may be more toxic even at therapeutic doses.

CLINICAL FACTORS INFLUENCING
THE TREATMENT OF ANXIETY IN THE ELDERLY

The decision to treat pharmacologically the anxious older patients depends on an appraisal of the severity of the anxiety symptoms, and the degree to which they interfere with function. In the elderly, as in younger adult patients, anxiety may interfere with social and interpersonal activity in the older patient resulting in a worsening of cognitive function. Anxiety in the elderly may also exacerbate physical illnesses and may be an unrecognized consequence of medical disorder. In the evaluation of the anxious elderly patient, therefore, the first task is to appraise the impact of the anxiety symptoms on social and emotional functioning or on the severity of a coexisting physical illness. Assuming that the elderly patient's anxiety symptoms are interfering with one or more of these functions, then the second clinical task is to weigh the severity of these symptoms against the potential toxicity of any anxiolytic treatment.

Older patients, as a group, are more sensitive to the potential toxicity of anxiolytic drugs. There are four factors that may predispose the older patient to this increased toxicity. These are age, comorbidity, polypharmacy, and reduced drug taking compliance.

1. *Age.* Effect of advanced age on the bio-availability and disposition of anxiolytic drugs are applicable. With advancing age, the central nervous system becomes more sensitive to the effects of anxiolytic drugs, so that older patients are more likely to develop central nervous system toxicity to anxiolytic doses that are nontoxic in younger adults. Hepatic metabolism and renal excretion also become less efficient so that some drugs accumulate and have prolonged pharmacological activity (Salzman, 1984b; Greenblatt, this volume). Drugs remain longer in the body and are likely to produce side effects. Although these generalizations apply to the elderly population as a group, persons over the age of 65 comprise a heterogeneous group in terms of physiologic status, emotional and physical functioning; being over the age of 65 does not guarantee a uniformity of drug response.

2. *Comorbidity.* Physical or emotional illness that exists concurrently with anxiety, may predispose the older patient to increased anxiolytic drug toxicity. For example, any central nervous system disorder (stroke, Parkinson's Disease, dementia) may increase central nervous system sensitivity to these drugs. Any disorder which compromises protein binding, hepatic metabolism, or renal clearance may also secondarily increase central nervous system sensitivity because of altered drug disposition.

3. *Polypharmacy.* The third factor that may increase toxicity of anxiolytic drugs in the elderly is the interaction of other medications taken concurrently by the older patient. On average, approximately one quarter of older persons living in the community take medication regularly, and older patients in a general hospital take an average of eight medications simultaneously (Salzman, 1984a). Many of these drugs, especially those with central nervous system properties may exacerbate the CNS toxicity of anxiolytic drugs. In the aging central nervous system with its presumed increased sensitivity to drug effects, toxic interactions with other medications may become evident even at doses that would not be considered toxic in younger adult patients. Some concurrent medications such as antidepressants, stimulants, and steroids may actually cause or exacerbate anxiety. There are also numerous pharmacokinetic interactions some of which may have toxic consequences in the elderly. Blood levels of benzodiazepine anxiolytics, for example, may be increased by concurrent treatment with cimetidine, or be reduced because of hepatic enzyme induction by other medication (e.g., steroids, anticonvulsants) (Salzman, 1984c).

4. *Compliance.* Noncompliance to drug prescribing schedules is frequent among older patients. Whether as a result of forgetfulness, confusion among different medications and dosing schedules, fearfulness, or personal beliefs about medications, older patients commonly take too much medication, or take too little. In either case over or under-dosing with anxiolytic drugs may lead to toxicity, or inadequate treatment of the symptoms of anxiety.

CLINICAL RECOMMENDATIONS

Recommendations for the Treatment of Anxiety with Benzodiazepines

Benzodiazepines are the anxiolytic of choice for most elderly patients and are frequently used both for the treatment of acute stressful situations, as well as for ongoing maintenance treatment. Older patients who take benzodiazepines for long periods of time, as a general rule, take approximately the dose that was originally prescribed, rarely escalate the dose and usually find the drugs helpful (Pinsker & Suljaga-Petchel, 1984). The predominant indication for prescription of the benzodiazepines to older patients is tension (88%); at least one quarter of older patients initially take benzodiazepines as part of treatment for a medical disorder.

Once the decision to prescribe an anxiolytic for an individual elderly patient has been made, an appropriate benzodiazepine must be selected from the many available. Short half-life benzodiazepines are usually recommended for older patients since they do not accumulate in the blood, are rapidly cleared from the circulation, and offer greater dosage flexibility. There are no data comparing the anxiolytic effect of the three short half-life benzodiazepines that are currently available: oxazepam, lorazepam, and alprazolam. In younger adults, rebound anxiety may be more intense following discontinuation of lorazepam or alprazolam, but there is no benzodiazepine discontinuance in the elderly.

There is a very large and consistent literature documenting the toxic effects of benzodiazepines in elderly patients. Unlike the treatment outcome studies, research on the toxic effect of drugs has been carefully controlled, and is, in most cases, methodologically sound. Four types of toxicity are common: sedation, cerebellar, psychomotor, and all cognitive, commonly occurring in older patients at doses lower than in younger adults (Salzman, 1989a). Although sedation may be helpful at bedtime, during the day can impair the functioning of older persons. Chronically sedated older people may become increasingly confused, belligerent and agitated. Cerebellar toxicity, manifested by ataxia, dysarthria, incoordination and unsteadiness obviously handicaps older people, many of whom already have tremor or difficulties with coordination. Psychomotor impairment in the older patient is characterized by slowed reaction time, diminished accuracy of motoric tasks, and impaired hand-eye coordination. Although there are limited data documenting the toxic effect of benzodiazepines on driving skills in the elderly, clinical experience suggest that older patients may be more susceptible to impairment of driving skills by benzodiazepines. Cognitive impairment is charac-

terized by an anterograde amnesia, diminished short-term recall, increased forgetfulness, and decreased attention. Such
cognitive impairment may resemble the early stages of a dementing illness, as well as normal age-related impairment in
cognitive function. Some cognitively impaired older patients
who take benzodiazepines for long periods of time, may actually be experiencing progressively increasing benzodiazepine
induced cognitive toxicity. The cognitive impairment, is reversible, however, so that discontinuance of benzodiazepines may
be associated with an improvement in memory, tension, and
concentration (Salzman 1989b).

The use of short half-life benzodiazepines predisposes the
older patient to risk of discontinuance symptoms. No data are
available to suggest that older patients, as a group, are more
likely than younger adults to develop discontinuance symptoms following abrupt termination of benzodiazepine use, nor
are there comparative data to suggest that the discontinuance
symptoms are more intense with older patients (Salzman,
1989c). However, clinical experience suggests that older patients may become frightened by some of their discontinuance
symptoms, and that at least some older patients continue to
take benzodiazepines on a chronic basis in order to avoid rebound and withdrawal symptoms.

Treatment of Anxiety With
Non-Benzodiazepine Medications

Several classes of drugs other than the benzodiazepines are
also used to treat anxiety in older patients, although they have
been used with less frequency and with less predictable response. These include buspirone, beta blockers, antidepressants, and neuroleptics. (A recent report also suggests that
meprobamate is still used by some elderly patients [Hale et al.,
1988]).

1. *Buspirone.* As indicated in Table 10.6, there are three studies
documenting the efficacy of buspirone in anxious elderly patients.
These research studies demonstrate therapeutic equivalence of this

drug with the benzodiazepines. The side effect profile suggests that there may be less sedation with buspirone. Clinical experience with buspirone in the elderly patient, however, is still relatively sparse so that recommendations regarding indications or contra-indications for its use are still tentative. Buspirone has been reported effective in controlling severe agitation and disruptive behavior and dementia; one case of tardive dyskinesia has been reported (Strauss, 1988).

2. *Beta blockers.* Information regarding the effects of beta blockers for the treatment of anxiety or disruptive behavior comes from its use with younger anxious patients, with mentally retarded patients, or among elderly patients with serious neurologic dysfunction. As with younger patients, therapeutic doses of beta blockers in older patients may substantially improve disruptive behavior, but there are no clinical trials of the use of beta blockers in anxious elderly outpatients who are otherwise free from neurologic, emotional, or physical disease (Salzman, 1989a). The effect of beta blockers in reducing autonomic symptoms associated with anxiety (e. g., sweating, tachycardia, palpitations) have also been recommended for older patients but there are no research data or even clinical reports of the use of benzodiazepines for the control of such symptoms in anxious elderly outpatients who are otherwise physically and neurologically well.

3. *Antidepressants.* Antidepressants have been reported effective in treating anxiety in young adult outpatients, and have demonstrated efficacy in the control of panic disorder as well. Like the beta blockers, however, there are neither research data nor published clinical experience using either tricyclic antidepressants or MAO inhibitors to treat anxiety in the elderly. Given the observation that anxiety and depression commonly co-exist in older patients, there may be a special use for antidepressants in such mixed affective symptom pictures. However, there are no data suggesting that antidepressants are especially useful for such patients, or more useful than single drug antianxiety treatments (e. g., with benzodiazepines). Antidepressants, probably due to their anticholinergic properties have been reported to impair cognitive function in patients, and it is likely that older patients would be more susceptible to this toxic effect because of age related reductions in CNS acetylcholine (Salzman, 1984c).

4. *Neuroleptics.* A review of research studies has documented the effectiveness of neuroleptics for the treatment of severe agitation in the elderly (Salzman, 1988). This agitation is usually secondary to central nervous system organic impairment such as dementia. However, the use of neuroleptics for the treatment of subjective anxiety states, especially in the elderly, has never been demonstrated. Given the potential toxicity of neuroleptics (extrapyramidal movements, anticholinergic, sedation), that neuroleptics should not play a major role in the treatment of anxious elderly patients.

CONCLUSIONS

Benzodiazepines are therapeutic for the treatment of symptoms of anxiety in older patients, and when anxiety compromises normal functioning of the older patient, the benefits of benzodiazepine treatment outweigh the potential toxicity. This is especially true when anxiety accompanies physical illness or other emotional disorders, or is a result of extreme stress due to life circumstances. Conversely, the toxicity of benzodiazepines may outweigh any potential benefits for the older patient whose symptoms are not severe, do not interfere with normal daily functioning, and which may be treated by nonpharmacologic means. When benzodiazepines are indicated, short half-life drugs are preferred, low doses are suggested, and treatment should be for brief periods.

Anxiety in the elderly may also be treated by drugs other than the benzodiazepines. Buspirone may be useful but more experience is needed; beta blockers may have limited usefulness in this population. The use of antidepressants, although sometimes recommended for younger adults, is less certain than the use of these other medications, and antidepressant toxicity may outweigh any potential therapeutic benefit. Neuroleptics are not recommended for the outpatient treatment of anxiety, but may be especially beneficial for inpatient treatment of severe agitation.

Despite the wide spread use of benzodiazepines in the elderly, there is limited research data upon which the foregoing clinical recommendations are based, and it is apparent that further controlled research studies would be helpful. Future research studies should take into consideration the following elements:

1. Diagnosis of Anxiety. Anxiety, as a subjective mood state, must not be confused with agitation, depression, hyper-adrenergic states, toxicity from medication, secondary consequences of other illness, or neurologic or organic impairment.

2. A placebo control must be included.

3. In addition to careful attention to dose, blood levels should be obtained whenever possible in order to correlate therapeutic and toxic effect with circulating drug levels.

4. Outcome criteria should be designed for the older anxious patient, and not simply be adapted from studies with younger adults.

5. Attention should be paid to the heterogeneity of the older age group. Very old anxious patients should be distinguished from the elderly. Studies of the effects of the antianxiety agents in the elderly should not be blended into studies of heterogeneous populations of all age groups.

6. Careful studies of discontinuance of benzodiazepines determining the minimum dose and duration of treatment necessary to produce dependence is very important.

7. Continuation of studies elucidating the toxicity of antianxiety agents in the elderly are critical, especially the long-term effects of anxiolytics on cognition and memory.

COMMENTARY

1. There are no data to suggest differences among benzodiazepines in terms of producing clinical toxicity. Accumulation of long half life benzodiazepines may predispose such toxicity. This is a result of the accumulation rather than any intrinsic specific property of the drug at the receptor site.

2. There is (and should be) substantial concern about possible increases in automobile accidents among elderly people who are taking benzodiazepines even at nontoxic therapeutic doses. Existing data cannot be used to draw conclusions for two reasons: a. One cannot assume that drivers (of any age) who receive benzodiazepines are comparable to drivers who do not receive benzodiazepines—the underlying disorder may compromise driving function; b. Although you cannot demonstrate a direct cause of benzodiazepines on auto accident in the elderly, they may represent an additional increased risk factor. The data in young people suggest that steady therapeutic doses of benzodiazepines do not impair driving skills. Driving is impaired, however, with acute increases in doses, with acute dosing in people who have not previously taken benzodiazepines, or when benzodiazepines are mixed with other sedative hypnotics such as alcohol. These findings, however, have not been specifically examined in the elderly. There may be a gradual deterioration in the driving skills of elderly long term users of therapeutic doses of benzodiazepines. One must ask whether such gradual deterioration is any different from changes in the driving skills over time of an elderly person who does not take benzodiazepines.

   3. Benzodiazepines have little role in the management of severe agitation and dementia. Short half life benzodiazepines may play a minor role in the management of these behavioral disorders. This is different than for treatment of the anxious outpatient elderly person for whom neuroleptics play no role and benzodiazepines are superior.

   4. Patterns of benzodiazepine discontinuance in the elderly do not differ from patterns in the young. However, older persons' subjective experience of discontinuance from benzodiazepines may be worse and may explain the older patients' greater reluctance to discontinue benzodiazepines than younger patients. There are few data for this however, and this information mostly comes through clinical observation.

   5. Rebound symptoms in the elderly, like those in younger patients, may be a significant clinical problem. In elderly patients who take triazolam for sleep, it is common to take a second triazolam four or five hours after the first dose has been taken. This may represent treatment of rebound symptoms due to rapidly declining blood levels, or may represent a psychologic dependence or both.

   6. Benzodiazepines are an increase risk in sleep apnea. There are no data to suggest whether this risk is worse in elderly than in young people.

REFERENCES

Allen, R. M. (1986). Tranquilizers and sedative/hypnotics: Appropriate use in the elderly. *Geriatrics, 41,* 75–88.

Ancill, R. J., Embury, G. D., MacEwan, G. W., et al. (1987). Lorazepam in the elderly—a retrospective study of side effects in 20 patients. *J of Psychopharm, 2,* 126–127.

Ayd, F. J. (1957). The treatment of anxiety, agitation, and excitement in the aged. A preliminary report on trilafon. *JAGS, 5*, 1–4.

Ayd, F. J. (1960). Tranquilizers and the ambulatory geriatric patient. *JAGS, 8*, 909–914.

Bareggi, S. R., Nielsen, N. P., Leva, S., et al. (1986). Age related multiple dose pharmacokinetics and anxiolytic effects of delorazepam (chlordesmethyldiazepam). *Int J Clin Pharm Res, 6*, 309–314.

Beber, C. R. (1971). Treating anxiety and depression in the elderly: A double blind crossover evaluation of two widely used tranquilizers. *JFMA, 58*, 35–38.

Beers, M., Avorn, J., Soumerai, S. B., et al. (1988). Psychoactive medication use in intermediate-care facility residents. *JAMA, 260*, 3016–3020.

Carskadon, M. A., Seidel, W. E., Greenblatt, D. J., et al. (1982). Daytime carryover of triazolam and flurazepam in elderly insomniacs. *Sleep, 5*, 361–371.

Chesrow, E. J., Kaplitz, S. E., Breme, J. T., et al. (1962). Use of a new benzodiazepine derivative (valium) in chronically ill and disturbed elderly patients. *JAGS, 10*, 667–670.

Chesrow, E. J., Kaplitz, S. E., Vetra, H., et al. (1965). Blind study of oxazepam in the management of geriatric patients with behavioral problems. *Clinical Medicine*, 1001–1005.

Covington, J. S. (1975). Alleviating agitation, apprehension, and related symptoms in geriatric patients: A double blind comparison of a phenothiazine and benzodiazepine. *Sthrn Med J, 68*, 719–724.

Crook, T. (1982). Diagnosis and treatment of mixed anxiety depression in the elderly. *J Clin Psychiatry, 43*, 35–43.

Cutler, N. R., & Narang, P. K. (1984). Implications of dosing tricyclic antidepressants and benzodiazepines in geriatrics. *Psychiat Clin of N Am, 7*, 845–861.

Dawson-Butterworth, K. (1970). The chemopsychotherapeutics of geriatric sedation. *JAGS, 17*, 97–114.

Deberdt, R. (1977). Oxazepam in the treatment of anxiety in children and the elderly. *ACTA Psychiatric Suppl., 274*, 104–110.

DeLemos, G. P., Clement, W. R., & Nickels, E. (1965). Effects of diazepam suspension in geriatric patients hospitalized for psychiatric illnesses. *JAGS, 13*, 355–359.

Epstein, L. J. (1978). Anxiolytics antidepressants and neuroleptics in the treatment of geriatric patients. In M. A. Lipton, A. DiMascio, and K. F. Killam (Eds.), *Psychopharmacology: A generation of progress*. New York: Raven Press.

Exton-Smith, A. N. (1962). Tranquilizers and sedatives in the elderly. *Practitioner, 188,* 732–738.

Exton-Smith, A. N., Hodkinson, H. M., Cromie, B. W., et al. (1963). Controlled comparison of four sedative drugs in elderly patients. *Brit Med J,* 1037–1040.

Fancourt, G., & Castleden, M. (1986). The use of benzodiazepines with particular reference to the elderly. *Brit J Hosp Med, 35,* 321–326.

Goldstein, B. J. (1967). Double-blind comparison of tybamate and chlordiazepoxide in geriatric patients. *Psychosomatics, 8,* 334–337.

Greenblatt, D. J., Harmatz, J. S., & Shader, R. I. (1978). Factors influencing diazepam pharmacokinetics: Age sex and liver disease. *Int J Clin Pharmacol, 16,* 177–179.

Greenblatt, D. J., Divoll, M., Harmatz, J. S., et al. (1981). Kinetics and clinical effects of flurazepam in young and elderly noninsomniacs. *Clin Pharmacol and Therapeu, 30,* 475–486.

Hale, W. E., May, F. E., Moore, M. T., et al. (1988). Meprobamate use in the elderly. *JAGS, 36,* 1003–1005.

Halliday, A. R., & Mihlay, E. (1966). A controlled evaluation of two dose levels of oxazepam compared to placebo. *J New Drugs, 6,* 124.

Hershey, L. A., & Kim, K. Y. (1988). Diagnosis and treatment of anxiety in the elderly. *Rational Drug Therapy, 22,* 1–6.

Jenike, M. A. (1983). Treating anxiety in elderly patients. *Geriatrics, 38,* 115–119.

Jones, T. H. (1962). Chlordiazepoxide (librium) and the geriatric patient. *J Am Geriat Soc, 10,* 259–263.

Kanowski, S. (1986). Sleep disturbances and agitational states in the elderly. Therapeutic possibilities and limitations in West Germany. *Acta Psychiatry Scand Supple 329, 73,* 77–80.

Kirven, L. E., & Montero, E. F. (1973). Comparison of thioridazine and diazepam in the control of nonpsychotic symptoms associated with senility double blind study. *JAGS, 21,* 546–551.

Koepke, H. H., Gold, R. L., Linden, M. E., et al. (1982). Multicenter controlled study of oxazepam in anxious elderly outpatients. *Psychosomatics, 23,* 641–645.

Kraus, J. W., Desmond, P. V., Marshall, J. P., et al. (1978). Effects of aging and liver disease on disposition of lorazepam. *Clin Pharmacol and Therapeu, 24,* 411–419.

Larson, E. B., Kukull, W. A., Buchner, D., et al. (1987). Adverse drug reactions associated with global cognitive impairment in elderly persons. *Annals of Intern Med, 107,* 169–173.

Lehmann, H. E., & Ban, T. A. (1969). Chemotherapy in aged psychiatric patients. *Canad Psychiat Ass J*, *14*, 361–370.

Levine, S., Napoliello, M. J., Domantay, A. G. (1989). Open study of buspirone in octogenarians with anxiety. *Human Psychopharmacology*, *4*, 51–53.

Lynch, T., Power, P., & Prasad, H. C. (1981). Comparison of oral and rectal diazepam (valium) in the treatment of insomnia associated with anxiety in the elderly. *J of Irish Colleges of Physicians and Surgeons*, *11*, 73–75.

Lyndon, R. W., & Russell, J. D. (1988). Benzodiazepine use in a rural general practice population. *Aust NZ J Psychiatry*, *22*, 293–298.

Mellinger, G. D., Balter, M. B., & Uhleuhuth, E. H. (1984). Antianxiety agents; duration of use and characteristics of users in the USA. *Can Med REs Opinion* (supplement), 21–35.

Merlis, S., Koepke, H. H. (1975). The use of oxazepam in elderly patients. *Dis Nerv Syst*, *5*, 27–29.

Nakra, B. R. S., & Grossberg, G. T. (1986). Management of anxiety in the elderly. *Comprehensive Therapy*, *12*, 53–60.

Napoliello, M. J. (1986). An interim multicentre report on 677 anxious geriatric outpatients treated with buspirone. *Brit J Clin Practice*, *40*, 71–73.

Parry, H. J., Balter, M. B., Mellinga, G. D., Cisin, I. H., & Manheim, D. I. (1973). National patterns of psychotherapeutic drug use. *Arch Gen Psychiatry*, *28*, 769–783.

Petrie, W. M. (1983). Drug treatment of anxiety and agitation in the aged. *Psychopharm Bulletin*, *19*, 238–246.

Pinsker, H., & Suljaga-Petchel, K. (1984). Use of benzodiazepines in primary care geriatric patients. *JAGS*, *32*, 595–597.

Pomara, N., Stanley, B., Block, J., et al. (1984). Adverse effects of single therapeutic doses of diazepam on performance in normal geriatric subjects: Relationship to plasma concentrations. *Psychopharmacol*, *84*, 342–346.

Pomara, N., Stanley, B., Block, R., et al. (1985). Increased sensitivity of the elderly to the central depressant effects of diazepam. *J Clin Psychiatry*, *46*, 185–187.

Ray, W. A., Griffin, M. R., Schaffner, W., et al. (1987). Psychotropic drug use and the risk of hip fracture. *NEJM*, *316*, 363–369.

Roberts, R. K., Wilkinson, G. R., Branch, R. A., et al. (1978). Effect of age and parenchymal liver disease on the disposition and elimination of chlordiazepoxide (librium). *Gastroenterology*, *74*, 479–485.

Robinson, D., & Napoliello, M. J. (1988). The safety and usefulness of buspirone as an anxiolytic in elderly versus young patients. *Clin Therapeutics, 10,* 740–746.

Sallis, J. F., & Lichstein, K. L. (1982). Analysis and management of geriatric anxiety. *Int'l J Aging and Human Development, 15,* 197–211.

Salzman, C. (1984a). Overview in C. Salzman (Ed.). *Clinical geriatric psychopharmacology* (pp. 3–17). New York: McGraw-Hill.

Salzman, C. (1984b). Psychotropic drug dosages and drug interactions. *Clinical geriatric psychopharmacology* (pp. 201–216). New York: McGraw-Hill.

Salzman, C. (1988). Treatment of agitation anxiety and depression in dementia. *Psychopharm Bulletin, 24,* 39–42.

Salzman, C. (in press, 1989a). Recent advance in geriatric psychopharmacology in American Psychiatric Association. *Annual update in psychiatry.* Washington: American Psychiatric Press Inc.

Salzman, C. (1989b). Improvement in cognitive function in elderly nursing home residents when benzodiazepines are withdrawn. Unpublished data.

Salzman, C., et al. (1989c). American Psychiatric Association Task Force in Benzodiazepine Dependency, Toxicity, and Abuse. Washington: American Psychiatric Press Inc.

Salzman, C., & Shader, R. I. (1974). Psychopharmacology in the aged. *J Geriatric Psychiatry, 7,* 165–184.

Salzman, C., & van der Kolk, B. A. (1984c). Treatment of depression in C. Salzman (Ed.), *Clinical geriatric psychopharmacology* (77–115). New York: McGraw-Hill.

Sanders, J. F. (September 1965). Evaluation of oxazepam and placebo in emotionally disturbed aged patients. *Geriatrics,* 739–746.

Shader, R. I., & Greenblatt, D. J. (1982). Management of anxiety in the elderly: The balance between therapeutic and adverse effects. *J Clin Psychiatry, 43,* 8–18.

Singh, A. N., & Beer, M. (1988). A dose range finding study of buspirone in geriatric patients with symptoms of anxiety. *J Clin Psychopharmacol, 8,* 67–68.

Spiers, C. J., Navey, F. L., Brooks, D. J., et al. (1986). Opisthotonos and benzodiazepine withdrawal in the elderly. *Lancet, 2,* 1101.

Stotsky, B. A., & Borozne, J. (1972). Butisol sodium vs. lithium among geriatric and younger outpatients and nursing home patients. *Dis Nerv Syst, 33,* 254–267.

Strauss, A. (1988). Oral dyskinesia associated with buspirone use in an elderly woman. *J Clin Psychiatry, 49,* 322–323.

Tewfik, G. I., Jain, V. K., Harcup, M., et al. (1970). Effectiveness of various tranquilizers in the management of senile restlessness. *Geront Clin, 12,* 351–359.

Thompson, T. L., Moran, M. G., & Nies, A. S. (1983). Psychotropic drug use in the elderly. Part I. *NEJM, 308,* 137–138.

Tobias, C. R., Turns, D. M., Lippmann, S., et al. (1988). Psychiatric disorder in the elderly. *Postgraduate Medicine, 83,* 313–319.

Turnbull, J. M., & Turnbull, S. K. (1985). Management of specific anxiety disorders in the elderly. *Geriatrics, 40,* 75–82.

Welborn, W. S. (1961). A trial of a new tranquilizing agent in geriatric patients. *Psychosomatics, 2,* 1–3.

Wilson, P. G. (1982). Anxiety and depression in elderly and dying patients. Symposium on Clinical Pharmacology of Symptom Control. *Medical Clinics of North America, 66,* 1011–1016.

Winkelman, N. W. (1971). Haloperidol as a treatment of anxiety in psychoneurotic patients. *Curr Therapeu Research, 13,* 451–456.

Cognitive Toxicity of Benzodiazepines in the Elderly

11

Nunzio Pomara, Dennis Deptula,
Rajkumar Singh, and Cherry Ann Monroy

The development of benzodiazepines represents a psychopharmacological milestone in the treatment of anxiety and insomnia. The benzodiazepines are more efficacious and considerably safer than their pharmacologic predecessors—the barbiturates and meprobamate. Consequently, benzodiazepines have become widely prescribed with as many as 20% of women and 10% of men taking one of these medications in a given year (Curran & Golombok, 1985).

Despite their efficacy and relative safety, the benzodiazepines' addictive and abuse potential warrants caution in prescribing these drugs for extended periods. Additionally, these drugs have adverse effects on memory, attention and psychomotor functions which may impair a patient's ability to perform their normal routine (driving, working, operating machinery, etc.). This chapter will selectively review studies of adverse effects of benzodiazepines on cognitive and psychomotor functions with particular focus on the elderly.

175

THE EFFECTS OF BENZODIAZEPINES
IN THE YOUNG

As reviewed elsewhere (Curran, 1986; Kleinknecht & Donaldson, 1975; Taylor & Tinklenberg, 1987) administration of single doses of most benzodiazepines has been shown to impair performance on a variety of tasks in nongeriatric subjects. Benzodiazepines have been shown to impair learning of new information (memory), attention, arousal, as well as to generally slow performance on motor tasks. While it is the sedative effects which may be most apparent to the clinician, Ghoneim and colleagues (1981) have concluded that diazepam's most profound adverse CNS effect is on memory. Furthermore, it has been suggested that the sedative and memory effects of benzodiazepines may be at least partially dissociable, that is, the adverse memory effects are not completely secondary to sedation (McKay & Dundee, 1980).

Benzodiazepines typically lead to peak impairment 1 to 3 hours following administration with durations of effects ranging from 3 to 24 hours (Taylor & Tinklenberg, 1987). The duration of impairment of single doses does not necessarily correspond to the elimination half life and may be more closely related to their lipophilicity which influences the distribution half life.

Although the acute adverse effects of initial single doses of benzodiazepines on cognitive functions are well documented, the relevance of these single dose studies to the clinical situation in which patients are administered multiple doses over time is questionable. The effects of multiple doses on cognitive performance have not been as adequately explored. In their review, Taylor and Tinklenberg (1987) concluded that the few studies available suggest that with repeated administration, some tolerance may develop to some adverse cognitive side effects, although the finding is not universal (Linnoila et al., 1983) It has been suggested that with regard to memory, partial tolerance may develop such that immediate recall is normalized but delayed recall remains impaired (Ghoneim et al.,

1981). Given that benzodiazepines are frequently given as hypnotics, it is important to note that even benzodiazepines administered h.s. have been shown to produce next day impairment (Hart et al., 1976; Johnson & Chernik, 1982; Mendelson et al., 1982).

To summarize, initial doses of virtually all benzodiazepines produce cognitive impairment in young individuals. There are some suggestions that with continued administration, partial tolerance to some of those adverse effects on performance may develop.

THE EFFECTS OF BENZODIAZEPINES IN THE ELDERLY

In general, the elderly are thought to be more sensitive to the adverse effects of psychotropic drugs on task performance. Additionally, given normal age associated decline in cognitive and psychomotor functions, and the elderly's increased vulnerability to various types of fractures and accidental falling (Overstall et al. 1977), the adverse effects of these drugs on task performance in the elderly is of particular clinical relevance. As seen in Table 11.1, the overwhelming majority of studies of elderly subjects have found that both single and multiple doses of benzodiazepines induce significant cognitive impairment.

Reviewing the effects of diazepam on task performance, a single 10 mg dose has been shown to result in psychomotor performance and attentional impairment. When given in multiple doses over an 11 to 14 day period, diazepam has been found to impair memory (Salzman et al., 1975) and psychomotor performance (Gagnon et al., 1977; Salzman et al., 1975) of the elderly, as well as to increase sedation (Salzman et al., 1983). In the only study of clorazepate, no acute effects of a single dose was found (Scharf et al., 1985).

When administered at night for 3 to 14 days, benzodiazepines have generally been found to induce significant next day effects in most (Carskadon et al., 1982; Cook et al., 1983; Fillin-

Table 11.1 Performance Effects of Benzodiazepines in Elderly Individuals: Studies Without Young Controls

Reference	Population (N)	Drug, dose (mg)	Condition of administration	Effects
Carskadon et al., 1982	Insomniacs (13)	Flurazepam (15)[a] Triazolam (0.25)	hs × 3	Impaired auditory vigilance (FL). No effects on memory.
Cook et al., 1983	Geriatric Inpatients (58)	Temazepam (20)[a] Nitrazepam (5)	hs × 7	Psychomotor & attentional impairment (T,N).
Crome et al., 1985	Female Inpatients (7)	Temazepam (20)	hs × 7	No psychomotor effects after nights 1 and 7
Fillingim, 1982	Insomniacs (75)	Flurazepam (30)[a] Temazepam (30)	hs × 4	Self rated daytime sedation Increased (FL) Decreased (T)
Gagnon et al., 1977	Medically ill pts (21) Elderly volunteers (38)	Diazepam (5)[a] Halazepam (20, 40)	tid × 3 days, then bid × 11 days	Impairment on Tandem Walk (HZM 40) and manual dexterity (DZM, HZM 20, 40)
Linnolia & Viukari, 1976	Psychogeriatric (20) Insomniacs	Nitrazepam (10)[a]	hs × 14	Memory & psychomotor impairment in a.m. at end of treatment
Linnoila et al., 1980	Psychogeriatric (20) (mild dementia)	Lorazepam (2)[a] Oxazepam (30) Temazepam (20)	hs × 7	No drug effects on memory and orientation

178

Study	Population (n)	Drug (dose)	Regimen	Findings
Morgan, 1982	Elderly volunteers (11)	Nitrazepam (5)[a]	hs × 8	Increased errors in psychomotor task following night 8 but not night 1
Murphy et al., 1982	Insomniacs (16)	Nitrazpam (2.5) Triazolam (0.125)	hs × 5	Card sorting task impaired following night 5 but not night 1 (N)
Nikaido et al., 1987	Elderly volunteers (16)	Diazepam (5, 20, 15)[a]	single dose (3 weeks apart)	Psychomotor and attention task impairment (DZM 10, 15) Memory not assessed.
Salzman et al., 1975	Elderly volunteers (38)	Diazepam (12)[a]	Daily × 14 days	Memory and psychomotor impairment. Older showed higher rated fatigue
Salzman et al., 1983	Elderly volunteers (24)	Diazepam (2) Oxazepam (10)	tid daily × 14 days	Increased self rated sedation (DZM, OZM). (DZM effects longer)
Scharf et al., 1985 Viukari et al, 1978	Elderly volunteers (43) Mild Dementia (17) (Heterogeneous)	Clorazepate[a] (3.75, 7.5) Flurazepam (15)[a] Fosazepam (60) Nitrazepam (5)	Single dose hs × 7	No effects on memory No effects on memory (FL) Psychomotor impairment (N, FO)

[a]Placebo controlled.

179

gim, 1982, Linnoila et al., 1980; Morgan et al., 1982; Murphy et al., 1982; Viukari et al., 1978), but not all studies (Crome et al., 1985; Linnoila et al., 1980). Nighttime doses have been found to induce psychomotor impairment, attention and memory impairment as well as to increase sedation. Interestingly, some studies with nitrazepam have suggested that in the elderly, there is greater next day impairment following five and eight nights of treatment than after one night of treatment (Morgan et al., 1982; Murphy et al., 1982). This may suggest that within the elderly, tolerance may not develop to some of the next day adverse effects on performance, at least not within an 8 day period.

COMPARISON OF THE PERFORMANCE EFFECTS ON YOUNG AND ELDERLY

From the above review it is clear that most benzodiazepines affect the performance of both young and elderly individuals. Given the increased susceptibility of the elderly to adverse drug reactions (Hurwitz, 1969) and the elderly's tendency to have decreased clearance of benzodiazepines (Crooks et al., 1976) the elderly could be expected to be more sensitive to the adverse performance effects of these drugs on cognitive functions.

As illustrated in Table 11.2, adverse effects surveys of patients treated with diazepam, chlordiazepoxide, flurazepam, and nitrazepam have consistently found that the elderly show increased drowsiness, confusion, ataxia, and fatigue compared to young patients (Boston Collaborative Study, 1973; Greenblatt et al., 1977; Greenblatt & Allen, 1978).

Similarly, as shown in Table 11.3, in studies in which benzodiazepines were utilized for preoperative procedures, the elderly have been found to require lower doses to achieve adequate relaxation (Giles et al., 1978; Reidenberg et al., 1978). The elderly have also been found to have greater self-rated sedation (Kanto et al., 1981) and greater memory impairment (Korttila

Table 11.2 Survey of Adverse Effects of Oral Benzodiazepines

Reference	Population (N) mean age (yrs.)	Drug dose (mg/day)	Effects
Boston Collaborative Drug Surveillance Program, 1973	Medical Inpatients (2274) Heterogeneous (52.8)	Diazepam (variable) Chlordiazepoxide (variable)	Increased drowisness Elderly > Young
Greenblatt et al., 1977	Medical Inpatients (2542) Heterogeneous (54.5)	Flurazepam (variable)	CNS Depression[a] Elderly > Young
Greenblatt & Allen, 1978	Medical Inpatients (2111) Heterogeneous (57.0)	Nitrazepam (variable)	CNS Depression[a] Elderly > Young

[a]Drowsiness, confusion, ataxia, fatigue (especially with higher dose).

Table 11.3 CNS Effects of Benzodiazepines in Pre-operative Procedures

Reference	Population (N) (mean age)	Drug dose (mg) route	Effects
Reidenberg et al., 1978	Cardiac pts. for cardio-version (23) (63.9)	Diazepam (3–70) IV	Elderly required lower dose for adequate sedation.
Giles et al., 1978	Pts. for endoscopy (19) (50)	Diazepam (5–110) IV	Elderly required lower dose for adequate relaxation
Korttila et al., 1978	Bronchoscopy pts. (79) (55)	Flunitrazepam (0.01 mg/kg) IV	Memory impairment Elderly > Young
Kanto et al., 1981	Surgical pts. (20), Epidural Anaesthesia (51)	Flunitrazepam (0.015 mg/kg) IV	Self & Experimenter rated sedation Elderly > Young
Clark et al., 1982	Cystoscopy pts. (128) (66.9)	Diazepam (10) po vs. Temazepam (20) po	Both drugs impaired visuomotor coordination

et al., 1978) than young in response to preoperative treatment with benzodiazepines.

While surveys and preoperative studies have suggested that the elderly may be more sensitive than young to the adverse cognitive and psychomotor effects of benzodiazepines, experimental studies have yielded inconsistent results. (See Table 11.4.) Examining the acute effects of a single 2.5 mg dose of diazepam in a double blind study, Pomara et al. (1985) reported that a single 2.5 mg dose of diazepam impaired memory and psychomotor performance in elderly but not young. Similarly, when administered for seven nights, ketazolam was found to result in next day impairment in balance in elderly but not young subjects (Bonnet & Kramer, 1981). In contrast, Hinrichs and Ghoneim (1987) found that a single diazepam dose (0.2 mg/kg; mean dose = 13.4 mg) impaired memory and attention equally in young, middle age, and elderly individuals. Swift et al. (1985) also found that two 10 mg doses of diazepam (one h.s., one the following AM) resulted in similar impairment in young and elderly subjects. Also, elderly subjects administered flurazepam for 15 nights did not differ from young in the rating of self-rated sedation the following day. (Greenblatt et al., 1981).

In summary, there is ample evidence that benzodiazepines induce cognitive and psychomotor impairment in elderly subjects. There are suggestions that the elderly may show increased sensitivity to these effects, but the data are equivocal. The small sample size employed in many studies and failure to use placebo controls, make interpreting the results difficult. In addition, the question of tolerance development has not been adequately explored, particularly in the elderly.

THE EFFECTS OF BENZODIAZEPINES IN THE ANXIOUS

For some time, it has been believed that excessive levels of anxiety impair performance (Easterbrook, 1959; Rapaport

Table 11.4 Performance Effects of Benzodiazepines in Elderly Individuals: Studies With Young Controls

Reference	Population (N)	Drug, dose (mg)	Condition of administration	Effects
Bonnet & Kramer, 1981	Young Insomniacs (10) Elderly Insomniacs (12)	Ketazolam (30)	hs × 7	Next day balance performance impaired in elderly but not young.
Briggs et al., 1980	Young Normals (10) Elderly Normals (10)	Temazepam (20)[a]	hs × 1	Psychomotor impairment Elderly > Young
Castleden et al., 1977	Young Normals (10) Elderly Normals (10)	Nitrazepam (10)	hs × 1	No psychomotor effects at 4 and 11 hrs. post-drug.
Greenblatt et al., 1981	Young Normals (9) Elderly Normals (9)	Flurazepam (15)	hs × 15	Self-rated sedation increased in young and elderly.
Hinrichs & Ghoneim, 1987	Young (12) Middle (12) Elderly (12)	Diazepam[a] (0.2 mg/kg)	single dose	Impairments in attention, recall and other higher cognitive functions. Not age related.
Pomara et al., 1985	Young (12) Elderly (12)	Diazepam[a] (2.5)	single dose	Memory and psychomotor impairment in elderly only. Increased sedation in elderly.
Swift et al., 1985	Young (11) Elderly (12)	Diazepam[a] (10)	2 doses hs & a.m.	Impairment in attention & coordination in both. Memory not assessed.

[a]Placebo controlled.

et al., 1968). Consequently, it is conceivable that anxious patients may be less vulnerable to the detrimental effects of anxiolytics on performance and could actually show improvement in performance in response to benzodiazepine administration. However, as shown in Table 11.5, only one study reviewed assessed the effects of anxiolytics specifically in anxious elderly (diagnostic criteria were not specified). In this study, lorazepam, but not clobazam, a benzodiazepine derivative tested in Europe, was found to impair memory in elderly anxious patients (Paes de Sousa et al., 1981). Similarly, in primarily non geriatric patients in controlled single dose (Lucki et al., 1987) and multiple dose (Linnoila et al., 1983) studies, diazepam induced significant deficits in patients with anxiety disorders. Less well controlled studies in which dose was adjusted by clinical need have also reported that chronic benzodiazepine administration is associated with task performance impairment in anxious patients (Angus & Romney; Lucki et al., 1986; Olajide & Lader, 1987; Salkind et al., 1979). In contrast to these reports suggesting that benzodiazepine induce deficits in anxious patients, Barnett et al., (1981) have reported that some measures of short term memory of college students with high self-rated anxiety was improved by 5 mg of diazepam whereas in low anxiety subjects, the drug induced performance decrements. Similarly, clobazam, a benzodiazepine derivative tested in Europe, has also been found to produce less impairment in highly anxious volunteers than volunteers with low anxiety. However, Hartley et al. (1982) failed to find differential effects of diazepam on response latencies on a memory task.

Hodges and Spielberger (1969) have made the distinction between "state" anxiety, a transitory state, and "trait" anxiety, a relatively stable trait. They noted that state and trait anxiety were not unusually differentiated on most anxiety scales. They demonstrated that on a digit span task, poor performance was associated with high state anxiety but not trait anxiety. In this context, it is interesting to note that in the study reporting that the short term memory of high anxiety volunteers was improved by diazepam (Barnett et al., 1981) subjects were rated

Table 11.5 Performance Effects of Benzodiazepines in Anxious Individuals

Reference	Population age range	(N)	Drug, dose (mg)	Condition of administration	Effects
Angus & Fomney, 1984	Anxious insomniacs (21–74)	10	Diazepam (5–30)[b]	> 5 days	Memory impairment
Barnett et al., 1981	Anxious Students High vs. Low (18–25)	24	Diazepam (5)[a]	single dose	memory improvement in High Anxious. Impairment in Low Anxious Group
Hartley et al., 1982	Anxious Students Non Anxious Students (18–38)	8 8	Diazepam (5)[a]	single dose	Slowing of retrieval from semantic memory in both groups
Linnoila et al., 1983	Anxious Patients ($\bar{x}$ = 29.1) Normal volunteers ($\bar{x}$ = 29.0)	30	Diazepam (5, 10)[a]	single dose-all subjects (tid × 21 days for anxious subjects only)	Psychomotor and attention impairment in both (10 mg). Psychomotor & attention impairment after 21 days in anxious. No tolerance noted.
Lucki et al., 1986	Various Anxiety Disorders (on drug) 26–70) GAD (drug free) ($\bar{x}$ = 38.6)	43	Diazepam (5–20)[b] Lorazepam (1–10) Clorazepate (3.75–15) Alprazolam (0.75–6)	Chronic vs. Acute Challenge	Chronic treatment decreased arousal relative to unmedicated pts. Acute challenge impaired delayed recall.
Lucki et al., 1987	GAD Patients (19–60)	39	Diazepam (5)[a] Buspirone (5, 10)	single dose	Impaired delayed recall (D)
Olajide & Lader., 1987	GAD Patients (24–57)	24	Diazepam (10–30)[b] Buspirone (10–30)	21 days	Mild psychomotor impairment (D)
Paes deSousa et al., 1981	Anxious Patients (above 65)	30	Lorazepam (1 mg tid) Clobazam (10 mg tid)	4 weeks	Impaired delayed recall
Salkind et al., 1979	Anxious Patients (15–65)	55	Diazepam (5–10)[b] Clobazam (10–20 tid)	14 days	Psychomotor and attentional impairment

[a]Placebo controlled.

186

using a state anxiety scale. In contrast, the studies of psychiatric patients with anxiety disorder found that benzodiazepines induce impairment. In order to be diagnosed as having an anxiety disorder, there is typically a history of a person being anxious (trait anxiety) but that does not necessarily imply the patient was more anxious than controls when tested for a study (state anxiety). Therefore, it seems possible that benzodiazepines may improve performance only in subjects who are highly anxious during the actual test sessions.

PRELIMINARY FINDINGS

In summary, benzodiazepines have been shown to produce deficits in memory, attention, and psychomotor performance. While there are suggestions that the elderly may be more sensitive to these adverse effects, the findings of controlled studies are equivocal. In addition, only a few studies in the elderly have assessed memory, a clinically important cognitive function on which the benzodiazepines have profound effects. Additionally, it is unknown whether the elderly develop tolerance to these adverse effects and whether the presence of anxiety modulates these effects. In order to address these questions, we are conducting a study on the effects of benzodiazepines on memory, attention, and psychomotor functions comparing young and elderly patients with and without anxiety disorders. This study assessed the acute effects of diazepam, a widely prescribed benzodiazepine, by administering a battery of tests (including tests of memory, attention and reaction time) at baseline, 1.5 and 3 hours following drug administration. It also tested the next day effects following one week and three weeks of treatment. Finally, the study rechallenged the subjects with diazepam after 3 weeks of treatment to assess whether tolerance develops to the acute adverse performance effects of the drug.

Each of the 45 normal young (age range 19–35 years) and 45 normal elderly (age range 60–79 years) were administered single placebo, 2.5 mg and 10 mg diazepam doses on 3 separate

weeks to assess the acute drug effects on performance. Subsequently, subjects were randomly distributed into three
groups—receiving either placebo, 2.5 mg or 10 mg diazepam
h.s. for three weeks. On the last day (after 3 weeks) of the study,
subjects were rechallenged with the same dose they had been
receiving to assess tolerance.

Preliminary analysis suggests that 10 mg doses of diazepam
induced profound deficits acutely in memory, attention and
reaction time in both age groups. Taking the mean of all tests,
(age-normed) the elderly, but not young, showed deficits in
response to a single 2.5 mg dose ($p < .05$). Figure 11.1 summar-
izes the effects of 10 mg of diazepam vs. placebo in the study.
As shown in the figure, a single 10 mg diazepam dose induced
significant deficits in both groups with a trend for the elderly
to show greater impairment ($p < .06$). When administered
chronically at night, both age groups showed comparable
next day impairment in performance. Similarly, when rechallenged, both groups showed similar deficits. Notice the magnitude of decline from baseline (0 hours) is significantly less in
the rechallenge than challenge, suggesting that some degree
of tolerance develops to the acute effects following 3 weeks
of treatment. However, since the rechallenge baseline is
lower because of next day impairment of chronic treatment,
the overall levels of impairment produced by chronic treatment and a single 10 mg dose is comparable to the initial 10 mg
dose.

Therefore, these results imply that an initial dose may
produce somewhat greater performance decrements in normal elderly than young. Additionally, one and 3 weeks of h.s.
treatment with 10 mg diazepam produced comparable next
day deficits in both groups and that only partial tolerance
develops to the drugs acute effects following 3 weeks of
treatment. We are currently extending the study to include
both young and elderly patients with generalized anxiety disorder (GAD) to ascertain whether GAD modulates the adverse
effects of diazepam on memory and psychomotor performance.

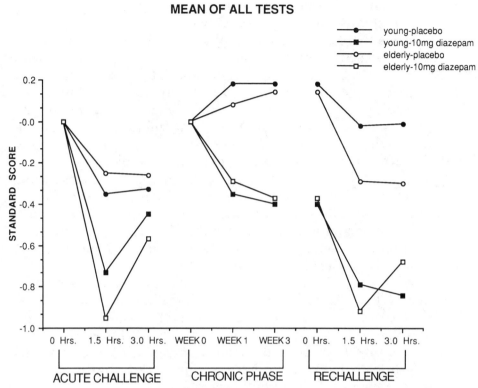

FIGURE 11.1 Effects of diazepam on the standardized mean of all tests administered following an initial single dose (acute challenge), chronic hs treatment (chronic phase) and subsequent rechallenge (rechallenge)
Mean of All Tests.

CONCLUSIONS

Administration of both single and multiple doses of most benzodiazepines impair a wide range of cognitive functions including memory, attention, and psychomotor skills. While partial tolerance may develop to some of these adverse effects, some deficits seem to persist after several weeks of administration. Similarly, when administered repeatedly only at night, next day impairment is frequently detectable.

While there are some suggestions that the elderly may show increased sensitivity to the adverse effects of benzodiazepines on performance, the data are equivocal. Our own preliminary findings have suggested that the elderly may show increased sensitivity to the adverse effects of a single diazepam dose on some measures, but not after receiving multiple doses. In addition to the possibility of increased sensitivity to adverse cognitive effects, it is important to note that the elderly's baseline level of performance on most cognitive tasks is considerably lower than that of young (Hinrichs & Ghoneim, (1987). Consequently, even if benzodiazepines produce comparable impairment in the young and elderly, it may be more noticeable and of greater clinical significance in the elderly patient whose functioning is already compromised.

While the performance of individuals with high state anxiety may be less adversely affected by benzodiazepines than others, the bulk of the evidence suggests that anxious patients are not immune to these adverse cognitive effects. However, performance effects of benzodiazepines on well diagnosed anxious elderly patients have not been adequately examined and further research is needed in this area.

Given the large number of different benzodiazepines available for clinical use, it would be of great importance to know whether some benzodiazepines induce less cognitive toxicity in the elderly than others. This is particularly true in light of the fact that currently prescribed benzodiazepines differ with respect to the rate of absorption, distribution and elimination half life and the relative affinity for central benzodiazepine receptors. Since aging is accompanied by an increase in the volume of distribution for lipid soluble substances such as benzodiazepines, and by a reduction in the rate in which certain benzodiazepines undergo hepatic biotransformation and metabolism, aging may alter the cognitive effects of both single and multiple doses of benzodiazepines. While theoretical arguments could be made to advocate for the use of medications with a shorter elimination half life (3- hydroxy and triazolo compounds) rather than those with a longer elimination half line (2) keto compounds), there are few systematic comparisons of these drugs' adverse performance effects, at least within the elderly. Somewhat inconsistent with this assumption, Salzman (1983) demonstrated that the 2 mg diazepam tid (longer half life) and 10 mg oxazepam (short half life) produced comparable self-rated sedation in elderly subjects. This study highlights the need for further research on the relationship between the pharmacokinetic and pharmacodynamic properties of benzodiazepines and their performance effects.

COMMENTARY

1. Tolerance develops to the cognitive impairment effects.

2. Pharmacokinetics in the very old (75–90) are not different from pharmacokinetics in young elderly (60–75). Both groups however are markedly different kinetically from younger adults.

3. The Pomara data are in a sample of mean age 67. This may not represent the truly elderly population.

4. It should be acknowledged that it is very difficult to control psychopharmacology research studies and control cognition studies in the elderly.

REFERENCES

Angus, W. R., & Romney, D. M. (1984). The effect of diazepam on patients' memory. *Journal of Clinical Psychopharmocology*, 4(4), 203–206.

Barnett, D. B., Taylor Davies, A., & Desai, N. (1981). Differential effect of diazepam on short term memory in subjects with high or low level anxiety. *British Journal of Clinical Pharmacology, 11*, 411–412.

Bonnet, M. H. & Kramer, M. (1981). The interaction of age, performance and hypnotics in the sleep of insomniacs. *Journal of the American Geriatric Society, 29*, 508–512.

Boston Collaborative Drug Surveillance Program (1973). Clinical depression of the central nervous system due to diazepam and chlordiazepoxide in relation to cigarette smoking and age. *New England Journal of Medicine, 288,* 6, 277–280.

Briggs, R. S., Castleden, C. M., & Kraft, C. A. (1980). Improved hypnotic treatment using chlormethiazole and temazepam. *British Medical Journal, 1,* 601–604.

Carskadon, M. A., Seidel, W. F., Greenblatt, D. J. & Dement, W. C. (1982). Daytime carry over of triazolam and flurazepam in elderly insomniacs. *Sleep, 5*(4), 361–371.

Castleden, C. M., George, C. F., Marcer, D., & Hallet, C. (1982). Increased sensitivity to nitrazepam in old age. *British Medical Journal, 1,* 10–12.

Clark, G., Erwin, D., Yate, P., Burt, D., & Major, E. (1982). Temazepam as premedication in elderly patients. *Anaesthesia, 37,* 421–425.

Cook, P. J., Huggett, A., Graham-Pole, R., Savage, I. T., & James, I. M. (1983). Hypnotic accumulation and hangover in elderly inpatients: A controlled double-blind study of temazepam and nitrazepam. *British Medical Journal, 286,* 100–102.

Crome, P., Gain, R, Suri, A. C., & Dawling, S. (1985). Temazepam in elderly women: Single and multiple dose kinetics and effects on psychomotor performance. *British Journal of Clinical Pharmacology, 19,* 583p.

Crooks, J., O'Malley, K., Stevenson, I. H. (1976). Pharmacokinetics in the elderly. *Clinical Pharmacokinetics, 1,* 280–296.

Curran, H. V. (1986). Tranquillising memories: A review of the effects of benzodiazepines on human memory. *Biological Psychology, 23,* 179–213.

Curran, H. V. & Golombok, S. (1985). *Bottling It Up.* London: Faber & Faber.

Easterbrook, J. A. (1959). The effect of emotion on cue utilization and organization of behavior. *Psychological Review, 66,* 183–201.

Fillingim, J. M. (1982). Double-blind evaluation of temazepam, flurazepam and placebo in geriatric insomniacs. *Clinical Therapeutics, 4,* 369–380.

Gagnon, M. A., Langlois, Y., Boghen, D. R., & Verdy, M. (1977). Effects of halazepam and diazepam on the motor coordination of geriatric subjects. *European Journal of Clinical Pharmacology, 11,* 443–448.

Ghoneim, M. M., Mewaldt, S. P., Berie, J. L., & Hinrichs, J. V. (1981). Memory and performance effects of single and 3 week administration of diazepam. *Psychopharmacology, 73,* 147–151.

Giles, H. G., MacLeod, S. M., Wright, J. R., & Sellers, E. M. (1978). Influence of age and previous use on diazepam dosage required for endoscopy. *Canadian Medical Association Journal, 118*, 513–514.

Greenblatt, D. J., & Allen, M. D. (1978). Toxicity of nitrazepam in the elderly: A report from the Boston Collaborative Drug Surveillance Program. *British Journal of Clinical Pharmacology, 5*, 407–413.

Greenblatt, D. J., Allen, M. D., & Shader, R. I. (1977). Toxicity of high-dose flurazepam in the elderly. *Clinical Pharmacology and Therapeutics, 21*, 355–361.

Greenblatt, D. J., Divoll, M., Harmatz, J. S., MacLaughlin, D. S., & Shader, R. I. (1981). Kinetics and clinical effects of flurazepam in young and elderly non-insomniacs. *Clinical Pharmacology and Therapeutics, 30*(4), 475–486.

Hart, J., Hill, H. M., Bye, C. E., Wilkenson, R. T., & Peck, A. W. (1976). The effects of low doses of amylobarbitone sodium and diazepam on human performance. *British Journal of Clinical Pharmacology, 3*, 289–298.

Hartley, L. R., Spencer, J., & Williamson, J. (1982) Anxiety, diazepam and retrieval from semantic memory. *Psychopharmacology, 76*, 291–293.

Hinrichs, J. V., & Ghoneim, M. M. (1987). Diazepam, behavior, and aging: Increased sensitivity or lower baseline performance? *Psychopharmacology, 92*, 100–105.

Hodges, W. F., & Spielberger, C. D. (1969). Digit span: An indicant of trait or state anxiety? *Journal of Consulting and Clinical Psychology, 33*(4), 430–434.

Hurwitz, N. (1969). Predisposing factors in adverse reactions to drugs. *British Medical Journal, 1*, 536–539.

Johnson, L. C., & Chernik, D. A. (1982). Sedative-hypnotics and human performance. *Psychopharmacology, 76*, 101–113.

Kanto, J., Kangas, L., Aaltonen, L. & Hilke, H. (1981). Effect of age on the pharmacokinetics and sedative effect of flunitrazepam. *International Journal of Clinical Pharmacology Therapy and Toxicology, 19*, 400–404.

Kleinknecht, R. A., & Donaldson, D. (1975). A review of the effects of diazepam on cognitive and psychomotor performance. *The Journal of Nervous and Mental Disease, 161*(6), 399–411.

Korttila, K., Saarnivaara, L., Tarkkanen, J., Himberg, J. J., & Hytonen, M. (1978). Effect of age on amnesia & sedation induced by flunitrazepam during local anaesthesia for bronchoscopy. *British Journal of Anaesthesia, 50,* 1211–1218.

Linnoila, M., Erwin, C. W., Brendle, A., & Simpson, D. (1983). Psychomotor effects of diazepam in anxious patients and healthly volunteers. *Journal of Clinical Psychopharmacology, 3,* 88–96.

Linnoila, M., & Viukari, M. (1976). Efficacy and side effects of nitrazepam and thioridazine as sleeping aids in psychogeriatric inpatients. *British Journal of Psychiatry, 128,* 566–569.

Linnoila, M., Viukari, M., Lamminisivu, U., & Auvinen, J. (1980). Efficacy and side effects of lorazepam, oxazepam and temazepam as sleeping aids in psychogeriatric inpatients. *International Pharmacopsychiatry, 15,* 129–135.

Lucki, I., Rickels, K., Giesecke, M. A., & Geller, A. (1987). Differential effects of anxiolytic drugs, diazepam and buspirone, on memory function. *British Journal of Clinical Pharmacology, 23,* 207–211.

Lucki, I., Rickels, K., & Geller, A. M. (1986) Chronic use of benzodiazepines and psychomotor and cognitive test performance. *Psychopharmacology, 88,* 426–433.

McKay, A. C., & Dundee, J. W. (1980). Effect of benzodiazepines on memory. *British Journal of Anaesthesia, 52,* 1247–1257.

Mendelson, W. B., Weingartner, H., Greenblatt, D. J., Garnett, D., & Gillin, J. C. (1982). A clinical study of flurazepam. *Sleep, 5,* 350–360.

Morgan, K. (1982). Effect of low-dose nitrazepam on performance in the elderly. *The Lancet, 1,* 516.

Murphy, P., Hindmarch, I., & Hyland, C. M. (1982). Aspects of short-term use of two benzodiazepine hypnotics in the elderly. *Age and Ageing, 11,* 222–228.

Nikaido, A. M., Ellinwood, E. H., Heatherly, D. G., & Dubow, D. (1987). Differential CNS effects of diazepam in elderly adults. *Pharmacology Biochemistry & Behavior, 27,* 273–281.

Olajide, D., & Lader, M. (1987). A comparison of buspirone, diazepam, and placebo in patients with chronic anxiety states. *Journal of Clinical Psychopharmacology, 7,* 148–152.

Overstall, P. W., Exton-Smith, A. N., Imms, F. J., Johnson, A. L. (1977). Falls in the elderly related to postural imbalance. *British Medical Journal, 1,* 261–264.

Paes de Sousa, M., Figuiera, M. L., Loureiro, F., & Hindmarch, I. (1981). Lorazepam and clobazam in anxious elderly patients. Clobazam: Royal Society of Medicine International Congress and Symposium. London: Academic Press Inc. And Royal Society of Medicine. Series No. 43, 119–123.

Pomara, N., Stanley, B., Block, R., Berchou, R. C., Stanley, M., Greenblatt, D. J., Newton, R. E., & Gershon, S. (1985). Increased sensitivity of the elderly to the central depressant effects of diazepam. *Journal of Clinical Psychiatry, 46,* 185–187.

Rapaport, D., Gill, M. M., & Schafer, R. Diagnostic Psychological Testing. Vol. 1. Chicago: Year Book Publishers, 1945. (Republished: Rev. Ed., New York: International Universities Press,, 1968).

Reidenberg, M. M., Levy, M., Warner, H., Coutinho, C. B., Schwartz, M. A., Yu, G., & Cheripko, J. (1978). Relationship between diazepam dose, plasma level, age, and central nervous system depression. *Clinical Pharmacology & Therapeutics, 23,* 371–374.

Salem, S.A.M., Kinney, C.D., & McDevitt, D.G. (1982). Pharmacokinetics and psychomotor effects of nitrazepam and temazepam in healthy elderly males and females. *British Journal of Clinical Pharmacology, 13,* 601–602.

Salkind, M. R., Hanks, G. W., & Silverstone, J. T. (1979). Evaluation of the effects of clobazam, A 1, 5 benzodiazepine, on mood and psychomotor performance in clinically anxious patients in general practice. *British Journal of Clinical Pharmacology 7,* 113s–118s.

Salzman, C., Shader, R. I., Greenblatt, D. J., & Harmatz, J. (1983). Long vs short half-life benzodiazepines in the elderly. *Archives of General Psychiatry, 40,* 293–297.

Salzman, C., Shader, R. I., Harmatz, J., & Robertson, L. (1975). Psychopharmacologic investigations in elderly volunteers: Effect of diazepam in males. *Journal of the American Geriatrics Society, 23,* 451–457.

Scharf, M. B., Hirschowitz, J., Woods, M. & Scharf, S. (1985). Lack of amnestic effects of clorazepate on geriatric recall. *Journal of Clinical Psychiatry, 46,* 518–520.

Schatzberg, A. F., & Cole, O. J. (1987). *Manual of Clinical Psychopharmacology* (pp. 139–171). Washington, D.C.: American Psychiatric Press, Inc.

Swift, C. G., Ewen, J. M., Clarke, P., & Stevenson, I. H. (1985). Responsiveness to oral diazepam in the elderly: relationship to total and free plasma concentrations. *British Journal of Clinical Pharmacology, 20,* 111–118.

Taylor, J. L., & Tinklenberg, J. R. (1987). Cognitive Impairment and benzodiazepines. Meltzer, H. Y. (Ed.), *Psychopharmacology: The Third Generation of Progress* (pp 1449–1454). New York: Raven Press.

Viukari, M., Linnoila, M., & Aalto, U. (1978). Efficacy and side effects of flurazepam, fosazepam, and nitrazepam as sleeping aids in psychogeriatric patients. *Acta Psychiatrica Scandinavica, 57,* 27–35.

Cognitive-Behavioral Treatment of Anxiety in the Elderly: A Proposed Model

12

Paul R. McCarthy, Ira R. Katz,
and Edna B. Foa

Epidemiological data suggest that the anxiety disorders of primary significance in the elderly are likely to be the phobias, often with components representing exaggerations of rational concerns, generalized anxiety, and mixed anxious-depressive states. In contrast, the onset of both obsessive-compulsive and panic disorders appear to be relatively rare in later life. In current clinical practice, pharmacotherapy is the most common form of treatment for symptoms of anxiety. Though there is increasing evidence that use of benzodiazepines by older patients is associated with significant morbidity including excess sedation, cognitive impairment, falls, and vulnerability to withdrawal symptoms, anxiolytic benzodiazepines and related medications are used by approximately 12% of the elderly (Gurland, Copeland, Kuriansky et al., 1983). Psychotherapy or behavioral therapy, in contrast, is essentially without risk. However, there has been little research designed either to develop specific therapies for anxiety in the elderly, or to evaluate the efficacy of existing nonpharmacological treatments. This chapter reviews established psychosocial treatments for anxiety with specific emphasis on the elderly and makes recommendations for future research.

TECHNIQUES OF BEHAVIORAL TREATMENT

Early behavior therapists viewed all types of pathological fear as essentially equivalent, sharing common mechanisms for their acquisition and maintenance. Consequently, early studies of treatment outcome involved anxiety disorders of heterogeneous origin (e.g., Gelder, Marks, & Wolff, 1967). Later attempts to define differences between anxiety disorders led to the use of more symptomatically homogeneous populations. This chapter is based upon the current DSM-III-R classification of anxiety disorders. Because there has been little systematic research on the psychological treatment of anxiety in the elderly, this chapter will review relevant studies conducted in younger adults. It will focus on behavioral and cognitive-behavioral treatment because studies using these approaches constitute most of the available literature on controlled trials of the efficacy of psychosocial treatment for anxiety. The emphasis will be on two specific types of treatment: exposure based procedures and anxiety management techniques (Foa, Rothbaum, & Kozok, 1989). Available evidence suggests that exposure techniques are particularly beneficial when the anxiety disorder involves excessive avoidance; the treatment aims to both activate and modify a patient's set of fearful beliefs. AMT is used when anxiety pervades daily functioning, and there is a greater need to manage fear. In general, AMT treatments have been found superior for more reality-based types of fears, such as the rape-related fears of a rape survivor (Foa, Rothbaum, & Kozak, 1989).

Exposure Techniques

All exposure-based treatment approaches require the patient to confront fear. Confrontation procedures can be subdivided on several dimensions including the medium of presentation (imaginal vs. in vivo), the duration of the exposure (short vs. long), and the desired level of arousal during the exposure (low vs. high). When organized in this way, systematic desensitization (Wolpe, 1958) is representative of a treatment using imaginal exposures of brief duration and minimal arousal. Conversely, *in vivo* exposure, or flooding (Marks, 1972), represents a technique using prolonged exposures to actual feared items at high levels of anxiety.

Systematic desensitization as outlined by Wolpe (1958) was the first clearly delineated behavioral exposure technique. It consists of presenting the patient with short scenarios that involve confrontation with feared situations or objects. A series of fear-relevant scenes are established ranging in perceived threat from minimal (e.g., seeing a picture of a snake) to maximal (e.g., holding a snake). They are arranged hierarchically, with the least fearful one being presented first. The patient is then instructed to imagine a verbally-presented scene as clearly as possible for a brief period. Concurrent relaxation procedures are used to intentionally minimize anxiety. Scenes continue to be repeated until they are no longer capable of eliciting anxiety to the patient (desensitization) and then the next scene is presented. This continues until the hierarchy is completed. There are several other forms of desensitization, including gradual confrontation with actual feared situation (in vivo exposure). An alternative treatment procedure, flooding, involves exposures which *begin* with highly feared stimuli, are prolonged, and elicit high levels of anxiety. These exposures are continued in a treatment session until some degree of anxiety reduction has occurred (habituation). As with systematic desensitization, flooding can be employed either in imaginal or in vivo forms.

Anxiety Management Techniques (AMT)

In contrast to exposure treatment techniques which activate fear and promote habituation, AMT seeks to reduce anxiety through the development of skills to *control* fear. The behavioral and cognitive-behavioral treatments that are most commonly included as part of AMT are progressive muscle relaxation (e.g., Bernstein & Borkovec, 1973) and controlled breathing (e.g., Clark, Salkovskis, & Chalkley, 1985). In addition to reducing overall muscle tension, these procedures more generally affect the autonomic nervous system, reducing sympathetic responses (e.g., decreased pulse, respiratory rate, and blood pressure). A cognitive-behavioral treatment component is also included as part of AMT treatment for the purpose of correcting maladaptive patterns of thought and behavior. Several of the most frequently used cognitive-behavioral components include positive self-talk and imagery (Meichenbaum, 1974), cognitive restructuring (e.g., Ellis, 1977), social skills training (e.g., Becker, Heimberg, & Bellack, 1987), and distraction techniques such as thought stopping (Wolpe, 1973). For example, one particularly successful AMT package was used for treatment of victims of rape or other violent crimes who suffered post-traumatic stress disorder. The treatment components included progressive muscle relaxation, controlled breathing, thought stopping, cognitive restructuring, positive self-talk, and imagery, provided over eight sessions; significant reductions in anxiety and depression were found (Foa, Rothbaum, & Kozak, 1989).

TREATMENT OF SPECIFIC ANXIETY DISORDERS

In this section, we discuss studies of treatment for simple phobia and generalized anxiety, the disorders that are most common in the elderly.

Simple Phobia

Numerous studies have examined the effectiveness of systematic desensitization (SD) as a treatment for simple phobias. This treatment has been found superior to other forms of individual and group psychotherapies (e.g., Gelder, Marks, & Wolff, 1967). It has been documented that phobics who failed to benefit from traditional psychotherapy improved when treated with SD

(Gelder & Marks, 1968). Desensitization treatment often includes homework assignments requiring the in vivo confrontation of feared stimuli to augment imaginal exposure. Such augmentation may be critical. Only a 50% transfer to real life situations was observed when imaginal SD was used without in vivo homework assignments (Barlow, Leitenberg, Agras, & Wincze, 1969).

Another technique similar in form to SD, imaginal flooding, has also been effective in the treatment of simple phobias. SD and imaginal exposure have been found to be equally effective for treatment of phobias (Marks, Boulougouris, & Marset, 1971; Gelder, Bancroft, Gath et al., 1973; Crowe, Marks, Agras, & Leitenberg, 1972), but in vivo, graded exposure was found significantly more effective than SD (Crowe, Marks, Agras, & Leitenberg, 1972) or imaginal exposure (Barlow, Leitenberg, Agras, & Wincze, 1969) for simple phobics. As summarized by Mathews (1978). "the available evidence suggests that direct exposure is always superior with simple phobics" (p. 399). More recent studies demonstrating the efficacy of in vivo exposure procedures have been conducted with height and with driving phobics (Williams, Dooseman, & Kleinfield, 1984; Williams, Turner, & Peer, 1985).

Generalized Anxiety Disorder (GAD)

Previously labeled "free floating anxiety," generalized anxiety disorder (GAD) has lacked a well tailored behavior therapy treatment. The few existing interventions used for this pervasive anxiety problem focused on the anxiety responses themselves. SD was used as a means of teaching patients to cope better with anxiety, rather than as a counter-conditioning technique (Goldfried, 1971). A technique similar to SD, called Anxiety Management Training (AMT), required exposure to stressful situations and the rehearsal of techniques to manage anxiety (Suinn & Richardson, 1971). Treatment studies that use procedures such as AMT share the basic assumption that GAD results from deficits in the overall management of anxiety, rather than from conditioned fear to nondangerous stimuli. Within such treatment programs, therefore, patients are exposed to threatening situations to learn more effective ways of managing anxiety.

Recently, new treatment programs for GAD have been designed and studied. In an early pilot study, a modification of Suinn and Richardson's AMT was compared to a no-treatment period using a multiple baseline design (Jannoun, Oppenheimer, & Gelder, 1982). The AMT program included self-monitoring of anxiety, reading information on anxiety, muscle relaxation, and the use of positive self-statements. As expected, AMT was found to be significantly more effective in reducing anxiety. Patients continued to use their acquired skills even after the termination of treatment. This pilot study provided the basis for a larger treatment outcome study in which patients were randomized into either AMT or wait-list groups (Butler, Covington, Hibbert, Limes, & Gelder, 1987). Improvements were found for the AMT treatment group on all recorded anxiety measures and were maintained at three and six month follow-ups. Although no improvements occurred for subjects in the wait-list group, they improved to levels equivalent to the treatment group after receiving AMT.

An alternate form of treatment for GAD, based on Meichenbaum's stress inoculation therapy (Meichenbaum & Turk, 1973) and Beck's cognitive therapy for anxiety (Beck, Emery, & Greenberg, 1985), has been developed and studied in comparison to the wait-list control condition. Patients received a treatment package which included progressive muscle relaxation, EMG biofeedback, and a cognitive-behavioral therapy (Barlow, Cohen, Waddell et al., 1984). A significant reduction in anxiety was found; GAD and panic disordered patients responded equally well. The authors note that although patients with panic disorder responded primarily to relaxation, those with GAD benefitted more from the cognitive intervention. Treatment gains were maintained at three and 12 month follow-ups.

Most recently, Borkovec, Mathews, and colleagues (Borkovec, Mathews, Chambers et al., 1987) have begun a program of clinical research to identify common active ingredients in cognitive-behavioral treatments for GAD. In an initial study, they compared cognitive therapy plus relaxation, nondirective therapy plus relaxation, and relaxation alone. Although all treatments produced therapeutic gains, cognitive treatment plus relaxation showed the greatest reduction in anxiety. In a second study of patients with GAD, Borkovec and Mathews (1987) again compared cognitive therapy to a nonspecific therapy adding a coping desensitization condition closely related to AMT. All groups showed improvement from pretreatment, but no differences between groups were found either immediately following treatment or at follow-up. The magnitude of the treatment effect found in this study was comparable to previous studies (e.g., Barlow, Cohen, Waddell et al., 1984; Butler, Covington, Hibbutt et al., 1987). Because all treatment conditions in this study included instruction in relaxation, relaxation itself may have been the most potent treatment component. In support of this interpretation, significant correlations between relaxation practice and therapist ratings of anxiety were found across all groups. Furthermore, patients who paradoxically experienced anxiety while practicing relaxation (relaxation-induced anxiety) did not improve as much as the others.

Similarly, Blowers, Cobb, and Mathews (1987) compared the clinical outcome of GAD patients receiving nondirective counseling, a version of AMT (including relaxation and cognitive therapy), or a wait-list control group. Very few differences in outcome were found between treatment conditions. However, the AMT treatment group, but not the group receiving nondirective treatment, was found to be significantly improved as compared with wait-list controls. These findings, comparable to those of Borkovec and Mathews, further support the hypothesis that GAD patients are deficient in more general anxiety management skills.

APPLICABILITY OF EXISTING METHODS FOR TREATING ANXIETY IN THE ELDERLY

There is considerable evidence supporting the efficacy of behavioral and cognitive-behavioral treatments of depression in the aged. Some of these studies have also evaluated the effects of these treatment procedures on concurrent general anxiety in elderly depressed patients. Steuer, Mintz, Hammen et al. (1984) compared the effectiveness of a cognitive-behavioral therapy and a psychodynamic therapy in a study in which a group of 20 elderly depressed patients was divided equally into groups receiving either of the two treatments over a nine month period. They found that depression and anxiety were responsive to both forms of treatment. Thompson, Gallagher, and Breckenridge (1987) evaluated the relative efficacy of three types of treatment, behavioral, cognitive, and brief psychodynamic, for major depression in elderly patients and found all three treatments yielded equally positive effects for reducing depression and anxiety. All groups were improved significantly in comparison to a wait-list control group.

Only a few studies to date have directly evaluated the effects of established treatments for anxiety in the elderly. Evidence for both the efficacy of treatment and the beneficial effects of a reduction in symptoms of generalized anxiety comes from a series of papers by Yesavage and co-workers. Yesavage, Rose, and Spiegel (1982) found that instruction in progressive muscle relaxation facilitated recall memory on a list learning task in elderly subjects with high trait anxiety. In a later study, Yesavage and Jacob (1984) examined the interaction between relaxation and subsequent instruction on a mnemonic strategy in improving name-face recall in elderly subjects. In this study, recall did not improve following relaxation alone, but greater recall was found following the combination of relaxation and mnemonic training; improved recall was associated with lower anxiety, worry, and ratings of cognitive interference. Another study (Yesavage, 1984) compared improvement in name-face recall in an experimental group that received relaxation training before mnemonic instruction with a control group that received nonspecific pretreatment. They found that relaxation improved the ability of older subjects to benefit from mnemonic training and that the degree of improvement correlated with the decrease in the level of anxiety. A more recent study (Yesavage, Sheikh, Tanke, & Hill, 1988) found that the benefits of relaxation occurred specifically in subjects with high pretreatment levels of anxiety. The authors concluded that anxiety can interfere with learning and with performance on tests of attention and memory in the elderly, and, further, that this negative effect can be reduced via instruction in relaxation.

Further evidence suggesting that behavioral and cognitive-behavioral treatments are effective for anxiety problems in the elderly is found in case reports. One such case report examined the efficacy of a behavioral treatment developed for younger adult obsessive-compulsives with a 67 year old patient with a 45 year history of this disorder. Rowan, Holburn, Walker, and Siddique (1984) found almost complete elimination of ritualistic behavior following an eight session treatment program. Their treatment emphasized both in vivo exposure and response prevention. Treatment gains were maintained at 18 month follow-up. Hussain (1981) reported the treatment of four elevator phobic residents of a nursing home. An AMT treatment package utilizing instruction in relaxation, positive self-talk and imagery, and in vivo exposure was employed. At two month follow-up, all four residents were able to ride the elevator with minimal anxiety. In yet another case report, Thyer (1981) used graded in vivo exposure with a 70 year old dog phobic. Of particular interest in this case is the extensive avoidance that had developed in the three years since this patient was attacked by a dog. Due to her fear of dogs, she avoided going outside, and appeared agoraphobic in her avoidance of travel. Treatment for this patient included graded exposure, resulting in her ultimate contact with dogs and her being left alone to feed them. The size of the dog used, the relative closeness to the dog(s), and her proximity to the therapist (with therapist vs. alone) were dimensions along which exposures were graded. The patient's fear of dogs was eliminated and treatment gains were maintained at three and six month follow-ups. This case is illustrative of the importance of carefully evaluating the specific structure of an anxious patient's fear prior to treatment. As indicated, this patient's extensive avoidance of going out alone resulted in the appearance of agoraphobia. Merely performing exposures to outside places would have missed the essential aspect of this patient's fear.

In a study examining the importance of specifically targeting treatment to the symptoms experienced, Sallis, Lichstein, Clarkson et al. (1983) compared anxiety management training (Suinn & Richardson, 1971), a depression management treatment which combined pleasant events scheduling (Lewinsohn, 1975) and rational disputation (Ellis & Harper, 1961), and a placebo treatment which controlled for expectation but did not invoke "concepts or techniques relevant to the dimension of arousal" (p. 7). Twenty-four elderly subjects experiencing mild levels of depression and trait anxiety (determined psychometrically) were randomly divided into small groups (3 to 5 subjects per group), with two groups per treatment condition. Treatment groups met twice weekly for five weeks. Although all treatment conditions demonstrated reductions of depression and resting blood pressure from pre- to post-treatment, only the placebo group showed reduced trait anxiety. Treatment gains were found to be maintained at one month follow-up. Though these results suggest that a treatment's specificity for anxiety or depression may not be critical, further research with larger populations is clearly necessary.

TREATMENT RELEVANT DIFFERENCES IN ELDERLY

AMT holds promise as a treatment of choice for anxiety in the elderly. In contrast, there are several reasons to question the use of exposure for the treatment of simple phobias in late life. Early work by Eisdorfer and colleagues (e.g., Eisdorfer, 1968) demonstrated a striking decrement in cognitive performance related to anxiety in elderly subjects under test conditions in which stimuli were presented rapidly. The errors were primarily ones of omission, producing response rates below those found for slower stimulus presentations. These performance decrements were related to plasma levels of free fatty acids and were reversed by administration of the beta blocker propranolol, suggesting that this pattern of findings was related to increased autonomic arousal and sympathetic activity. Although LaRue and D'Elia (1985) have questioned whether the elderly are at increased risk for anxiety-related cognitive decrements, it appears that anxiety and high levels of autonomic arousal can have adverse effects on cognitive performance. As discussed above, the beneficial effects of relaxation on learning and memory have been shown in the elderly. Because all psychotherapies involve learning, the adverse effects of anxiety on cognitive performance may be relevant to the efficacy of treatment. Though they are highly effective in younger patients, forms of exposure that produce high levels of arousal may be less effective for the treatment of anxiety in the elderly. Conversely, because AMT produces less overall arousal, it may facilitate the learning of treatment relevant information. If the phobias of the elderly represent, in part, exaggerations of reality-based concerns associated with aging and increasing frailty (e.g., Bergmann, 1975), there is further reason to propose the use of AMT for treatment.

Although case studies suggest that exposure techniques may be used successfully with specific fears in aged individuals, this may represent a relative minority of this population. The elderly may commonly experience more generalized and reality-based fears. Therefore, treatments like AMT may be most appropriate for the elderly, both for patients with generalized anxiety and for many of those with simple phobia.

OBSTACLES FOR TREATMENT OF ANXIETY IN THE ELDERLY

Studies indicate that approximately 20 to 50% of the elderly may need or benefit from mental health services (MacDonald & Schnur, 1987). However, the gap between those in need and those receiving services is large; fewer than 20% of this group will receive such help. Barriers to psychological treatment for the elderly exist at multiple levels, including those attributed to the individual patient, the mental-health provider, and the primary care physician.

One common barrier lies within the individual. Many older persons in need of psychological service do not define their problems in psychological terms. Data on depression in the elderly suggest that with increasing age there is an increase in the somatic, relative to the psychological, symptoms of psychiatric illness (Gurland, 1976). Many of the elderly hold a highly stigmatized view of psychological problems, assuming that the diagnosis of such problems will lead to prolonged psychiatric care or even institutionalization (Fisher, 1985). Interestingly, Kulka and Tamir (1978) found, using survey methodology, that the majority (two-thirds) of older patients who did define their problems as being psychological in nature had sought and received mental health care. An individual patient's problems with mobility or the lack of available transportation to the delivery site of mental health services may also represent a barrier to treatment.

Other barriers may be attributed to the mental health provider. There are relatively few mental health professionals trained in treating the elderly with behavioral techniques. The mental health community as a whole is characterized by a lack of treatment experience with the elderly (Garfinkle, 1975). Possible "ageist" biases may contribute to provider-related problems. This bias may be embodied in the feeling that anxiety or depression in old age is "normal" and not in need of intervention. Additionally, even after recent increases, limitations in Medicare reimbursement can contribute to the apparent reluctance of providers to treat problems of mental health in the elderly.

An additional barrier to treatment with behavioral therapy programs may arise because many patients experiencing psychiatric symptoms seek treatment from their primary care physician and are more likely to receive pharmacotherapy rather than psychological care. The physician in a general medicine setting is subject to realistic time constraints on the services he can deliver. As a result of their training, primary care physicians may not be familiar with current approaches toward psychiatric diagnosis and may be biased toward physical explanations for psychological or psychiatric problems. Finally, the general lack of appropriate mental health referral resources available to the physician may affect his choice of treatments. Due largely to the ease of prescribing medication, the elderly patient is more often given a drug rather than a program of psychosocial treatment.

A MODEL FOR PSYCHOSOCIAL TREATMENT FOR ANXIETY IN THE ELDERLY

It is possible to propose a model for providing treatment that can minimize the impact of the above barriers. Given the higher level of contact for the elderly patients with their physicians, the most practical psychosocial treatment for anxiety may be one that can be administered in the primary medical care setting. Further, receiving such treatment in the primary physician's office may reduce any perceived stigma associated with entering the mental health system. In an attempt to limit service costs, treatments that can be appropriately delivered by paraprofessionals would be highly desirable. Both Marks (1981) and Thompson, Gallagher, Nies, and Epstein (1983) have examined the delivery of behavioral treatments by trained paraprofessionals and have found highly satisfactory results.

As previously indicated, AMT is a package of treatment components. Relaxation training and controlled breathing are, perhaps, the most potent and most common components of AMT. Both can be readily administered by a trained paraprofessional. The therapeutic benefits for anxiety individuals includes direct reduction of arousal levels and indirect enhancement of cognitive performance. While numerous effective forms of relaxation training exist, progressive muscle relaxation has been demonstrated to be especially effective in high trait anxious elderly (Yesavage, Rose, & Spiegel, 1982; Yesavage & Jacob, 1984). This technique involves the tensing and relaxing of major muscle groups throughout the body and has deep muscle relaxation as its goal. Only minor modifications in technique due to reduced mobility or flexibility may be necessary for older patients. Controlled breathing involves instruction and practice in slow, paced diaphragmatic breathing which is done through the nose (Clark, Salkovskis, & Chalkley, 1985). Because of this component's low physical demand, no modification seems necessary for this technique across age groups. Addition of cognitive-behavioral components to the AMT package is readily accomplished; these can also be provided for the elderly in the primary care setting.

This chapter suggests that AMT holds promise as a potentially safe and effective treatment for much of the anxiety seen in the elderly. Controlled research in this area is necessary. An initial study should evaluate both the efficacy of AMT in the elderly as well as its administration by paraprofessionals in a primary care setting. Research comparing the benefits and the adverse effects of AMT with those of a short acting benzodiazepine is also essential. Finally, a study evaluating the relative contribution of the components of AMT would help to develop a treatment that is efficacious for reducing anxiety in the disorder and, at the same time, cost effective.

COMMENTARY

1. There are very few elderly patients with agoraphobia and OCD.

2. Most elderly patients with these symptoms are referred to primary care physicians for medical type treatment.

3. The issue of diagnosis is raised again. Worrying does not necessarily mean the presence of GAD (although relaxation exercises can help worry—an alternative to benzodiazepines). Rather than look at definitions of disorders, it may be better to look at symptom patterns. We may be prisoners of a diagnostic system that is not entirely relevant to this population.

4. Elderly patients with panic attacks may be divided into two groups, those with early onset and those with late onset. Early onset patients have avoidance behaviors that are similar to younger people.

Late onset panic attacks is characterized by fewer avoidance behaviors.

5. The elderly may be a good population to treat with psychosocial treatment because of increased time availability, and increased medicare insurance. Relaxation techniques are useful in lower class elderly as well as middle class elderly. Cognitive therapies are also useful in the elderly.

REFERENCES

Barlow, D. H., Cohen, A. S., Waddell, M. J., Vermilyea, B. B., Kloski, J. S., Blanchard, E. B., & DiNardo, P. A. (1984). Panic and generalized anxiety disorders: Nature and treatment. *Behavior Therapy, 15*, 431–449.

Barlow, D. H., Leitenberg, H., Agras, W. S., & Wincze, J. P. (1969). The transfer gap in systematic desensitization: An analogue study. *Behaviour Research and Therapy, 7*, 191–196.

Beck, A. T., Emery, G., & Greenberg, R. L. (1985). *Anxiety disorders and phobias: A cognitive perspective.* New York: Basic Books.

Becker, R. E., Heimberg, R. G., & Bellack, A. S. (1987). *Social skills training for depression.* New York: Pergamon Press.

Bergman, K. (1975). Nosology. In J. G. Howells (Ed.), *Modern perspectives in the psychiatry of old age* (pp. 170–187). New York: Brunner/Mazel.

Bernstein, D. A., & Borkovec, T. D. (1973). *Progressive relaxation training.* Champaign, IL: Research Press.

Blowers, C. M., Cobb, J. P., & Mathews, A. M. (1987). Treatment of generalized anxiety disorders. A comparative study. *Behaviour Research and Therapy, 25*, 493–502.

Borkovec, T. D., & Mathews, A. M. (1987). Treatment of non-phobic anxiety disorders. Unpublished manuscript.

Borkovec, T. D., Mathews, A. M., Chambers, A., Ebrehimi, S., Lytle, R., & Nelson, R. (in press). The effects of relaxation training with cognitive therapy or non-directive therapy and the role of relaxation induced anxiety in the treatment of generalized anxiety. *Journal of Consulting and Clinical Psychology.*

Butler, G., Covington, A., Hibbut, G., Klimes, I., & Gelder, M. (1987). Anxiety management for persistent generalized anxiety. *British Journal of Psychiatry, 151*, 535–542.

Clark, D. M., Salkovskis, P. M., & Chalkley, A. J. (1985). Respiratory control as a treatment for panic attacks. *Journal of Behavior Therapy and Experimental Psychiatry, 16,* 23–30.

Crowe, M. J., Marks, I. M., Agras, W. S., & Leitenberg, H. (1972). Time-limited desensitization implosion and shaping for phobics patients: A cross-over study. *Behaviour Research and Therapy, 10,* 319–328.

Eisdorfer, C. (1968). Arousal and performance: Experiments in verbal learning and tentative theory. In G. A. Talland (Ed.), *Human aging and behavior* (pp. 189–217). New York: Academic Press.

Ellis, A. (1977). The basic clinical theory and rational-emotive therapy. In A. Ellis & R. Grieger (Eds.), *Handbook of rational-emotive therapy* (pp. 3–34). New York: Springer Publishing Co.

Ellis, A., & Harper, R. A. (1961). *A guide to rational living.* Hollywood: Wilshire.

Fisher, K. (1985). Survey shows aged hit harder by CMHE cuts. *APA Monitor, 16,* 24.

Foa, E. B., Rothbaum, B. O., & Kozak, M. J. (1989). Behavioral treatments of anxiety and depression. In P. Kendall & D. Watson (Eds.), *Anxiety and depression: Distinctive and overlapping features.* New York: Academic Press.

Garfinkle, R. (1975). The reluctant therapist. *Gerontologist, 15,* 138–141.

Gelder, M. G., Bancroft, J. H., Gath, D., Johnston, B. W., Mathews, A. M., & Shaw, P. M. (1973). Specific and non-specific factors in behavior therapy. *British Journal of Psychiatry, 123,* 445–462.

Gelder, M. G., & Marks, I. M. (1968). Desensitization and phobias: A cross-over study. *British Journal of Psychiatry, 114,* 323–328.

Gelder, M. G., Marks, I. M., & Wolff, H. (1967). Desensitization and psychotherapy in phobic states: A controlled inquiry. *British Journal of Psychiatry, 113,* 53–73.

Goldfried, M. R. (1971). Systematic desensitization as training in self-control. *Journal of Consulting and Clinical Psychology, 37,* 228–235.

Gurland, B. J. (1976). Aims, organization, and initial studies of the Cross-National Project. *International Journal of Aging and Human Development, 7,* 283–293.

Gurland, B. J., Copeland, J., Korionsky, J., Kelleher, M., Sharpe, L., & Dean, L. L. (1983). *The mind and mood of aging.* New York: Haworth Press.

Hussain, R. A. (1981). *Geriatric Psychology: A behavioral perspective.* New York: Van Nostrand Reinhold.

Jannoun, L., Oppenheimer, C., & Gelder, M. (1982). A self-help treatment program for anxiety state patients. *Behavior Therapy, 13,* 103–111.

Kulka, R., & Tamir, L. (1978, November). *Patterns of help-seeking and formal support.* Paper presented at the Annual Meeting of the Gerontological Society, Dallas, Texas, November.

LaRue, A., & D'Elia, L. F. (1985). Anxiety and problem solving in middle-aged and elderly adults. *Experimental Aging Research, 11,* 215–220.

Lewinsohn, P. M. (1975). The behavioral study and treatment of depression. In M. Hersen, R. M. Eisler, & P. M. Miller (Eds.), *Progress in behavioral modification* (Vol. 1) (pp. 19–64). New York: Academic Press.

MacDonald, M., & Schnur, R. (1987). Anxieties and American elders: Proposals for assessment and treatment. In L. Michelson & L. M. Ascher (Eds.), *Anxiety and stress disorders* (pp. 395–424). New York: Guilford Press.

Marks, I. M. (1972). Flooding and allied treatments. In W. Agras (Ed.), *Behavior modification: Principles and clinical applications.* Boston: Little and Brown.

Marks, I. M. (1981). *Cure and care of neuroses.* New York: Wiley Press, 256–275.

Marks, I. M., Boulougouris, J., & Marsett, P. (1971). Flooding versus desensitization in the treatment of phobic disorders. *British Journal of Psychiatry, 119,* 353–375.

Mathews, A. M. (1978). Fear reduction research and clinical phobias. *Psychological Bulletin, 85,* 390–404.

Meichenbaum, D. (1974). Self-instructional methods. In F. H. Kanfer & A. P. Goldstein (Eds.), *Helping people change.* New York: Pergamon Press.

Meichenbaum, D. H., & Turk, D. (1973). Stress inoculation: A skills training approach to anxiety management (pp. 189–217). Unpublished manuscript, University of Waterloo, Ontario, Canada.

Rowan, V. C., Holburn, S. W., Walker, J. R., & Siddique, A. (1984). A rapid multi-component treatment for an obsessive-compulsive disorder. *Journal of Behavior Therapy and Experimental Psychiatry, 15,* 347–352.

Sallis, J. F., Lichstein, K. L., Clarkson, A. D., Stalgaitis, S., & Campbell, M. (1983). Anxiety and depression management for the elderly. *International Journal of Behavioral Gerontology, 1,* 3–12.

Steuer, J. L., Mintz, J., Hammen, C. L., Hill, M. A., Jarvik, L. F., McCarley, T., Motoike, P., & Rosen, R. (1984). Cognitive-behavioral and psychodynamic group psychotherapy in treatment of geriatric depression. *Journal of Consulting and Clinical Psychology, 52,* 180–189.

Suinn, R., & Richardson, F. (1971). Anxiety management training: A non-specific behavior therapy program for anxiety control. *Behavior Therapy, 2,* 498–510.

Thompson, L. W., Gallagher, D., & Breckenridge, J. S. (1987). Comparative effectiveness of psychotherapies for depressed elders. *Journal of Consulting and Clinical Psychology, 55,* 385–390.

Thompson, L., Gallagher, D., Nies, G., & Epstein, D. (1983). Evaluation of the effectiveness of professionals and non-professionals as instructors of "coping with depression" classes for elders. *Gerontologist, 23,* 390–396.

Thyer, B. (1981). Prolonged *in vivo* exposure therapy with a 70 year old woman. *Journal of Behavior Therapy and Experimental Psychiatry, 12,* 69–71.

Williams, S. L., Dooseman, G., & Kleinfield, E. (1984). Comparative effectiveness of guided mastery and exposure treatments for intractable phobias. *Journal of Consulting and Clinical Psychology, 52,* 505–518.

Williams, S. L., Turner, S. M., & Peer, D. E. (1985). Guided mastery and performance desensitization treatments for severe agoraphobia. *Journal of Consulting and Clinical Psychology, 53,* 237–247.

Wolpe, J. (1958). *Psychotherapy by reciprocal inhibition.* Stanford, CA: Stanford University Press.

Wolpe, J. (1973). *The practice of behavior therapy.* New York: Pergamon Press.

Yesavage, J. A. (1984). Relaxation and memory training in 39 elderly patients. *American Journal of Psychiatry, 141,* 778–781.

Yesavage, J. A., & Jacob, R. (1984). Effects of relaxation and mnemonics on memory, attention, and anxiety in the elderly. *Experimental Aging Research, 10,* 211–214.

Yesavage, J. A., Rose, T. L., & Spiegel, D. (1982). Relaxation training and memory improvement in elderly normals: Correlation of anxiety ratings and recall improvement. *Experimental Aging Research, 8,* 195–198.

Yesavage, J. A., Sheikh, J., Tanke, E. D., & Hill, R. (1988). Response to memory training and individual differences in verbal intelligence and state anxiety. *American Journal of Psychiatry, 145,* 636–639.

Psychotherapy of the Elderly Anxious Patient

13

Frank A. Johnson

This chapter will review factors that are associated with anxiety in later life. Case descriptions of symptomatic or syndromic expressions of anxiety will be examined along with psychotherapeutic interventions used in their treatment. Some reflections and conclusions concerning the optimal psychotherapeutic treatment of older patients will include possible directions for future research.

PSYCHOTHERAPY OF THE ELDERLY

Content, Themes, and "Life-Review"

Knight (1986) has differentiated five content areas which require consideration in the treatment of older patients: *coping with chronic illness, death and dying, marriage, love and sexuality, understanding the aging process*, and considerations of *ethnicity*. He and other authors list the common themes of "loss," "increased dependency" and "existential approach of death." The significance of "Life Review" (also called "Reminis-

215

cence") has been strongly emphasized as integral to the psychotherapy of the aging patient. Identified by Butler (1963) and Pinkus (1968), the need to re-experience the past has been seen as indispensable. Both Pinkus and Butler promoted the use of autobiographies, pilgrimages to former settings, and reunions with former friends and associates. They also suggested that the patients compose a genealogy and recommended the use of scrap books, photo albums, letters, and other memorabilia to stir memories. Sharing this information with the psychotherapist was regarded as helpful in recognizing prior achievements, but also in identifying unfinished or conflictual areas requiring reinspection or further "working-through."

Resistance and counter-resistance to psychotherapy among the elderly has been reviewed by Silberschatz and Curtis (1989b). They point to the need for creating objective "plan compatibility" for treatment to succeed. They also summarize literature on challenging the therapist, which can arise at the outset of treatment as a persistent issue. This may be misinterpreted as a characterologic or "neurotic" impasse, rather than a transference "test" concerning how the clinician will react. They also cited Niederland's (1961) observation that older persons may show a resistance to improvement on the basis of a form of "survivor guilt"—not so much related to unconscious hostility, but to shame over outlasting their spouse, siblings, family, or friends.

Modifications in Technique

An essential element in the psychotherapy of the elderly is the need for some degree of flexibility and modifications in technique. This was evident in clinical reports from earlier in the century, but became stipulated in the geropsychiatric literature after the 1970s. Pfeiffer (1971) acknowledged what he called the "special psychologic needs of the elderly" as justifying *greater activity*, a *symbolic giving* from the therapist, and an *increased awareness of transference and counter-transference*. *More limited goals* in psychotherapy were also recommended, as well as the projection of a *positive counter-transference*. The therapist was encouraged to be more revealing, expressive, and demonstrative. Later commentators have accentuated the needs for *time-limited procedures* that take into account both the psychic limitations (for an arduous, open-ended process) and the economic resources necessary to sustain this. Awareness of this by the therapist coordinates with the older patient's awareness of "limited remaining time" (Cath, 1984).

Psychotherapy in Conjunction with Other Interventions

Psychotherapy with the elderly almost always includes dealing with medications given by the psychotherapist, other physicians, or purchased "over-the counter." The practitioner should be sophisticated concerning interactions among medications given by multiple physicians, and be aware of the need to calibrate and individualize dosages. If the therapist is not a physician, close coordination with other practitioners is essential in regard to management of dosage. Usually the psychotherapist is in the best position to estimate the cumulative effects that medications impose on the patient's sensorium or mood. Along with this goes a responsibility for the patient's physical health shared through consulting with other health professionals, talking with family members, and at times initiating requests for medical consultations—activities that rarely happen with younger patients.

CLINICAL CASES

The following vignettes were selected to illustrate the psychotherapeutic management of a range of older patients in whom anxiety was either predominant or a significant corollary symptom. All patients, were directly managed by the author or followed through supervision of post-graduate trainees. Cases were chosen from surveying older persons seen in individual psychotherapy during 31 years of practice at several different settings. In looking through the records of former patients an unanticipated finding emerged. *Not one case of uncomplicated acute or chronic anxiety syndrome was discovered; all instances of conspicuous anxiety were accompanied by other primary or secondary symptomatology.* Moreover, in examining the available charts, *virtually all patients revealed some anxious symptoms, albeit sometimes of slight significance.* Also, in reviewing the author's cases, it was interesting to note that *the most common presenting psychiatric diagnosis in this age group was some form of depressive condition.* The cases selected here are not representative, but were chosen to display a range of disorders where anxiety was prominent. All patients have, of course, been disguised.

Case One - Pseudodementia: Anxiety, Simple Phobia, and Depression

Mrs. Polly Whitmore was a 76-year-old retired office worker referred with complaints of anxiousness, insomnia, and concerns about decline in memory, along with fears about attending church and going to social gatherings. There was a positive family history for suspected Alzheimer's Disease in her maternal grandmother, maternal aunt, mother, and older brother. She had been widowed three years previously, and phobically avoided going to church or places that reminded her of her husband. She had had a bilateral radical mastectomy for carcinoma of the breast fifteen years previously. Two married children resided nearby.

The patient was the younger of two children. Both her mother and maternal aunt were devout Christian Scientists. When she was 5, her grandmother moved in with her family because of progressive dementia. No explanation was furnished concerning her peculiar behavior. While the patient was in high school her grandmother died. Toward the end of college, her maternal aunt began to show severe problems with memory, which required hospitalization in a state facility. Because of her religious background, the patient had been explicitly trained to think that illness was due to "spiritual" causes, e.g., illness came because one was not devout. Also when someone died, there was an implication that the person perhaps had not prayed enough, or had insufficient faith. She was totally unfamiliar with scientific patho-physiological explanations of illness. After she married, her own mother began to show serious memory lapses. She subsequently required domiciliary care and died. A "crisis in faith" developed when concerns about her childrens' health led her to abandon Christian Science. Later, her husband reluctantly allowed her to work when her younger child left for college. Her older brother developed symptoms of severe memory loss when he was 68, followed by a swift decline and death by age 73. Two years following this the patient was unexpectedly widowed.

In interview she was an attractive, patrician woman whose chief complaint was that she was "worried about getting Alzheimer's." Baseline cognitive testing showed above normal intelligence without decline in calculation, constructional or psychomotor tasks. Her mental status showed a slightly lowered mood, along with an obsessional concern about "things she forgot": such as appointment times, correspondence, checking balance, or scores of ball games. Her insomnia was mild and surrounded the unresolved loss of her husband. Anxiety was concentrated on fears about dementia, and its implications for her children and grandchildren. She also experienced severe trembling and fear and difficulty breathing when attending funerals, going to church, or to parties at her country club.

Initially, she was seen weekly for a period of six months. Sessions focussed around the anger toward her mother whom she retrospectively saw as passive, weak, and unavailable to her. She particularly resented not getting factual information about the physiology of the body, or concerning the nature of her grandmother's and aunt's illnesses. She was also angry at her husband for not allowing her more independence, and distressed at the suddenness of his death, which left her with unanticipated responsibilities. She formed a strong working alliance, and rapidly showed symptomatic improvement, without medication. By confessing the "secret" ways in which she still "spoke" to her dead husband, she was able to discharge both her embarrassment and anger. She came to grips with some of the phobic dreads she had about revisiting places they had previously attended partly through reducing her "pretended" conversation with him.

In her efforts to construct a genealogy (on my request) she rehabilitated relations with "lost" cousins, and deepened those with younger kin. Repeated testing at six-month intervals showed no decline in intellectual functioning and acted to diminish her concern about memory loss. She also became aware that difficulties in remembering "what to do," were partly a result of solitary living. After three months she began attending places that she had previously avoided. Insomnia disappeared as she discussed the realistic sadness of being alone after living with other people for over 75 years. On the basis of her genealogy and the results of testing, she was advised of the likelihood that there was an "autosomal dominant condition" in her family from which both she and her progeny had apparently been spared.

She was seen monthly for an additional year and then only intermittently. In 1988 she had a recurrence of metastatic carcinoma, and over a six-month period rapidly declined despite chemotherapy. She had two appointments late in her illness. One was to discuss her recognition that "this time I know that I am going to die." On her final visit she complained of feeling bored. "I just seem to be sitting around in my living room waiting for the end!" I suggested that she dictate an *oral history* for her family on audio cassette tapes, which she did. Several months later, I was notified of her death by her daughter.

This case is representative of older persons who feel they are losing their cognitive skills—with or without prior family history of dementia. Most of these patients have some concurrent depression—sometimes of a severe nature. These symptoms are often intensified by widowhood, incomplete mourning, and solitary living. Previously highly organized and perfectionistic persons are especially prone to "pseudodementia" in their exaggeration of the significance of normal, senescent forgetfulness. This particular patient was seen early and responded well to a positive transference, cathartic reminiscence and various interpretations. These clarified her negative (ambivalent) reaction toward her mother, Christian Science and to the loss of her husband. Like many people who unexpectedly begin living solitary lives, part of her "memory loss" was due to the lack of someone to interact with and share daily experience, mull over the past and plan for the future. Based on the good, former working alliance the patient returned for several final sessions which were focused on existential and practical aspects of dying.

Case Two - Early Senile Dementia Alzheimer's Type Accompanied by Depression and Acute Anxiety

Malcolm Petit was a 61-year-old executive self-referred for treatment of declining memory of two years duration. This was accompanied by a moderate depression, confusion and recent episodes of anxiety. He "secretly" obtained work-ups at two different Alzheimer Clinics, both of which confirmed insidious and serious memory loss. Recently, he had become lost while travelling on the subway, and experienced terror and hyperventilation while trying to find his way to the office. When he first noticed declining memory, he was seven years into a happy second marriage, and had two very young children.

During his childhood he had lived in Berlin, where his father was a commercial attache. He attended German schools before he and his mother returned to the U.S. in 1939. His mother's health deteriorated and he was sent to live with a Japanese American physician who was a college friend of his father. While finishing high school, he fell in love with the physician's 16-year old daughter. His romance was interrupted as he left for college in 1941, and the family was sent off to an internment camp the following spring. Shortly thereafter, he was inducted into the Army. His "childhood sweetheart" subsequently died of tuberculosis, and almost at the same time, he was notified that his father had been executed in Vichy, France for "spying." Following the war, he completed college, married, had one son, and established himself as a freelance writer. As his son entered college he and his wife divorced amicably, whereupon he traveled to South America and "started a new life." He accepted a position in a regional office of an international brokerage house and after 7 years rose to an important executive position. At age 54 he had married a 37-year-old Colombian woman.

In interview he was a well-dressed, genial man with excellent verbal skills, but some obvious "word searching." Although presenting in a natural and self confident manner, he showed increased tension, moved about in his chair and sighed frequently. He seemed only moderately depressed—demonstrated by some long pauses in the conversation when he became misty-eyed. The immediate psychotherapeutic problems concerned (a) how to deal with his anxiety and mild depression, (b) how to contend with the conscious and unconscious denial concerning realistic cognitive decline, and (c) how to facilitate his objectively dealing with his wife and business associates. He was seen weekly for two months and produced a detailed life-history. Conflicts emerged in his hostility concerning the loss of his father and childhood sweetheart. Discussing these losses reactivated feelings of being deprived of his father's companionship during his early life, and of his mother's nurturance due to a series of physical illnesses. His current depression centered on his recognition of progressive loss of cognitive skills.

A positive transference was readily established on the basis of common age and avocational interests (German *lieder*). Each visit began as if it were the first. He would disclose the nature of his symptoms, his fear of being discovered, and his rationalization that he was only experiencing the "usual problem of early aging." He then would ask me, "Well, but what do *you* think?" I repeatedly and gently stated that the evidence of psychological testing, and his current symptoms indicated a progressive and severe loss of recent memory. Antidepressant medication was considered, but not given because he did not show vegetative symptoms or signs of a fixed depression.

After several months, on the patient's suggestion, his wife came in for an appointment to provide her with an explanation of what was happening. This constituted a breakthrough in his denial, and allowed him to begin talking about the need for medical retirement. Repeated recommendations had been made that *he* take the initiative in broaching his problem to his superiors. He finally did this, and was promptly given medical leave, followed by his early retirement on the basis of SDAT. Thereafter, he was seen every four to six weeks, concerning adaptational problems regarding his family, the containment of hostility, and planning for the future. He eventually moved to a border town in California that permitted his wife more socialization and provided inexpensive child care. No medications were required. The patient continued to show a high capacity for lively and intelligent conversation. As he poignantly said, "Doctor, I'm not 'nuts.' I feel the same inside as I always did. I think I know everything that is going on in this room. I just can't *remember* anything."

This case illustrates the successful use of psychotherapy in early SDAT. Despite his severe recent memory loss, resolution of denial and depression were achieved through conventional investigation of conflicts underlying the threat of illness. This then led to a realistic working through of the social, economic and family adaptations following his decision to retire. Despite his manifest inability to remember from week to week details of what we had discussed before, there was a detectable (and strong) *emotional continuity* despite his problems in accessing *cognitive* memory. Both my office and myself became increasingly familiar to him. Like many people with early dementia, he showed a staunch denial which only slowly yielded to realistic acceptance of his infirmity. Following the practical negotiation of retirement and relocation, more severe memory loss made travel impractical—something that commonly happens as even supportive therapy becomes less feasible in progressive dementia. The effectiveness, however, of early intervention is demonstrated by this patient's case.

Case Three - Depression Accompanied by Simple Phobias and Anxiety

Ursula Potter was a 68-year-old widow of a politician who, following her husband's death ten years previously, had become

severely depressed, was hospitalized for 3 months, and treated
with antidepressants. Recently, following a severe viral infection, she again became anxious and depressed, began to avoid
contact with people, and experienced recurrent thoughts concerning "how she had wasted her life." She also had moderate
insomnia and loss of appetite. Her most debilitating symptoms
were those of severe apprehension in preparation for leaving
home or in attending obligatory social functions. This anxiety
would focus on past events when the patient felt embarrassed or
afraid of having to make small talk. Eventually she became
frightened of operating her car, and a younger sister agreed to
drive her to the psychotherapist.

In interview, she was a stylish, attractive woman looking
younger than her stated age. She was alert and spoke in a
determined voice, but seemed on the verge of crying. She
launched into a critical discussion of her married life centering
on anger about not having fulfilled herself. She had been married directly following college to a young lawyer who did not
want children. She was closely involved in her husband's politi-
cal life, and when she was 45, discovered that he was having a
liaison with a close friend of hers. Although their marriage
straightened out, it continued to be haunted by the treacherous
affair. Her husband subsequently died of a myocardial infarction at age 59. Following the rehash of his affair, her anger
broadened toward his preventing their having children, not
allowing her to accept interesting employment and spending 34
years "telling her what to do." She was furious at his leaving his
inherited estate to be managed by an associate whom she
described as "a complete, simpering idiot." She was also jealous
of her younger sister who had led a "charmed life."

The patient was begun on imipramine, 50 mg tid and seen
twice a week for 8 weeks. She made considerable improvement; insomnia diminished as self-recriminatory thoughts re-
ceded. She had a showdown with her sister and resumed driving. After four months she discontinued medications while I
was on vacation. She also sold some family property and in-
vested the proceeds into a mutual fund. She became heavily

involved in both volunteer and recreational activities. She was thereafter seen in monthly therapeutic sessions for an additional year before terminating. Following this, she travelled to Europe and thereafter, kept in contact by sending holiday cards.

This case illustrates the precipitation of a depressive reaction that recapitulated the incomplete mourning based on unresolved anger toward her dead husband. Her symptoms of anxiety and insomnia responded rapidly to catharsis plus anti-depressant medicine. Incomplete resolution of previous losses is not an uncommon complaint among elderly patients. Also, as in this case, some patients seem to crave an opportunity to redress past failures and disappointments, at times concerning very "ancient history." In this patient's recovery the opportunity to review her "past" led to the capacity to change her "present." The release from a dependent relationship to her little sister plus her reinvestment in new activities helped to turn around the former anxious, hostile dependency. Gaining economic and symbolic independence from her husband's trust was also helpful in refuting his posthumous control.

Case Four—Paraphrenia, Anxiety, and Early Dementia

Ina Gottlieb was a 78-year-old, childless widow, referred because of severe anxiety concerning "people" who she was seeing in the mirrors of her apartment for the past three months. She also had a 2 year history of gradually losing facility with recent memory, and a need to search for words to describe common objects. The patient had attended two years of college and then worked for an investment firm as a commodities analyst. She married at 35 and became the Mary Poppins of her family, both for the children of her siblings and later for her grand nieces and nephews. She retired in her mid-sixties and was widowed shortly thereafter. As her old neighborhood deteriorated, the family prevailed on her to come to the West Coast and live in a nearby life care facility. Upon relocation, her moderate cognitive symptoms became exaggerated.

When first interviewed, she was a well dressed, extremely pleasant, intelligent woman who was alert, but highly apprehensive. Her anxiousness centered on concerns about seeing women in the mirrors of her bathroom, hallways, and in the reflections of certain pictures hanging in her living and dining rooms. She did not recognize "these people," even though they were always wearing her clothes. Gradually she developed the conviction that these women were actually "living in the walls," and were intent on stealing her things and terrifying her. She had a good fund of general information, but showed definite word-searching problems, and deficiencies in recent memory. She also had difficulty making simple calculations, but was oriented to time and place, and could recall recent social events with reasonable clarity. Symptoms of *paraphrenia* were confined to her own apartment. Psychological testing confirmed a definite early dementia.

During a "house call" accompanied by her nephew, she "introduced" us to the inhabitants who lurked in her bathroom, and living areas. When told that these "people" were images of herself, she was polite but unconvinced. With her cooperation several mirrors were removed, and some of the larger pictures covered with newspaper. She was also treated palliatively with small doses of haloperidol (0.5 mg bid). The family was outstanding in taking her on trips, providing diversions during the daytime and telephoning her frequently. Her panic concerning these apparitions diminished, although she was worried that the managers of her facility might learn about their presence. In shouting at these creatures she finally drew the attention of her neighbors, and eventually the managers. During the following year, she became increasingly preoccupied, and began to show more severe memory loss and disconnection from her environment. Additional house calls were made to supervise the daytime nursing help and recheck her functional capacity. Finally, she was hospitalized for two-and-a-half weeks (treated by another psychiatrist) and given three modified electroshock treatments. These reduced the obsessional preoccupations, but produced increased confusion. Returning to her apartment, she required increasing day and evening care, and finally was transferred to a skilled care facility. Subsequently she was seen several times—mostly to be sure there was no toxic or pharmacologic stress that might be aggravating her baseline dementia. Her dementia gradually became more profound, and after several months she passed away due to the effects of a large cystic ovarian tumor.

When first contacted, the patient was treated as a mild, monosymptomatic case of paraphrenia. She was initially managed with supportive psychotherapy, environmental manipulation (covering the mirrors) and low dosages of neuroleptic. As her dementia increased, family and ancillary help were added to sustain independent living. Referral to another clinician and a short course of electroshock was then attempted in a vain effort to rehabilitate functioning. This case required great flexibility including "house calls," frequent telephone contact, and close liaison with the family and other practitioners. Her case is included here to illustrate that supportive psychotherapeutic work may yield to other interventions and management in the face of deterioration of a clinical condition. She also represents an excellent example of where the cooperation of family members potentiates both the understanding and effective treatment of the patient.

Case Five—Anxiety and Reactive Depression in Terminal Carcinoma

Rebecca Tulliver was a 68-year-old widow of a physician seen in an inpatient consultation requested by her oncologist because of increasing depression, nocturnal anxiety attacks, "non-compliance," and statements of hopelessness. Carcinoma of the breast had been treated 13 years previously through radical mastectomy and radiation. Subcutaneous and pleural metastases recurred when she was 65, and were treated with chemotherapy. During the succeeding three years she lost weight, had less energy, and did not respond to additional chemotherapy. Recently she had developed icterus and incurred a pathological fracture of the humerus. The oncologist recommended beginning chemotherapy with an experimental medication. Her internist was negativistic, and said that her condition "was hopeless," and that she "wanted to be left alone to die." The clinical difference of opinion between her oncologist and internist was also reflected in her family. Her older daughter felt that "she should not give up, and should give the new medication a chance." Her younger daughter felt that having to go through another course of treatment was purposeless, and would only make her more miserable. The nursing staff was divided in their opinion; some of them treated her as a petulant, uncooperative child, while others tried to protect her from the more critical physician and nursing staff.

The patient had grown up in St. Louis and received a masters degree in mathematics prior to locating in Hartford where her husband practiced as a general surgeon. She had two children during her early 30's, and resumed working as an insurance actuary after they entered high school. She was very active in the community and had always masterminded the financial and social affairs of the family.

Her panic attacks, anger, and acute depression were clearly related to the sudden loss of ability to direct her own life, and to the controversy regarding her medical care. It was also evident to her that she was near the end of her life; the loss of control at this point was especially demeaning and terrifying to her. Despite an initial reluctance, she requested continuing the consultation. She complained that nobody wanted to talk to her about *dying*, but instead everybody seemed to want to talk to her about *living*. She faced this with me by ventilating her apprehension about death, which she knew was swiftly approaching. She was also able to state how furious she was that everyone was quibbling about what to do with her, rather than considering what she might want to do with herself. Upon her recommendation, I met with the daughters and was able to tell them what she wanted to do. The older daughter called me the following day and agreed that her mother's wishes should be followed. Also after reading my notes in the chart, her oncologist backed off and suggested that she only be given analgesia, intravenous fluids, and other supporting measures. Her anxiety symptoms diminished although she continued to awaken in mild states of disorientation and fear, possibly aggravated by morphine-sulphate. Arrangements were made to transfer her to a convalescent hospital. Before she left, she thanked me for helping her regain control of the situation, and also for being able to discuss her feelings about imminent death.

This case illustrates the development of severe focal anxiety due to the indecision concerning the management of her terminal illness. It also reflected her inability to talk to family or physicians about her own mortality and her sense of loss of control. This case illustrates the need to deal with the collective anxieties of various family members and professionals who were involved in their own despair and sense of helplessness in the midst of caring for this brave and independent older woman.

Case Six—Adjustment Disorder, Panic, and Suicide Attempt

Bruce Dowling was an 82-year-old-fruit tree farmer referred by his internist following a serious suicide attempt. He was brought up on a ranch in midland California, married in 1921 and had four children. His business thrived as he diversified into raising grapes for local wineries. His marriage had always been cordial but cool. After reaching 60 his wife gravitated toward church work and declined engaging in sex, travelling, or in doing "adventurous" things. Through participation in a charitable foundation, he met a 56-year-old separated woman. Their friendship deepened, and they periodically spent clandestine vacations together. After five years their special relationship began to invite suspicion. Finally, his oldest son ran into his father and "woman-friend" while they were sharing Sunday breakfast in a local motel. A family conference was held where the father was chastised, embarrassed, and made to feel guilty. At that same time his "lover" became remorseful and decided that they should never see each other again. Directly following this, the patient made an attempt on his life using a vacuum cleaner hose connected to his automobile tailpipe. The hose disengaged and he

was rushed to a local hospital where arrangements were made
for a psychiatric consultation.

In interview he presented as a handsome, phlegmatic but
tremulous man who looked 62 rather than his actual age of 82.
He was embarrassed about "causing trouble" and chagrined
that he had not died. Although he had felt despondent and
angry at the time of his suicide attempt, his symptoms in the
hospital were for severe anxiety. In addition to insomnia,
sweating, and obsessional thoughts about his lover, he experienced a series of classical anxiety attacks, which were related
to trying to devise a solution, such as "running away together."
These featured a fear that he was going to die from some
physical cause. Although feeling sincerely guilty, he felt hope-
lessly in the grips of "the most important love of my life." He
found himself obsessed with thoughts about her beauty, her
poise, and her sensuality. Speaking to him several times in the
hospital gave me reassurance that he would not make another
suicide attempt. His level of apprehension diminished with a
decrease in sweating, palpitations, and labored breathing. He
was placed on chlordiazepoxide (25 mg tid) and scheduled for
outpatient psychotherapy. He was followed for three outpatient visits, and began to deal productively with realistic
alternatives. The psychotherapeutic aim was to analyze some
of the repressed emotional ingredients in his romance that led
to its perilous inflation and dangerousness. Discussing his clandestine relationship with a third party rapidly brought it into
perspective, and helped him to look more cross-sectionally at
his whole life. Interestingly, his wife was not shocked at his
having a romance; in fact she had felt guilty because of her
own avoidance of sex. As the patient speculated, she might
have even adjusted to a divorce. However, his sons were not so
lenient, and were furious at their father for what he had done.
He continued to be subjected to family conferences where he
was castigated and shamed. Also, his sons became distrustful
of the psychotherapy, insofar as it was apparently not being
devoted to his punishment and "repentance." Because of this
they brought pressure on the patient, and he missed several

appointments. Finally he wrote a letter saying that it was impossible for him to tolerate the pressure from the family, and he essentially was "caving in" (his term) to their demands.

This case illustrates the development of acute anxiety related both to the terror of discovery, and fear of loss of a romantic love object in an elderly man, whose conflicts about this nearly resulted in his death. Attempts to investigate this psychotherapeutically were initially successful but aborted because of family pressures. Anxiety was modified by the objectification of events that brought some of the unconscious determinants out into his awareness. As in an adolescent "crush," the secretive, forbidden passion and the unlikelihood of realistic solution all combined to produce the combination of intense exhilaration and anxiety (Kaplan & Johnson, 1978). Sudden deprivation of this was accompanied by external shaming, combining to produce intense pressure on this patient.

This gentleman was seen in the early 1960s at a time preceding the common use of family psychotherapeutic techniques. In retrospect a more advantageous situation would have been created had the therapist interviewed other family members, and gained their support and cooperation. This would have allowed the sons to deal with their inflated rage in a more reasonable (and nonoedipal) manner. Also the wife would have been given the opportunity for gaining more information about herself, instead of being buried in the pity and righteous indignation of her sons.

Case Seven—Major Depression, Anxiety, and Suicide Attempt in Longstanding Somataform Disorder

Allen Harvard was an 85-year-old retired furniture store manager admitted after a nearly successful suicide attempt through an overdose of accumulated sedatives. The patient had been widowed three years previously, but denied this was a problem. However, he had been noticed to become more listless, lacking in energy, and absorbed in chronic somatic complaints concerning the lower intestinal track. He had been hospitalized in 1940

for depression secondary to a business slump and received elec-
troconvulsive therapy (ECT) with prompt improvement. He had
a longstanding history of severe somatic complaints, sequentially involving the genito-urinary tract, nasal sinuses, and lower
intestine. He had been in a serious automobile accident at 55 in
which he incurred a laceration of the liver. For the past 20 years
he suffered episodes of severe colonic spasms, right lower quad-
rant pain, with alternating diarrhea and constipation. He had
been seen by numerous gastro-enterologists and diagnosed as
having "irritable bowel syndrome." I first saw him in consultation in the hospital to evaluate his current psychiatric condition.

In interview he was a casually dressed gentleman who was
obviously sad but making determined efforts to be congenial
and cooperative. He said he had never attempted suicide before, but for the last three months lost interest in watching
sports, fishing, playing cards, or socializing. He had become
very discouraged by multiple physical symptoms. He stated
that he felt "life was not worth living." He complained of feeling
very anxious, and worried about falling. His conversation centered around descriptions of pains and spasms in his lower
abdomen. He expressed concerns about "something growing
down there."

A series of antidepressants were tried but each produced
serious postural hypertension. He was placed on low dosage of
Alprazolam (0.25 mg tid) but not given evening sedation. His
somatizations became increasingly prominent and he developed the conviction that he had "stomach cancer." He repeatedly stated "he wished we had let him die." He was transferred
to another hospital in order to receive a short course of electroshock treatment. Three treatments produced a slight euphoria
and a prompt cessation of his somatized delusion, but left him
confused. Despite the advice of his family he signed out of the
hospital, but agreed to be followed in supportive psychotherapy.

The patient was the second of five children and was always
noted for his "pleasant personality" and ability to get along with
people. Beginning in late adolescence he had a succession of

genito-urinary symptoms following treatments for gonorrhea. During his 30's and 40's he had chronic sinusitis that involved multiple visits for medications, drainage, and diathermy. However, his most serious cluster of physical symptoms followed his automobile accident at age 55 and centered on gastro-intestinal complaints. He was married at 32 to a dietician; they had one child. He worked in retail sales and was well respected. He was an excellent card player and retained a high interest in sports. He insisted that he had adapted well to his wife's death. He said "at my age you expect things like that; nobody lives forever."

The slight confusion following ECT cleared rapidly. Upon my encouragement he resumed socializing with friends, playing cards, and going fishing. My meetings with him became inter-mittent, usually coincident with a flare-up of his irritable colon symptoms. On these occasions he would dramatically describe the character of his stools, the location of pains, the timing of spasms, the amount of flatulence—all addressed to me for purposes of seeking my opinion. Characteristically, he would also complain of "nervousness" and apprehension about "what these symptoms might mean." His pattern was to call every 2–3 months, and to come in twice a year. Sessions always began with a detailed account of his abdominal symptoms. During this communication I listened carefully, asked questions, and jotted down notes. I was careful to deny any expertise (as a pseudogastroenterologist), but cooperated with him in decid-ing what *he* might do to seek additional consultation. He was emphatic about not wanting to be on any psychotropic medica-tion.

I was usually able to change the topic of conversation and discuss either past events or recent interactions with friends or family. He would only grudgingly admit to psychological prob-lems, and then would say they were due to "his bowels." He periodically made appointments with new diagnosticians (in-ternists, enterologists) as a way of handling his more intense anxieties. Meanwhile, I continued to see him and remained in contact with his two regular specialists who had faithfully followed him in the past.

Supportive psychotherapy in this case demanded listening attentively to the somatizations that the patient wished to discuss. He chiefly saw his difficulties as associated with gastrointestinal symptoms and complaints. Emotional features were regarded as "secondary" by him. By accepting this, the psychotherapist was able to offer reassurance, and go on to discuss other matters. Talking about the past readily distracted him from current problems and became an important repository of shared information. He was seen once every six weeks but would telephone periodically to ask for advice, or sometimes just "to say hello." Coaxing him to resume his previous activities was also crucial in his rehabilitation. No "depth" interpretations were made. A positive, cooperative transference was used to reassure him about his capability of either overcoming or enduring his symptons.

One of the biggest counter-transference problems in these situations focuses on the boredom and sense of futility in listening to what seems to be endless recitations about colons, feces, "gas," "stabbing pains," and peristaltic rushes. Not being able to psychologize such intestinal narratives is a cruel deprivation for the average psychotherapist, but must be endured in order to help the patient through catharsis (literal as well as symbolic). A positive transference is also essential to facilitate temporary improvement. Also, perhaps needless to point out, these individuals keep returning unless they tire of the therapist.

Case Eight—Anxiety, Rage, and Depression in a Dependent Personality

When first seen, "Buck" Nelson was a 65-year-old retired Air Force Colonel who was referred through an Alzheimer's Clinic for treatment of crying spells and difficulty in coping with his wife's rapidly advancing dementia. In interview he was a muscular man who did not look his age; he was tense and pent-up in his affect—as if trying not to cry. Initially laconic, and blunt in his conversation, he relaxed and began to recite his intense disappointment regarding the deteriorating health of his wife. Anxiousness was shown by sweating, moving about in his chair, breathing "hard" and repetitiously twisting a handkerchief in his hands. Emotion was copious and took the form of mixtures of crying and expression of anger about "being in this goddamn situation." During the past year and a half, he had taken over preparing meals, laying out clothing, transporting his wife to various physicians and supervising her life down to the last detail. He was furious with having to do all of this at this point in his life. He was also angry at the fact that this situation elicited so much emotion in him. He complained that "he never cried like this before."

He had grown up in Minneapolis as the elder of two sons, and was close to his mother. His father was physically abusive to the entire family. On several occasions he was directly combative with his father, which resulted in his being ejected from home. (As he spoke with "pride" about being independent since age 15, he cried copiously). He finished high school in 1939, entered the service and was trained as a combat pilot serving in the European Theatre as a Wing Commander. At the end of the war he married an Air Force Officer; they had two children, and he elected to stay in the service. After sponsored college training he rose to positions of increasing responsibility before retiring in 1969. By his own admission, he had been an authoritarian husband and father, but unlike his own father "tried to be fair." He was known as a tough, but good natured person and officer. He had a close and extremely dependent relationship with his wife, who was responsible for running the family and finances. Following retirement, he settled in California and became a consultant to a small aerospace firm, while his wife worked in a bank. After ten years they both stopped working and began what they hoped would be a "real retirement" with plans for extensive touring, playing golf, and enjoying life together. His wife's symptoms of forgetfulness and confusion developed shortly after this.

A strong transference was established on the basis of a "cohort effect" and a common interest in military aircraft. In psychotherapy the primary problem was his inability to accept these misfortunes and moreover, to deal with the copious emotion that accompanied these inescapable emotions. Historical reminiscence was helpful in bringing earlier feelings of rage and depression to consciousness. The most poignant of these centered around the tender feelings he had for his mother, his father's abuse of her and the futility he felt in trying to protect her. He was able to recall crying about this as a youngster and also later at the time of her death. He also remembered crying when he had to write letters to widows and family members of young men that had been shot down during the war. This again was accompanied by a rage at the circumstances under which they died, and about the question as to "why was this all necessary?"

His anxiety, which was quite manifest, began to be understood as resulting from his unsuccessful efforts to contain and control both his aggression, and his crying. The connection between anger and depression was in regard to the *injustice* or unfairness in his witnessing his wife's slow death through Alzheimer's. Gradually his more conscious acceptance of both anger and sadness seemed to be helpful, along with a catharsis about past and present events. During later appointments it became evident that he had been exceedingly dependent on his wife, and that part of his anger was related to the violent switch in roles, as he was now totally responsible for domestic and social life of the family. This "switch" unmasked his own dependency needs, and released the anger and depression about being kicked out of his home as an adolescent. He also began to realize how much her symptoms distressed him. He said "he had always hated people who were stupid and couldn't do things," and found that his wife's dementia at times automatically unleashed his anger and disgust. He also felt relieved in being able to discuss the unspeakable wish that she would die as soon as possible (although he always disavowed any fantasies about killing her). Both his anxiety and his crying diminished but did not disappear. He also gradually became troubled by the dependency implication of "having to see a shrink." He discontinued treatment after 6 months (17 sessions) because of his partial improvement, desire to save money, and problems commuting to my office (75 miles away).

This was an example of supportive psychotherapy in a person who never would have sought treatment except for the circumstances of his spouse's decline. The reversal of dependency and deferment of retirement pleasure re-exacerbated a long buried furor and sadness connected with both wartime and juvenile life-experience. Reconnecting his present symptoms with the past was *partly* effective in reducing his symptoms. Although partially relieved, the experience of discussing his feelings eventually became threatening and he discontinued treatment. It is not uncommon to see male caregivers become emotionally depleted at having to undertake domestic responsibilities late in life. For unusually dependent men (or women) such responsibilities may appear awesome. In supportive psychotherapy, interpretation about characterologic problems is useless. However, helping the patient plan to redistribute chores or merely to commiserate with their difficulty may often be helpful.

SUMMARY

General Considerations of Dynamic and Supportive Treatment

The preceding cases demonstrate mixtures of supportive and investigative (dynamic) psychotherapy applied to a range of conditions in which *anxiety* was prominent. Although none of these cases was studied using instrumented measurements of pre- and post-treatment, objective clinical improvement occurred in each instance, albeit to various degrees. Symptoms of anxiety were responsive in most cases to the establishment of therapeutic alliance, catharsis accompanying the "backward drift" (Glover, 1956), and interpretations concerning the life-historical nature of recent conflict. A variety of environmental manipulations were also promoted, especially in the more supportive treatment.

For patients at any age, the dynamic treatment of acute or chronic anxiousness is directed at examining both hidden and obvious life-historical events which presumably constitute the "psychic components" of the contemporary anxiety experience. It is common that the *events* have not been forgotten, but rather that the *affects* have been sealed off. Dynamic psy-

chotherapy thus attempts to promote an emotional re-experience and interpretation of these earlier situations. If done
accurately, this permits the redistribution of some of the currently experienced (uncomfortable) feelings back into the past,
and moreover to examine a variety of feelings (outside of
terror) which accompanied the earlier trauma. Among the
emotions uncovered during the review of the past are anger,
embarrassment, guilt, and feelings of futility or helplessness.
Psychotherapy also should examine recent object relations,
especially those events may be associated with promoting anxiety. Also, the cultivation of a positive transference allows for
more permissive "use" of the transference as a fulcrum for
improvement (Johnson, 1989). As in some of the earlier as-
sumptions of derived psychoanalytic procedures (Deutsch and
Murphy, 1960), such a use of transference is more a factor of
not questioning (i.e., not "investigating") positive transference
than "manipulating" the transference.

In all cases, the use of "Reminiscence" was invaluable toward diminishing the adverse "cohort effect" of differential
age between the therapist and patient and providing the basis
for selective interpretations and interventions.

Although many research questions remain to be answered
concerning psychiatry in this age group, a large volume of case
reports testify to the feasibility of engaging older persons in
various forms of psychological treatment, either as an adjunct
or a primary approach to a range of clinical conditions. Older
people are reported to have increased life-historical perspective, motivation to achieve change expeditiously and, usually
down-to-earth expectations for improvement. As in any age
group, older persons show varying capacities for participation
in psychotherapy. In the cases reported here, mixtures of dynamic and supportive psychotherapy were useful in reducing
or eliminating symptoms of anxiety. Moreover, in most cases,
anxiety was only a corollary symptom to more serious underlying disorders (of depression, somatization, paraphrenia, or dementia).

Life-historical and recent determinants relating to anxiety
are usually readily discoverable, and may be helpful in provid-

ing relief through a combination of insight and catharsis. However, anxiety connected to longstanding Somatoform Disorders (as in Case 7) does not remit in the face of interpretation. However, it may be responsive to the influence of a positive transference, with or without the use of anxiolytics or, in some cases, antidepressives. Similarly, the convictions about ideas of reference in paraphrenia are ordinarily unshakable through interpretation. However, the psychotherapist may be successful in lowering the anxiety level or even in advising environmental changes that reduce the symptomatology—again, with or without medication.

The need for therapeutic flexibility in this age group takes into account the realistic, status and functional characteristics of persons in our society. As with most adolescents, these patients want and need *some degree of natural association* with the therapist. This often involves more overt emotional responsiveness from the therapist and disclosure of a modicum of realistic information. In the author's experience such limited responsiveness serves to delineate the "therapeutic barrier" just as effectively as *total* nonresponsiveness does in younger and middle aged adults in a psychoanalytic situation. The kind of information divulged concerns therapist's reactions to sporting events, news items or a shared area of interest, e.g., German lieder or military aircraft of WW II. Although restricted in length and consciously monitored, such disclosure is in the genre of normative "small talk," devised to affirm positive feelings, mutuality and egalitarian acceptance rather than provide penetrating insights into the reality of the therapist's private world, that might indeed compromise the therapeutic relationship.

Other modifications evolve naturally: Patients will often require longer to walk to the office from the waiting room. Therapists may assist an arthritic 80-year old in taking off her coat, or arising from her chair at the end of the hour. Telephone contact is commonly used to check on reactions to medication or even partly substitute for an office visit in persons who are infirm. House calls and hospital visits may be imperative in order to continue treatment during periods of illness or following accidents.

Modification of fee may be a consideration in some older patients, most of whom subsist on Social Security, and a small fixed income. Although short-term psychotherapy for serious acute psychiatric conditions may be covered by Medicare or private insurance, prolonged out-patient psychotherapy for adjustment reactions, psychoneurosis, or character disorders usually is not sustained beyond a few visits. The therapist may then be faced with the decision to reduce fee (on a sliding scale), refer to a public clinic, or try to mobilize the patient's acceptance of the regular fee, perhaps for an estimated, time-limited procedure.

In emphasizing the need to consider modifications with some older patients the author may inadvertently have introduced bias, through implying that more traditional approaches are not often appropriate. Such is not the case. Some patients in this age group adapt well to investigative psychotherapies (or psychoanalysis) taking place over extended periods of time and providing an opportunity for symptomatic and cognitive changes based on insight and analysis of resistance and transference. Eloquent examples of these are available in the literature (Pollack, 1982; Nemiroff & Colarusso, 1985) testifying to the satisfactory use of more standard techniques. In fact, over-consideration of modifications on an *a priori* basis may constitute a form of negative countertransference representing an unconscious prejudice toward other persons ("ageism") (Lannon, 1989).

Pharmacologic Considerations and Behavior Techniques

Virtually all patients in this age group enter psychotherapy already taking medications for either physical and/or psychological problems. Each case demands careful assessment in regard to changing dosage levels, switching to different medications and (all too frequently) in weaning patients away from the injudicious, chronic use of sedative/hypnotics. In this author's experience, many patients arrive in treatment already over-medicated. The reduction or elimination of certain medications is enhanced by the support and insight provided by expressive psychotherapy.

The author shares Marmor's (1971) speculation that repetitious interpretations, subtle persuasion, and shared "reality-testing" can be understood according to *behavioral principles* involving identification, reinforcement, reward and learning. Several of the cases reported here had mild phobic symptomatology which yielded to a combination of interpretations, positive transference, and the gradual assumption of regular activity. More refractory phobic symptoms, if prominent, indicate the need for referral to behavioral specialists who may attempt to desensitize the patient through more direct behavioral techniques.

Themes and Issues in Psychotherapy

Physical Health is a prominent issue in the treatment of elderly persons, both as a realistic concern and symbolically in the form of psychic associations, somatizations, or at times denial of physical symptomatology. In acute conditions, it generally takes an older person longer to recover from incidental illness. Often viral infections, uncomplicated fractures, or elective surgery may be looked on as "just *one more unacceptable thing*" which can seriously destabilize the person's composure or desire to continue living.

In this age group, *mourning reactions* are routine and involve normal grieving following a recent bereavement. Usually this is responsive to solicitous "listening" and consolation. Delayed and protracted states of mourning that surface in an anxious depression surrounding a loss of significant person many years previously are more difficult to handle. In some instances a rehashing and working through of psychological issues not faced following the original loss can be effectively done.

All older patients talk about the realistic issue of mortality, usually in a matter-of-fact manner. Two of the cases presented here involved serious suicide attempts. Neither of these persons was overtly or severely depressed. Typically this makes the suicidal risk more ominous, since others are not alert to the possibility. In having more acceptance of dying, the elderly patient may decide to "cash in" more out of resignation, or out of temporary furor than a fixed depression or sense of chronic desolation. In contrast, patients who are more openly anxious and depressed, call attention to themselves in a way that may lead to treatment and distraction from their suicidal preoccupations.

It is also challenging for the psychotherapist to deal with the existential issues of loneliness, boredom, and loss of meaning that occur in some older people. Even in persons having a network of family and friendly connections, there still may be despondency and boredom with solitary living, and the desolation encountered as spouses, companions, family and friends, succumb to age, medical disease or accident. Psychotherapeutically, these losses may be dealt with directly in terms of their past and present significance. The transference may furnish a transitional relationship, but must be eventually replaced by reinvestment in other persons and activities.

The need to discuss the immanence of death was present in two of the cases reported here. Medical practitioners especially, tend to regard death as a "grim reaper" and an enemy of the patient and therapist. Physicians find it hard to "give up." This makes it difficult to face the needs that patients may have to talk about actually dying. Patients are often more prepared to die than their health personnel or families are to lose them. The issue of dying may become exclusively delegated to psychotherapists, with the implication that this subject is taboo with other medical personnel, and an un-warranted burden on the family "who are not prepared for this."

Other themes susceptible to psychotherapeutic intervention are connected to the physiologic lowering of zestful appetites (eating, engaging in sex, "exploring," relating to people). Some of this decline is realistically based. It is harder for most older (or younger) people to prepare and enjoy eating, if they are not sharing meals. Also the former consolation and excitement of close tactile comfort and sensuality often are dealt with through denial. Moreover, it is all too easy for persons in this age group to rationalize having fewer social contacts and finding younger people "boring" or banal. This invariably feeds into diminished self esteem which in a circular way diminishes even further the numbers of contacts. The psychotherapist attempts to make the person aware of this cycle, and if possible to break it.

RESEARCH POSSIBILITIES

One of the most interesting findings discovered by reviewing this present author's past cases was the fact that *NONE* of the elderly patients seen in over 30 years of practice showed "pure" acute or chronic anxiety *as a primary uncomplicated disorder.* Explanations for this should be sought through epidemiological and clinical research. Are there fewer instances of clinically significant anxiety among older people, or do they merely tend to show combined displays of symptomatology? These and other questions might be asked.

In general, there are a number of conceptual and practical problems in performing systematic psychotherapy research with elderly persons. First of all, anxiety as a free-standing or even predominating symptom in the elderly is rare; most cases represent combinations of various symptoms. Also, the measurable (subjective and objective) manifestations of anxiety often respond swiftly to various interventions or even time, suggesting a high but nonspecific tendency to improve. Goode and Kleinman (1985, p. 322) raised some researchable questions about anxiety disorders that investigate a number of factors relating to cross-cultural differences and commonalities, including questions regarding differential risk. These could readily be applied to populations over 65.

Silberschatz and Curtis (1989c) have summarized some of the problems and deficiencies of empirical studies concerning psychotherapy of the elderly. Anecdotal case studies, although useful, generally are preselected in favor of "positive results," rarely use verifiable process criteria and are often unrepresentative of the general elderly population. Even the "Clinical

Trials Method" may display a "false uniformity" in patient selection and obscure the inevitable variation in supposedly homogenous treatment methods ("behavioral," "dynamic," "cognitive"). These authors endorse a "Case-Specific" method requiring (a) an *individualized program for treatment* based on discrete aspects of the patients' current problem and background; (b) use of *process measures* that fit the patient's problem and character style; and (c) *outcome measures*, that are specifically coordinated with the customized treatment "program" and specified "process variables" (Illustrated in Weiss et al., 1986; Silberschatz & Curtis, 1989c).

Two other areas of research might be suggested. First, understanding and correlating the interconnection between anxiety and other symptoms in presenting in elderly patients could be of both clinical and epidemiological interest. Second, the issue of utilization of psychotherapy by older persons could be investigated through studying the referral tendencies among nonpsychiatric physicians (psychologists, other physicians, other health personnel), in their reactions to clinically anxious older persons. By examining the attitudes of these practitioners and the actual patterns of response to symptoms of anxiety, the background which underlies decisions concerning treatment or referral could be illuminated. Specifically, it might be learned *why* and *when* referring consultants: (a) treat anxiety with medication, (b) recognize anxiety as a signal of significant psychological problem and/or (c) refer to a psychotherapist.

ACKNOWLEDGMENTS

Some of this clinical work was conducted during a NIMH Senior Development Award in Geropsychiatry (# MH 18 312-02). The author wishes to thank Dr. Jared Tinklenberg and Mrs. Helen Davies of the Geropsychiatric Rehabilitation Unit of the Palo Alto Veteran's Administration Medical Center for their longstanding cooperation. Earlier versions of this chapter were reviewed by Drs. Leon Epstein, John Curtis, George Silberschatz, Richard Lannon and F. Pierre Johnson.

REFERENCES

American Psychiatric Association. (1987). *Diagnostic and statistical manual of mental disorders*, Third edition, Revised (DSM-III-R). Washington, D.C.: American Psychiatric Association.

Beitman, B. D., Goldfried, M. R., & Norcross, J. C. (1989). The movement toward integrating the psychotherapies: An overview. *American Journal of Psychiatry, 146*, 138–147.

Butler, R. N. (1963). The life review: An interpretation of reminiscence in the aged. *Psychiatry, 26*, 65–76.

Butler, R. N., & Lewis, M. I. (1973). *Aging and mental health: Positive psychosocial approaches*. St. Louis: C. B. Mosely & Co.

Cath, S. H. (1984). A psychoanalytic hour: A late-life awakening. In L. N. Lazarus (Ed.), *Clinical Approaches to Psychotherapy with the Elderly* (pp. 147–172). Washington, DC: American Psychiatric Press.

Curtis, J. (1989). (Private communication).

Deutsch, F., & Murphy, W. (1960). *The clinical interview*. New York: International Universities Press.

Dohrenwend, B. P., Shrout, P. E., Egri, G., & Mendelsohn, F. S. (1980). Non-specific psychological distress and other dimensions of psychopathology. *Archives of General Psychiatry, 37*, 1229–1236.

Erickson, E. H. (1959). *Identity and the life cycle. (Psychological Issues* Monograph #1). New York: International Universities Press.

Frank, J. (1961). *Persuasion and healing: A comparative study of psychotherapy*. Baltimore: Johns Hopkins Press.

Freud, S. (1926). *Inhibitions, symptoms and anxiety*. Standard Edition. Volume 20. London: Hogarth Press (1959).

Glover, E. (1956). *The technique of psychoanalysis*. New York: International Universities Press.

Goldfarb, A. I., & Schepps, J. (1954). Psychotherapy of the aged. *Psychosomatic Medicine, 16*, 182–192.

Good, B., & Kleinman, A. M. (1985). Culture and anxiety: Cross-cultural evidence for the patterning of anxiety disorders. In A. H. Tuma and J. Maser (Eds.), *Anxiety and the anxiety disorders* (pp. 297–324). Hillsdale, NJ: Lawrence Erlbaum Associates, Publishers.

Gorman, J. M., Leibowitz, M. R., Fyer, A. J., & Stein, J. (1989). A neuroanatomical hypothesis for panic disorder. *American Journal of Psychiatry, 46*, 148–161.

Gould, R. (1978). *Transformation: Growth and change in adult life.* New York: Simon and Shuster.

Gray, J. A. (1985). Issues in the neuropsychology of anxiety. In A. H. Tuma and J. Maser (Eds.), *Anxiety and the anxiety disorders* (pp. 5–26). Hillsdale, NJ: Lawrence Erlbaum Associates, Publishers.

Horowitz, M. (1985). Anxious state of mind induced by stress. In A. H. Tuma and J. Maser (Eds.), *Anxiety and the anxiety disorders* (pp. 619–632). Hillsdale, NJ: Lawrence Erlbaum Associates, Publishers.

Izard, C. E., & Blumberg, S. H. (1985). Emotion theory and the role of emotions in anxiety in children and adults. In A. H. Tuma and J. Maser (Eds.), *Anxiety and the anxiety disorders* (pp. 109–130). Hillsdale, NJ: Lawrence Erlbaum Associates, Publishers.

Johnson, F. A. (1981). Ethnicity and interaction rules in counseling and psychotherapy: Some foundational considerations. In A. J. Marsella and P. Pederson (Eds.), *Cross cultural counseling and psychotherapy* (pp. 91–138). Elmsford, NY: Primadon Press.

Johnson, F. P. (1989). (Private communication).

Kaplan, E. A., & Johnson, F. A. (1978). The function of adolescent crushes. *Human Sexuality, 12*, 57–70.

Kastenbaum, R. (1964). *New thoughts on old age.* New York: Springer.

Kierkegaard, S. (1980 [1877]). *The concept of anxiety.* Princeton, NJ: Princeton University Press.

Knight, B. (1986). *Psychotherapy with older adults.* Beverly Hills, CA: Sage Publication.

Lannon, R. (1989). Private communication.

Lazarus, R. S., & De Longis, A. (1983). Psychological stress and coping in aging. *American Psychologist, 38*, 245–254.

Levinson, D. J. (1980). Toward a conception of the adult life course. In N. Smelser and E. Erickson (Eds.), *Themes of work and love in adulthood* (pp. 260–290). Cambridge: Harvard University Press.

Link, B., & Dohrenwend, B. P. (1980). Formulation of hypotheses about the true prevalence of demoralization in the United States. In B. Dohrenwend et al. *Mental Illness in the United States* (pp. 114–130). New York: Praeger.

Maddox, G. L. (1979). Sociology of later life. *Annual Review of Sociology, 5*, 113–135.

Marin, R. S. et al. (1988). A curriculum for education in geriatric psychiatry. *American Journal of Psychiatry, 145*, 837–843.

Marmor, J. (1971). Dynamic psychotherapy and behavior therapy. *Archives of General Psychiatry, 24,* 22–29.

Myers, W. A. (1984). *Dynamic therapy of the older patient.* New York: Jason Aronson.

Nemiroff, R. A., & Colarusso, C. A. (1985). *The race against time: Psychotherapy and psychoanalysis in the second half of life.*

Niederland, W. G. (1961). The problem of a survivor. *Journal of the Hillside Hospital, 10,* 233–247.

Pfeiffer, E. (1971). Psychotherapy with elderly patients. *Postgraduate Medicine, 50,* 254–258.

Pincus, A. (1970). Reminiscence in aging and its implication for social work practice. *Social Work, 15,* 47–53.

Pollack, G. H. (1982). The mourning-liberation process and creativity: The case of Nathe Kollwitz. *Annual of Psychoanalysis, 10,* 333–356.

Rechtsheffen, A. (1959). Psychotherapy with geriatric patients: A review of the literature. *Journal of Gerontology, 14,* 73–89.

Rosow, I. (1976). Status and role change through a life span. In R. Binstock & E. Shanas (Eds.), *Handbook of aging and the social sciences* (pp. 62–93). New York: Van Nostram Reinholt.

Scherer, K. & Ekman, P. (Eds.). (1984). *Approaches to emotion.* Hillsdale, NJ: Lawrence Erlbaum Associates Publishers.

Silberschatz, G., Curtis, J., & Nathans, S. (1989a). Using the patient's plan to assess progress in psychotherapy. *Psychotherapy, 26,* 40–46.

Silberschatz, G., & Curtis, J. (1989b, in press). Time-limited psychodynamic therapy with older patients. In W. A. Myers (Ed.), *New techniques in the psychotherapy of older patients.* Washington, DC: American Psychiatric Association.

Silberschatz, G., & Curtis, J. (1989c). Research on the psychodynamic process in the treatment of older persons. In N. E. Miller (Ed.), *Psychodynamic research perspectives on development, psychopathology and treatment in later life.* New York: International Universities Press.

Tuma, A. H., & Maser, J. D. (1985). *Anxiety and the anxiety disorders.* Hillsdale, NJ: Lawrence Erlbaum.

Vaillant, G. T. (1977). *Adaptation to life.* Boston: Little, Brown.

Weiner, H. (1985). The psychobiology and pathophysiology of anxiety and fear. In A. H. Tuma and J. Maser (Eds.), *Anxiety and the anxiety disorders* (pp. 333–354). Hillsdale, NJ: Lawrence Erlbaum Associates, Publishers.

Weiss, J., Sampson, H., & Mount Zion Psychotherapy Research
    Group. (1986). *The psychoanalytic process: Theory, clinical ob-
    servations, and empirical research.* New York: Guilford Press.
World Health Organization (1979). *International classification of dis-
    eases, injuries and causes of death.* Ninth Edition. (ICD-9) Ge-
    neva, Switzerland: WHO.

Frank Johnson was not a participant at the original conference,
so there is no commentary.

Issues for Future Research

V

Anxiety Rating Scales for the Elderly

14

Javaid I. Sheikh

Anxiety rating scales are variously used for screening, assessing the severity of symptoms, and to document effectiveness of various psychological and pharmacological therapeutic interventions. These scales were typically developed for and validated in younger people and their usefulness in older people is usually assumed though empirical data documenting such applicability is often lacking. The scales are primarily of two kinds: observer-rated and self-rated. Further, some of these scales are unidimensional, i.e., relatively pure measures of anxiety, whereas others are multidimensional, i.e., measuring anxiety as only one of the many domains.

This chapter will primarily focus on scales that are most widely employed and is thus representative only and by no means comprehensive. An attempt will be made to cover material published since the comprehensive review of this particular area by Salzman (1977), though it must be pointed out at the outset that his statement made a decade ago, "In nearly every case the conclusion is the same: further information is required to ascertain the validity of the scale for use in older populations" unfortunately, still seems to hold true. Finally, problems in geriatric anxiety assessment will be delineated, ways to document usefulness of the existing scales in older adults will be explored, and suggestions for an "ideal" geriatric anxiety assessment scale will be presented.

OBSERVER-RATED SCALES

Hamilton Anxiety Rating Scale (HARS)

This most popular observer-rated anxiety scale was designed to measure the severity of anxiety in patients already diagnosed as suffering from an Anxiety Disorder (Hamilton, 1959). It is a 14-item scale measuring psychic and somatic components of anxiety, with each item rated on 5 levels of severity from none (0) to very severe (4). Over the years, HARS has become the standard in the field, especially as a measure of change in clinical situations and in pharmacological research. There are some concerns, however, regarding HARS. For example, inclusion of 89 signs and symptoms under 14 headings with the possibility that severity of symptoms under the same heading might differ considerably from each other, can give rise to poor inter-rater reliability (Wang et al., 1976). In addition, there is insufficient homegeneity of items, especially somatic items (Maier et al., 1987). Further, there are no guidelines to separate side-effects of medications from somatic items on the scale.

Some modified versions of HARS provide better specificity (Snaith et al., 1982) as well as better internal consistency and discriminant validity between anxiety and depression (Riskind et al., 1987). Item structure permits differentiation between "panic anxiety" and "generalized anxiety" with proper instructions and scoring (Bech et al., 1986). No geriatric norms for HARS are available. Published studies in an elderly population are infrequent though some earlier studies seem to indicate limited sensitivity to change with active drug treatment (Salzman, 1977; Kochansky, 1979). Our own experience suggests that it is cumbersome to go through the list of 89 symptoms and the elderly tend to overendorse the somatic items. The usefulness of HAM-A in the elderly remains questionable.

Anxiety Status Inventory (ASI)

This is a 20-item scale designed by Zung (1971) to identify a primary anxiety disorder as well as to measure the severity of anxiety. It consists of 15 "somatic" and 5 "affective" items, on a 4-point scale from none (1) to severe (4). Unlike HARS, the rater is instructed to take the intensity, duration, and frequency of the symptom into account. Though the rater is asked to evaluate the status of anxiety symptoms for the past week, some items begin with "Have you ever," which can be a source of confusion if the rater is not cautious. Adequate reliability and predictive validity for this anxiety-screening device has been documented by Zung (1971). Geriatric norms are available for the self-rated version (SAS) of the ASI though published studies in elderly remain virtually non-existent.

SELF-RATED SCALES

Two types of instruments will be described under this category, "unidimensional" and "multidimensional."

Unidimensional Self-Rated Scales

State-Trait Anxiety Inventory (STAI)

Designed by Spielberger and associates (Spielberger et al., 1970), this most widely used instrument for measuring anxiety (Buros, 1985) provides operational distinction between anxiety as a transient emotional state (A-state), and anxiety as a relatively stable personality trait (A-Trait). The STAI consists of two 20 item scales, STAI-A-State scale and STAI-A-Trait scale, with four possible responses for each item. Both scales have shown high internal consistency (Spielberger, 1970) and predictive

Table 14.1 Commonly Used Anxiety Rating Scales

Scale	Description	Psychometrics	Time	Relevance to elderly	Comments
Hamilton Anxiety Rating Scale (HARS; Hamilton, 1959)	A 14-item observer-rated scale to measure severity of anxiety	Mixed reviews regarding internal consistency and interrater reliability	15–30 min.	No geriatric norms. Usefulness in geriatrics questionable	Most frequently used observer-rated scale
Anxiety Status Inventory (ASI; Zung, 1971)	A 20-item observer-rated scale to identify and measure severity of anxiety	Adequate reliability and predictive validity	5 min.	Geriatric norms for self-rated version	Recent use in drug trials limited
Self-Rating Anxiety Scale (SAS; Zung 1971)	A 20-item self-rating scale to identify and measure severity of anxiety	Adequate reliability and predictive validity	5 min.	Geriatric norms available	Useful as anxiety screening device
State-Trait Anxiety Inventory (STAI; Spielberger, 1970)	Two 20-item self-rating sets to distinguish between trait and state anxiety	High internal consistency and predictive validity	5 min. for each scale	Modified version with limited data in elderly available	Theory-derived and psychometrically sound; use in drug studies limited
Beck Anxiety Inventory (BAI; Beck et al., 1988)	A 21-item self-rating scale to measure severity of anxiety and to discriminate anxiety from depression	High internal consistency, test-retest reliability and discriminant validity	5 min.	No published norms in geriatrics	A new scale; to be used as a criterion and outcome measure
Profile of Mood States (POMS; McNair, et al., 1971)	Multidimensional, 65-item symptom/affect checklist that measures 6 mood states including anxiety	High consistency within different mood dimensions; good predictive validity	10 min.	No geriatric norms. Usefulness in geriatrics unproven	A sensitive measure of change in general populations
Hopkins Symptom Checklist (SCL-90-R; Derogatis, 1975)	Multidimensional, 90-item, 5-point Likert scale to measure 9 primary symptom dimensions of psychological distress including anxiety	High internal consistency, test-retest reliability and discriminant validity	15 min.	Geriatric norms under development. Published studies in geriatrics present	A sensitive measure of change in psychopharmacological studies

validity and have been used in medical and psychiatric populations to assess clinical anxiety. A children's version of the STAI, the STAIC (Spielberger, 1973) with a simpler format and vocabulary has been developed and was used successfully with some modification in a geriatric population (Patterson, O'Sullivan, & Spielberger, 1980; Patterson et al., 1982).

However, there are concerns about STAI's lack of specificity and discriminant validity as higher scores were found in depressed than in anxious patients (Barlow, Dinardo, Vermilyea, & Blanchard, 1986). Furthermore, this might not be the most preferable scale for drug studies as it does not ask about anxiety in the last week but only about how people are feeling "right now" (STAI-A-State) or "in general" (ATAI-A-Trait). It does seem particularly suited as a general measure of anxiety and in studies of psychological interventions.

The Self-Rating Anxiety Scale (SAS)

This is a 20-item self-rated version of the previously mentioned Anxiety Status Inventory (ASI), designed to identify a primary anxiety disorder as well as to measure the severity of anxiety (Zung, 1971). Like the ASI, it consists of 15 "somatic" and 5 "affective" items, on a 4-point scale from none or a little of the time (1) to most of the time (4). Patients are asked to respond to items as they applied to them within the past week. Highly reliable internal consistency and predictive and concurrent validity have been documented (Zung, 1980).

Preliminary data on geriatric norms (Zung, 1974) seemed to indicate higher baseline values in nonclinical populations 65 and older, compared to younger adults 20–64 years of age. Further data provided by Zung (1980) shows that baseline anxiety scores in older people are not significantly different from the younger adult population. This issue clearly needs further investigation. Published psychopharmacological studies using SAS with a geriatric population are virtually nonexistent.

Beck Anxiety Inventory (BAI)

A recently introduced (Beck et al., 1988) 21-item symptom
inventory, BAI is designed to measure the severity of anxiety in
psychiatric populations and to discriminate both "generalized
anxiety" and "panic anxiety" from depression. Respondents are
asked to rate the severity of each symptom "during the last
week including today" on a scale of none (0) to severe (3) and it
takes about five minutes to complete. Total score can range
from 0 to 63. Beck et al. (1988) report high internal consistency,
test-retest reliability and discriminant validity from depression
for BAI. No geriatric norms are available as yet. To quote the
authors (Beck et al., 1988) "Preliminary validity data support its
suitability for use in psychiatric populations as a criterion and
outcome measure."

Multidimensional Self-Rated Scales

Profile of Mood States (POMS)

A 65-item symptom/affect checklist measuring 6 primary
mood states: tension-anxiety, depression-dejection, confusion,
anger-hostility, vigor, and fatigue was designed by McNair and
associates (1971). Each item is rated on a 5-point scale from
"not at all" (0) to "extremely" (4) and the scale can usually be
completed within 10 minutes. The "tension-anxiety" subscale
contains items of somatic tension, psychomotor manifestations, as well as cognitive anxiety. Sound Psychometrics in
terms of high consistency within mood dimensions and test-
retest reliability along with predictive validity have been
documented (McNair et al., 1981). POMS has proven to be a
sensitive measure of change in both psychotherapeutic and
psychopharmacologic studies with younger people (Derogatis,
1987), but has shown rather limited sensitivity to change in
pharmacological studies with the elderly (Salzman, 1977). Further data in terms of its applicability to the elderly is being
awaited.

Hopkins Symptom Check List (SCL-90-R)

A very commonly used, 90-item, 5-point Likert scale is designed to measure psychological distress in terms of 9 primary symptom dimensions and 3 global indices of distress (Derogatis). The primary symptom constructs include somatization, obsessive-compulsive, interpersonal sensitivity, anxiety, hostility, phobic anxiety, paranoid ideation, and psychoticism. The standard time referent is "the past 7 days including today," though the time window is flexible for research purposes. It takes 15–20 minutes to complete, with older people taking closer to 20 minutes usually. High internal consistency within primary symptom dimensions and test-retest reliability along with high discriminant validity was reported by Derogatis (1983). SCL-90-R has shown to be very sensitive to therapeutic interventions in a broad variety of clinical and medical contexts, especially psychopharmacologic research. A 58-item version correlating highly with the 90-item version (Derogatis & Melisaratos, 1983) is available and probably preferable in the elderly due to its brevity. Geriatric norms are currently under development for SCL-90-R (Derogatis & Wise, 1989).

MISCELLANEOUS

As mentioned earlier, the intent is to provide a representative sampling of anxiety scales and so many other measures have been omitted from the review. Some of the more popular ones include Covi Anxiety Scale (Lipman, 1982), Multiple Affect Adjective Checklist-Revised (MAACL-R) (1983), Morbid Anxiety Inventory (MAI) (Bonn et al., 1971) and Taylor Manifest Anxiety Scale (TMAS) (1953). Needless to say, studies in the elderly with these scales are lacking. Some new scales with greater specificity within anxiety states, including Sheehan Clinician-rated Anxiety Scale, the Panic and Anxiety Attack Scale, and Marks and Sheehan Phobia scale (Sheehan, 1982) have proved to be useful in measuring their domains, though studies in the elderly are generally lacking.

Table 14.2 A Comparison of Self-Rated and Observer-Rated Scales

Self-rated	Observer-rated
Advantages	
1. Response comes from the source itself and not biased by observer perceptions.	1. Clinical judgement of a professionally trained person is available.
2. They provide economy of professional time	2. There is more flexibility in gathering information.
3. They can be easily administered and scored by computers.	
4. There are no concerns about interrater reliability.	
5. They usually take a short time to complete and can be used repeatedly to show effects of treatment.	
6. They can be used as screening aids for large populations.	
7. They can also provide useful data as mail responses.	
Disadvantages	
1. Misrepresentations in response can occur due to conscious distortion if that is desirable to the respondent. Other sources of response bias include a tendency to minimize or maximize feelings, and social desirability of certain responses	1. They require considerable expenditure of professional time and expense.
2. Misinterpretation of items by the respondents can occur due to multiple factors including education, social class, and ethnic background.	2. Even the most experienced clinicians can misperceive verbal and non-verbal cues.
3. There is a lack of flexibility in gathering information.	3. There is always the possibility of an inadequate interrater reliability (especially when raters are not trained using uniform criteria) within the same team or similar problems between different centers.

PROBLEMS OF MEASURING ANXIETY
IN THE ELDERLY

As mentioned previously, virtually all the existing anxiety instruments were designed for younger people. An important issue to resolve at this time is whether it is enough to carry out validation studies of the existing scales in the elderly or are there problems of measurement as well as manifestations of anxiety unique to older people which might necessitate specially designed scales for that population? Due to paucity of research in the area of geriatric anxiety it is not possible to come up with a definite answer at this time. However, there is some evidence suggesting affirmative answer to this question.

To begin with, it seems that psychiatric conditions can manifest different patterns across age groups. For example, depression might present as "pseudodementia" in the elderly (Wells, 1979) or somatic symptoms including sleep disturbances, decreased sexual desire, aches and pains, and a general sense of decreased energy might not indicate depression as positively in the elderly as they do in younger people (Yesavage et al., 1983). Are there manifestations of anxiety states in the elderly which might be different from younger people? Busse (1975) suggests that anxiety in the elderly may be expressed as bodily concerns. Salzman (1977) also suggests that distinction between anxiety and depression may become more blurred in the elderly as they might experience both early (anxiety) and late (depression) insomnia with or without these syndromes. This suggestion seems to be supported by data in our laboratory indicating that existing anxiety and depression rating scales show strongly positive correlation in the elderly (Sheikh, 1989) thus making it difficult to differentiate anxiety from depression. There is also some preliminary indication that the manifestations of panic disorder may be different in older people (Sheikh et al., 1988). It is also probable that increased medical co-morbidity in the elderly may lead to overendorsement of items on anxiety scales related to cardiac and respiratory problems. Finally, a tendency to deny psychopathology, a wish to give "socially desirable" and a general resis-

Table 14.3 Suggestions for Ideal Observer-Rated and Self-Rated Geriatric Anxiety Scales

Ideal Observer-Rated Scale	Ideal Self-Rated Scale
1. Should address multiple dimensions of anxiety, namely, cognitive, affective, behavioral, and physiological.	1. A maximum of 30 items with a large enough print for the elderly, with clear instructions on top of the form for subjects.
2. Should show discriminant validity between anxiety and depression.	2. Should require no more than 10 minutes to complete.
3. Should have items to measure panic attacks and anxiety separately.	3. Items should be worded in simple language to minimize bias of education, social status, and ethnicity.
4. Should have items to measure phobic symptoms.	4. Should cover items on cognitive, emotional, behavioral, and physiological components of anxiety.
5. Should have some flexibility for open-ended questions, especially, to discriminate from symptoms of medical co-morbidity.	5. Should have a yes-no format instead of complex gradations to minimize errors of measurement.
6. Should posses adequate psychometric properties, including geriatric norms.	6. Should be psychometrically sound with norms for the elderly and specific cut-off points.
7. Should show sensitivity to therapeutic interventions.	7. Should possess discriminant validity from depression.
	8. Should show sensitivity to therapeutic interventions.

tance to psychiatric evaluation in this population may lead to difficulties in accurate measurement of anxiety (Salzman, 1977).

CONCLUSION

With increasing sophistication of psychopharmacological treatments in the last two decades, sensitivity to drug-induced changes has become probably the most desired requirement for rating scales. Consequently measures of "state" anxiety are deemed more preferable as opposed to measures of enduring "trait" anxiety which were more popular until a couple of decades ago. As in other areas of psychiatric research, the development of anxiety rating scales has followed a trend from the more general measures of severity of anxiety to the more specific, and will continue to do so. Till we decide to pursue the goal of developing the "ideal" geriatric anxiety scale (see Table 14.3), progress needs to be made in various directions to accomplish somewhat less lofty goals. Firstly, a large scale validation study of the more popular existing anxiety scales needs to be carried out in both clinical and nonclinical populations of older people using structured diagnostic interviews as external criteria. Secondly, we need to develop measures which can differentiate anxiety from depression in the elderly on the one hand, and "generalized anxiety" from "panic anxiety" on the other. Thirdly, we need to develop measures to assess the severity of anxiety in the medically ill elderly. Fourthly, we need measures to assess types and severity of phobias in the elderly. Finally, as suggested by Finney (1985), we might need to combine psychological measures with physiological measures like heart rate and GSR in research on phenomenology of different anxiety states and their treatment.

COMMENTARY

1. Must be able to use a scale that can be used by patients with cognitive impairment. Especially important in the elderly since a large number of anxious elderly have cognitive impairment.

2. The tension between defining specificity of symptoms continues. Some people feel a need for high discrimination between anxious and depression symptoms and a rating scale. Others feel that this may not be necessary, and suggest relaxing the requirement for such discrimination and seeing symptoms more broadly and descriptively. May prefer to use a dysphoria scale rather than a specific anxiety or depression scale. This point of view is supported by the observation that if depression rating scales are deprived of anxious items, they will be deprived of many aspects of depression that need to be rated. As anxiety symptoms are part of depressive symptoms, they improve as the depression improves. The opposing point of view states that we need more specificity to assist diagnosis and treatment. Anxiety symptoms that cluster together, include autonomic systems and cognitive symptoms, as opposed to symptoms of depression that cluster together such as anhedonia, diurnal mood variation, early morning awakening, and suicidal ideation. For research purposes we need accurate assessment of symptoms.

3. We need a descriptive screening scale and then follow it up with a structured interview.

4. How do we measure change in the elderly. Need a multi-item scale with different terms. For example, worry may be better than the term anxiety. Need to interview elderly people and use their words to construct a new use of useful anxiety scale.

REFERENCES

Barlow, D. H., Dinardo, P. A., Vermilyea, B. B., Vermilyea, J., & Blanchard, E. B. (1986). Co-morbidity and depression among anxiety disorder: Issues in diagnosis and classification. *J Nervous and Mental Disease, 174,* 63–72.

Bech, P., Kastrup, M., & Rafaelsen, O. J. (1986). Mini Compendium of rating scales for states of anxiety, depression, mania, schizophrenia with corresponding DSM-III syndromes (pp. 1–37). *Acta Psychiatrica Scandinavica,* Supplementum 326, vol. 73.

Beck, A., Epstein, N., Brown, G., & Steer, R. (1988). An inventory for measuring Clinical Anxiety: Psychometric properties. *Journal of Consulting and Clinical Psychology, 56*(6), 893–897.

Bonn, J. A., Salkind, M. R., & Rees, W. I. (1971). A technique in the evaluation of psychotropic medication based on a patient demand schedule: Comparison of the efficacy of oxypertine, diazepam and placebo in anxiety. *Curr Ther Res, 13,* 561–567.

Derogatis, L. R. (1975). *The SCL-90-R.* Baltimore: Clinical Psychometric Research.

Derogatis, L. R. (1983). *SCL-90-R. Administration, scoring and procedures manual-II.* Baltimore: Clinical Psychometric Research.

Derogatis, L. R., & Melisaratos, N. (1983). The Brief Symptom Inventory. An introductory report. *Psychol Med, 13,* 595–605.

Derogatis, L. R., & Wise, T. N. (1989). In *Anxiety and Depressive Disorders in the Medical Patient* (p. 86). Washington, DC: American Psychiatric Press Inc.

Finney, J. C. (1985). Anxiety: Its measurement by objective personality tests and self-report. In A. H. Tuma & J. Maser (Eds.), *Anxiety and the anxiety disorders* (pp. 645–673). Hillsdale, NJ: Lawrence Erlbaum Associates, Publishers.

Hamilton, M. (1989). The assessment of anxiety states by rating. *Br J Med Psychol, 32,* 50–55.

Kochansky, G. E. (1979). Psychiatric rating scales for assessing psychopathology in the elderly: A critical review. In A. Raskin & L. Jarvik (Eds.), *Psychiatric symptoms and cognitive loss in the elderly* (pp. 125–156). Washington, D.C.: Hemisphere.

Lipman, R. S. (1981). Differentiating anxiety and depression in anxiety disorders: Use of rating scales. *Psychopharmacology Bulletin, 18* (4), 69–77.

Maier, W., Bullet, R., Philipp, M., & Isabella, H. (1988). The Hamilton Anxiety Scale: Reliability, validity and sensitivity to change in anxiety and depressive disorders. *J Affective Disorders, 14,* 61–68.

McNair, D. M., Lorr, M., & Droppleman, L. F. (1971/1981). EITS manual for the profile of mood states. San Diego: Educational and Industrial Testing Service.

Mitchell, J. V. R. (Ed.). (1985). *Buros Institute of Mental Measurements, Ninth Mental Measurements Yearbook.* Lincoln, NB: Univ of NB Press.

Patterson, R. L., Sullivan, M. J., & Spielberger, C. D. (1980). Measurement of state and trait anxiety in elderly mental health clients. *J Behavioral Assessment, 2,* 89–97.

Patterson, R. L., Dupree, L., Eberly, D. A., Dee-Kelley, C., O'Sullivan, M. L. & Penner, L. A. (1982). Overcoming deficits of aging: A behavioral treatment approach. New York: Plenum Press.

Riskind, J. H., Beck, A. T., Brown, G., & Steer, R. (1987).. Taking the measure of anxiety and depression: Validity of the reconstructed Hamilton Scales. *J Nervous and Mental Disease, 175*, 474–479.

Salzman, C. (1977). Psychometric rating of anxiety in the elderly. In *Diagnosis and treatment of anxiety in the aged, part II: Measurement of Anxiety* (pp. 5–21; available from Hoffman-LaRoche, Inc.). Proceedings of conference on 'Anxiety in the Elderly', cosponsored by Roche Laboratories and University of Arizona College of Medicine, in Tucson, Arizona, November, 1977.

Sheikh, J. J., Taylor, C. B., King, R. J., Roth, W. T., Yesavage, J. A., & Agras, W. S (1988). Panic attacks and avoidance behavior in the elderly (p. 225). Proceedings of the 141st Annual Meeting of the American Psychiatric Association, May 7–12.

Sheikh, J. I., Kilcourse, J., Gallagher, D., Thompson, L., & Tanke, E. (1989). Can we improve the specificity of anxiety and depression scales? Presentation at the 2nd Annual meeting of AAGP, Orlando, Florida.

Sheehan, D. V. (1982). Current concepts in psychiatry: Panic attacks and phobias. *N Eng J Med, 307*, 156–158.

Snaith, R. P., Baugh, S. J., Clayden, A. D., Husain, A., & Sipple, M. A. (1982). The Clinical Anxiety Scale: An instrument derived from the Hamilton Anxiety Scale. *Brit. J Psychiat, 141*, 518–523.

Spielberger, C. D., Gorsuch, R. C., & Lushene, R. E. (1970). Manual for the State-Trait Anxiety Inventory. Palo Alto, CA: Consulting Psychologists Press.

Spielberger, C. D. (1973). Preliminary test manual for the State-Trait Anxiety Inventory for Children ("How I Feel Questionnaire"). Palo Alto, CA: Consulting Psychologists Press.

Taylor, J. A. (1953). A personality scale of manifest anxiety. *J Abnorm Soc Psychol 48*, 285–295.

Wang, R. I. H., Wiesen, R. L., Treul, S., & Stockdale, S. (1976). A brief anxiety rating scale in evaluating anxiolytics. *J Clinical Pharmacology, 6*, 99–105.

Wells, C. E. (1979). Pseudodementia. *Am J Psychiatry, 136*, 895–900.

Yesavage, J. A., Brink, T. L., Rose, T. L., Lum, O., Huang, V., Adey, M., & Leirer, V. O. (1983). Development and validation of a Geriatric Depression Screening Scale: A preliminary report. *Journal of Psychiatric Research, 17,* 33–49.

Zuckerman, M. (1983). Manual for the Multiple Affect Adjective Checklist-Revised (MAACL-R). San Diego: Stanford Educational and Industrial Testing Service.

Zung, W. W. K. (1971). A rating instrument for anxiety disorders. *Psychosomatics, 12,* 371–379.

Zung, W. W. K. (1980). How normal is anxiety? *Current Concepts* (p. 12). Kalamazoo, MI: Scope Publications.

Anxiety in the Elderly: Research Issues

15

Jonathan O. Cole

Population surveys suggest that Generalized Anxiety Disorder and Panic Disorder and other anxiety disorders occur in individuals over 65 years of age, but at lower rates than in younger adults.

The core problem, however, is that many elderly patients have anxiety or agitation or both but their presentations do not neatly fit criteria for anxiety disorders as spelled out in DSM-III-R. Agitation as a symptom is even harder to define; the term covers a range of behaviors from a hyperaroused subjectively dysphoric state with visible jitteriness to demented restlessness to hypomanic intrusiveness. Something that can readily be called agitation occurs in the elderly in major depressive illness, in late life schizophrenia, mania, organic confusional or delirious states, dementia, withdrawal from alcohol or sedative drugs and as a result of akathisia due to neuroleptic drug administration.

Agitation would seem to be the behavioral manifestation of marked anxiety but it's by no means clear that this is so. For the purposes of this paper it seems sensible to consider that anxiety and agitation are separate phenomena which overlap in only a modest proportion of elderly patients.

If we had clearly effective drug therapies for both conditions in elderly patients, we could at least determine whether the same or different drugs were therapeutic for either or both and, then use clinical drug responsivity as a means of diagnostic classification. However, placebo controlled studies of anti-anxiety drugs in the anxious elderly are essentially nonexistent while studies in agitated elderly patients suggest modest response to both neuroleptics and benzodiazepines. Neither set of data is strong enough to support any clarifying leap into diagnostic classification.

The main features of research design for clinical drug trials and for studies comparing diagnostic groups with normal controls are well understood and reasonably straightforward. The study of anxiety in the elderly presents several special problems, however. In particular, the anxious elderly are not likely to present themselves for study or treatment. Agitation is more common, at least in elderly psychiatric inpatients, but occurs in a variety of diagnostic contexts and in patients who present urgent clinical problems. All this makes finding homogeneous patient samples suitable for placebo-controlled studies difficult.

Availability of elderly patients for studies is also compromised by the following: recruitment problems, presence of medical illness, presence of chronic symptoms with prior treatment attempts, polypharmacy, physical fragility, and drug sensitivity.

PROBLEMS RECRUITING ELDERLY RESEARCH SUBJECTS

In a psychiatric facility, even one with a good reputation, patients over 60 present for treatment almost exclusively as inpatients with serious depression or cognitive dysfunction with associated behavioral problems such as agitation, paranoid ideation, or inanition. Anxiety is likely to be seen only in the context of either major affective illness or dementia.

In addition, many elderly psychiatric inpatients have failed on a standard drug therapy prior to hospital admission, suggesting a degree of treatment resistance that may compromise research results. A few outpatients are referred for similar problems, usually by other psychiatrists for consultation because they have failed to improve on conventional therapies. This type of patient flow makes the execution of any type of drug trial or diagnostic study of anxiety in the elderly essentially impossible.

Attempts to recruit depressed elderly patients by newspaper advertisements may succeed in finding a few patients, but even antidepressant studies in the elderly are slow and laborious. In our experience, no patient who appeared to have a primary panic or anxiety disorder has responded to such ads. Major general medical centers also have difficulty recruiting older research subjects. Patients usually come for real or presumed medical problems, not for treatment of their anxiety.

It seems likely that the primarily anxious elderly either suffer without medical attention or are attached to one physician and are far less likely than younger patients to be willing to adventure further to a research clinic or a psychiatric clinic in search of potentially better treatment. In short, no matter how sophisticated the research design, execution is difficult in the absence of appropriate anxious patients.

Elderly patients with agitation, vaguely and broadly defined, are common on psychiatric inpatient wards but agitation is not a diagnosis and as noted, is present in dementia, schizophrenia, depression, and mixtures of these conditions. As one defines agitation with specific measurable behavioral characteristics and diagnostic context (e.g., moderate dementia of the Alzheimer's type), it becomes increasingly harder to recruit any substantial sample for study.

One can, of course, stratify any sample of agitated patients by diagnosis, thereby obtaining a larger, but more heterogeneous sample. For example, in order to compare agitation in psychotic depression that responds best to neuroleptics plus tricyclics, with agitated nonpsychotic depression that responds best to tricyclics alone and, also with agitation in dementia that responds best to neuroleptics alone, a very large subject sample will be needed, about as large for each diagnosis as one would need just to study that diagnostic group alone.

MEDICAL PROBLEMS

Perhaps a tenth of adult anxious or depressed patients will be disqualified for most drug studies by major medical problems. In elderly depressions, approximately one-third will have major medical problems and three-quarters will be on a variety of anti-inflammatory, antihypertensive, antidiabetic or gastrointestinal drugs for chronic conditions. In fact, medical illness and drug treatment is so common that any group of older people who are physically totally healthy and drug free but who are anxious or agitated will be hard to find and will differ clinically from a typical group of anxious elderly research subjects.

Use of an antianxiety drug by an older person does not necessarily indicate the presence of anxiety. Much of the antianxiety drug use in the elderly, as determined by prescription surveys, is for somatic problems. It is hard to determine whether a medically ill elderly person with pain, insomnia, and concern about his medical problems, who is receiving a benzodiazepine is being treated primarily for an anxiety disorder or for insomnia or muscle spasm.

Secondary anxiety, associated with illness in the elderly, doesn't fit well into DSM-III-R but appears to be common and warrants research study. However, there are also problems studying secondary anxiety in the elderly. Since such older patients rarely are seen by a psychiatrist, the site of the study might have to be in family practice or in internists' offices. It's not even known how and where such patients are begun on antianxiety drugs. If begun during hospital admissions for serious medical or surgical illnesses, a placebo-controlled antianxiety study becomes even more difficult. Also, most anxiety rating scales include a variety of physical symptoms. What if anorexia, shortness of breath, tremor, and frequent urination are all judged primarily due to real medical illness rather than to anxiety? Does one rate them as anxiety anyway or does the rater attempt to determine which physical symptoms are due to medical illness, which are anxiety, and which are more or less half and half?

Future studies of "anxiety" in elderly medical patients will require different diagnostic criteria than conventional psychiatric studies. For example, DSM-III-R duration requirements are inappropriate for short-term anxiety in the context of acute to subacute illness (e.g., coronary occlusion, hip fracture, recent diagnosis of a neoplasm). Treatment of chronic anxiety in the context of chronic arthritis, diabetes with complications, COPD, stroke, angina, etc., also needs to be studied. Some anxiety drugs may be more likely than others to affect cognition or coordination, whereas others may have effects on cardiac function; these differences are more important in studies of elderly patients.

In our experience, demented patients have even more medical problems than depressed elderly inpatients. The concept of "brain reserve," as a parallel to cardiac reserve, may be relevant: Elderly patients with borderline organic brain dysfunction from Alzheimer's Disease or Multi-infarct Dementia can rapidly develop major dementia through additional physical illnesses which would not faze a more cognitively intact or a younger patient.

CHRONICITY AND PRIOR TREATMENT

It seems likely that most anxiety disorders in the elderly are continuations of life-long illnesses rather than the sudden, late-life development of panic-agoraphobia, generalized anxiety, or social phobia in previously healthy individuals. This increases the likelihood that the elderly anxious patient will have been treated with medication, most likely for years with a low dose of a benzodiazepine. For either drug studies or biological studies of anxious patients, this means that the patient must be carefully tapered off the benzodiazepine with some probable increase in dysphoria before any study can be done. Some of these older patients will either refuse to stop the benzodiazepine or will be so uncomfortable that they drop out of the study before they are adequately drug free, at least from benzodiazepines.

For the agitated elderly patient with chronic schizophrenia or affective disorder, discontinuing long term prior psychiatric drug therapy may cause a recurrence or exacerbation of the disorder. Demented patients agitated enough to require hospitalization also are likely to have had some drug therapy during the period before admission. Agitation of any real severity is a major nursing care problem and withholding drug therapy or involving the patient in a study including the possibility of placebo treatment is sometimes clinically very difficult. A special, dedicated, well-staffed research ward may be required. Even though reliable treatment for agitation is lacking for the agitated demented patient, the clinical conviction that neuroleptics should be used may interfere with enrolling these patients in a research study!

In many jurisdictions, elderly patients unable to give informed consent because of dementia or psychosis require a court hearing and a court-appointed guardian before study medication can be administered. This generally poses both a time delay and a significant expense to the family, the state, or the research grant.

THE POLYPHARMACY PROBLEM

If, as I suspect, most antianxiety agents prescribed for the elderly are for patients with significant medical problems on a variety of nonpsychiatric drugs, then studies of the efficacy of antianxiety drugs need to be carried out in such medically ill patients. Such studies should require larger sample sizes for simple drug-placebo differences since the presence of a variety of other drugs may increase the variability of response.

THE HARD-TO-DIAGNOSE ELDERLY PATIENT

Elderly patients with subjective distress including elements of depression, anxiety, and cognitive dysfunction are more common than patients meeting criteria for panic disorder or generalized anxiety disorder. Furthermore, it is sometimes very difficult to tell pseudodementia from early true dementia unless the depression, anxiety, or both are relieved and the cognitive dysfunction concomitantly abates. In order to study drug effects on anxiety in the elderly, therefore, it seems better to set up criteria for the presence of anxiety symptoms of a given severity and to let depression, dementia, and even psychotic symptoms be measured at baseline and during the drug trial to see whether they also improve or worsen as anxiety improves.

It is still unclear whether or not all (or most) antidepressants are also effective in anxiety disorders and whether neuroleptics and antianxiety drugs are not effective in depression.

Given the heterogeneous presentations of distress in elderly psychiatric patients, it may be instructive to assign randomly all elderly patients to a benzodiazepine, a tricyclic, a neuroleptic, and placebo and see if diagnosis can be improved by examining the symptom patterns of patients who improve (or worsen) on each drug class.

THE FRAGILE ELDERLY PSYCHIATRIC PATIENT

It is often assumed that the elderly run higher blood levels on any drug dose, become confused more easily, develop worse orthostatic hypotension, more tardive dyskinesia, worse anticholinergic side effects, more tremor, etc., than younger patients do. Although these generalizations may well be true, I know of no confirming systematic studies. Furthermore, I suspect the "old old" have more problems associated with psychotropic drugs than the "young old." It is not clear whether increased sensitivity to drug side effects results from altered pharmacokinetic drug disposition or is due to changes in sensitivity to drugs in the brain or the periphery.

CONCLUSION

Anxiety symptoms and syndromes in elderly patients are sufficiently different from those in younger adult patients to warrant new approaches. The relative rarity of typical anxiety disorders, their relative unavailability for systematic study, and the common presence of concomitant medical illnesses and medical drug therapies all pose special problems. The presence of anxiety symptoms in patients with medical problems and mixed psychiatric pictures may be more common and require study more than standard anxiety disorders. A multi-dimensional or nondiagnostic approach may be more useful than single diagnostic categorization given the current stage of our knowledge.

Similar reasoning can be applied to agitation. If criteria for agitation are clear and usable, the patient's formal diagnosis can be used either as a stratification variable or as a predictor variable and drug studies of efficacy in agitation can then be carried out on diagnostically heterogeneous samples. For both anxiety and agitation trials in the elderly, if diagnosis is *not* a crucial inclusion criterion, then patient populations will become quite heterogeneous. This means that large-scale studies with careful sample descriptions will be required if meaningful results are to be obtained. Multicenter trials are likely to be required.

For studies of chronic, demented agitated patients, Veterans Administration facilities, state hospitals, and large nursing homes may suffice but the problems of discontinuing prior drug therapies, obtaining informed consent and sustaining staff and patients during placebo treatment remain major hurdles. And, the problem of how to most effectively manage acute agitation earlier in the course of dementia still would not be addressed by such studies.

As suggested above, more conventional studies of anxiety in the elderly without other psychiatric symptoms may be easier to do in medical facilities where anxiety associated with medical conditions is common. Despite my doubts about the possibility of finding enough elderly patients meeting standard criteria for generalized anxiety disorder, panic agoraphobia or social phobia, perhaps more aggressive and creative media campaigns including newspaper ads, TV appearances and ads, radio ads, and talk show appearances may yield enough symptomatic, physically healthy and amenable patients to do conventional drug trials in conventional diagnostic groups. Such studies, in fact, would be particularly instructive to determine if the elderly do or do not have similar drug responses and similar side effect profiles to those obtained in well-conducted studies in younger adult research samples.

Almost any reliable and valid information about drug efficacy and tolerance in the elderly, with anxiety or agitation whether young-old or old-old, would be a great improvement over current knowledge. Collaborative studies seem particularly promising since recruitment for any single study will be slow and the results of a multicenter study should be more generalizable. If the National Institute of Mental Health or the National Institute on Aging separately or together can plan, organize, and fund such studies, I believe the elderly and those who must prescribe for them will be most grateful.

COMMENTARY

1. Elderly people who have physicians as children are hard to attract into research studies.

2. We need to return to more clinical trial-treatment response driven post hoc diagnosis. The issue of pretreatment diagnosis is too unclear at this time.

3. It is still not clear that all antidepressants or all antianxiety drugs will cause the same response in all elderly patients. Therefore careful comparative trials are still indicated.

4. An example would be an empirical study of elderly dysphoric subjects: compare low toxicity traditional antidepressant (e.g., desipramine), a short half life traditional benzodiazepine for the elderly (e.g., oxazepam), and a placebo and see what symptoms respond. MAO inhibitors may also be useful drugs to treat anxiety in the elderly, although prescribing them to many elderly patients is a problem because of polypharmacy and compliance problems.

5. NIMH uses a system of "durable power of attorney" for people who may become cognitively impaired. You get the patient's permission to participate in studies before they are cognitively impaired and as they become progressively impaired, the designated guardian gives permission. This is probably not a useful technique for permission for drug studies however. If the study produced new information that was not available at the time the patient signed the consent, then the consent would be invalid.

6. Another difficult problem for doing drug studies with this population is that medicare will not pay for the cost of hospitalization if investigational drugs are used. This is a policy that should be reversed.

The Ideal Late Life Anxiolytic

16

Ben Zimmer and Samuel Gershon

Any meaningful discussion of the late-life pharmacotherapy of anxiety must first remind the reader of the nuances of anxiety phenomenology in late life as well as basic pharmacology of the agents being considered for its treatment. Unlike the primary affective disorder (major depressive disorders or bipolar affective disorders), primary anxiety disorders occur infrequently for the first time in late life. On the other hand, anxiety symptoms occur frequently in a variety of primary psychiatric disorders and as part of many primary medical conditions. The latter fact is potentially important for the elderly. It is also our experience that first episode anxiety in the elderly is often the manifestation of an organic condition. Indeed, particular behavioral complications such as agitation, sundowning, and the catastrophic reaction, are often discussed in connection with dementia.

A valid definition of anxiety and delineation of its underlying mechanisms are essential to address the question of what constitutes the ideal anxiolytic.

SOMATIC INTERVENTION IN ANXIETY

In an attempt to minimize the effects of stress and the dysphoria of tension and anxiety, man has historically pursued

277

relief through chemical agents. The oldest and most widely used sedative is alcohol. In the 1800s, bromide salts were introduced, and other sedative-hypnotic compounds, as well as opiates and belladonna were used to calm anxious patients (Harvey, 1980). From the early 1900s, the barbiturates enjoyed a long tenure, until their tolerance and overdose potential aroused concern. In the 1950s, the propanediol carbamates (e.g., meprobamate) became popular, until it became apparent that these compounds too had some highly undesirable characteristics (Baldessarini, 1980) similar to the barbiturates. During the last two decades, numerous other agents have been used with varying degrees of success to treat anxiety (Rickels, 1978; Edwards, 1981). Until recently it was felt that the greatest success has been achieved with benzodiazepines, but this class also has fallen short of the ideal (Table 16.1). Moreover, other classes of agents considered nontraditional must be considered when one addresses the issue of anxiolytics.

NEURAL SYSTEMS IMPLICATED IN ANXIETY

Competing evidence gathered from chemical and physical induction of anxiety in animal and man have clearly shown that the neurological basis of anxiety is complex (Gray, 1982) and cannot be attributed to a single system. It would seem that there are a number of interacting neural circuits that contribute to the final behavioral outcome so that it is to be expected that anxiety can be influenced pharmacologically by diverse agents such as alcohol, benzodiazepines, barbiturates, and tricyclic antidepressants (Donovan, 1988).

THE LOCUS COERULEUS

The locus coeruleus, a noradrenergic center located at the base of the fourth ventricle, clearly has been shown to play a major role in the control of anxiety. From electrical stimulation experiments in this area in humans and monkeys, producing

Table 16.1 Evolution of Pharmacologic Sedation

- Alcohol
- Bromide Salts
- Chloral Hydrate, Paraldehyde, Urethan, Sulfonal
- Opiates
- Belladonna Alkaloids
- Barbiturates
- Meprobamate
- Hydroxyzine, Scopolamine, Tybamate, Methaqualone, etc.
- Beta-adrenoreceptor Antagonists
- Antidepressants
- Neuroleptics
- Benzodiazepines

Source: Adapted from Gershon, S., Eison, A. S. The Ideal anxiolytic. *Psychiatric Annals*, 17(3), 159, 1987.

fear of imminent death in the former and increasing degrees of alertness in the latter, to pharmacologic stimulation of specific adrenergic autoreceptor antagonists with yohimbine and piperoxon, overactivity of this nucleus and its ascending noradrenergic system has been causally linked to the occurrence of anxiety attacks. Moreover, destruction of the locus in monkeys reduces the expression of anxiety, as do drugs depressing neural activity in the area and known to decrease human activity (Donovan, 1988).

Furthermore, preclinical data from studies in laboratory animals indicate that unremitting or uncontrollable stress leads to the development of Learned Helplessness, a stress induced temporary behavior syndrome resulting from the animals' lack of control over aversive experiences (Richardson & Richelson, 1984). Depression of motor behavior in the Learned Helplessness paradigm in rats has also recently been associated with a significant depletion of norepinephrine (NE) in the locus coeruleus. This depletion of NE in the locus coeruleus has been demonstrated in inescapably stressed animals at 90 minutes and 48 hours post-shock, but only slight depletions were found at 72 to 96 hours post-shock (Paul, 1988).

Other competing and possible biochemical causes of pathological anxiety or arousal may result from fluctuations in other
inhibitory neurotransmitters, including gamma-aminobutyric
acid (GABA), the most prevalent inhibitory neurotransmitter in
the brain, and adenosine. Indeed, the anxiogenic actions of
caffeine and methylxanthines are believed to be mediated by
the antagonism of adenosine at CNS adenosine receptors (Paul,
1988).

GABA AGONISM AND ANTAGONISM: LESSONS FROM LEARNED HELPLESSNESS

Benzodiazepines are considered to produce their central effects primarily by facilitating GABA neurotransmission, and
GABA is found in almost every brain region (Insel, Ninan, Aloi,
et al., 1984). Benzodiazepines work by binding to specific CNS
receptor sites, which are enriched in cortical and limbic-fore-
brain areas (Greenblatt, Shader, & Abernethy, 1983). The net
effect of the interaction of benzodiazepines with their receptors is to enhance the inhibitory neuronal properties of the
neurotransmitter, GABA. Paul (1988) recently and with facility,
summarized the functions of the benzodiazepine receptor:

> The benzodiazepine receptor is really a part of the GABA-
> receptor supramolecular complex, which is an oligomeric pro-
> tein consisting of at least four subunits that form a central
> chloride ion channel (Schofield, Darlison, Fujita, et al., 1987).
> GABA is known to increase the permeability of chloride ions
> through that chloride ion channel. When a benzodiazepine binds
> to its receptor, GABAergic neurotransmission is facilitated, and
> the rate of chloride ion transport across the neuronal membrane
> is increased. The heightened permeability of the cell to chloride
> ions decreases neuronal excitability by hyperpolarizing the
> neuronal membrane (Figure 16.1). Hyperpolarization of the
> neuronal membrane is believed to result in a decrease in the
> activity of brain regions involved in emotional expression, such
> as the hippocampus and the amygdala, thus resulting in a reduc-
> tion in arousal and anxiety. (Paul, 1988)

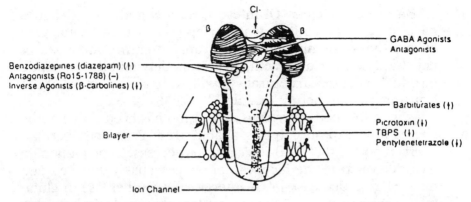

*TBPS = t-butylbiciclophosphorothianate.

Figure 16.1 The Benzodiazepine-GABA Receptor Complex*
Source: Paul, S. M. Anxiety and depression: a common neurobiological state?
Journal of Clinical Psychiatry *49(Suppl. 10): 13–16, 1988.*

In addition, in recent years a new class of "ligand" has come into focus in the area of benzodiazepine pharmacology. These are a group of compounds with anxiogenic and proconvulsant properties and diminish GABA activity. Moreover, because of the discovery of the high-affinity ligand benzodiazepine antagonist (Flumazenil [RO-15-1788]) that block both benzodiazepines and the above-mentioned anxiogenic ligands, the term inverse agonist was adopted. Thus, all three classes have been connected with this benzodiazepine receptor (Nutt & Linnoila, 1988).

A variety of other sedative-hypnotic drugs, including many barbiturates, also enhance GABAergic neurotransmission, as do alcohols such as ethyl alcohol (Suzdak, Schwartz, Skolnick, et al., 1986; Gershon & Eison, 1987; Burch & Ticku, 1980; Paul, Marangos, & Skolnick, 1981).

Moreover, other neuronal substrates including the serotinin (Gershon & Eison, 1987), dopaminergic (Gershon & Eison, 1987), septohippocompal (Gershon & Eison, 1987) systems have also been implicated in the action of anxiolytic agents. Interaction between the serotonin and dopamine systems and

GABA are more clear. Of interest, Kandel and his colleagues have studied synaptic activity in aplysia in great detail and believe that serotonin is the neurotransmitter mediating neuronal changes associated with chronic anxiety and that synaptic terminals become structurally modified to release more of the transmitter than before (Kandel, 1983).

As with the locus coeruleus, GABA too has been shown to be altered after exposure to inescapable stress. Petty and Sherman (1981) reported that GABA release was decreased and glutamate levels elevated in the hippocampi of inescapably shocked animals. Here a decrease in GABAergic and an increase in glutamatergic neurotransmission seemed to change the balance between excitatory and inhibitory neurotransmitters, resulting in a marked disinhibition of hippocampal activity.

While the specific binding of [^{3}H]-imipramine to the serotonin uptake pump in the cerebral cortex was interrupted in rats exhibiting learned helplessness (Sherman & Petty, 1984), the administration of tricyclic antidepressants reversed the biochemical and behavioral effects of inescapable stress in learned helplessness. In rats, for example, exposed to 45 minutes of inescapable shock, those sacrificed 1 to 4 days postshock showed a decrease in the calcium-dependent release of serotonin from neocortex and septal slices, as well as a decreased release of GABA from hippocampal slices. In contrast, those biochemical changes were reversed in inescapably stressed animals that received imipramine for 4 days before being sacrificed (Sherman & Petty, 1982).

Various biochemical substances have also been shown to induce the same learned helplessness response evoked by uncontrollable stress. Rats receiving one of the inverse benzodiazepine receptor agonists B-carboline ethyl esters, failed to acquire an escape response and exhibited a behavioral syndrome equivalent to that seen after a session of inescapable shock (Drugan, Maier, Skolnick, et al., 1985). Pretreatment of those rats with a benzodiazepine, however, completely prevented the development of learned helplessness elicited by B-carboline ethyl ester.

The chronic administration of reserpine, an antihypertensive depressogenic agent in man also facilitates the development of learned helplessness and induces a depression-like syndrome in animals. Reserpine increases the density of β-adrenergic receptors in the cerebral cortex of rats and enhances the ability of NE to stimulate the synthesis of cyclic adenosine-3'5' monophosphate (Sethy & Hodges, 1982). In contrast, chronic administration of imipramine significantly decreased β-adrenergic receptor density and the reserpine-induced increase in β-adrenergic receptors. The triazolobenzodiazepine, alprazolam, although not altering the density of β-adrenergic receptors alone (as was observed with tricyclic antidepressants), did attenuate the reserpine-induced up-regulation of cerebral cortical β-adrenergic receptors when chronically administered (Sethy & Hodges, 1982). According to Paul (1988) there seems to be a "continuum" model of anxiety-depression:

> In the early stages of the anxiety-depression syndrome, when the patient exhibits only anxiety or a mix of anxiety and depressive symptoms, benzodiazepines may be quite effective for ameliorating both symptoms when the firing rate of norepinephrine neurons in the locus coeruleus must be inhibited to prevent the neuro transmitter's depletion. When the depletion of neurotransmitters such as norepinephine and serotonin occur in critical "forebrain" areas with now a depressive presentation, the minor tranquilizers are no longer helpful and tricyclics, MAOI's and ECT may then be required. (Paul, 1988) (See Figure 16.2.)

NON-BENZODIAZEPINES

A number of pharmacologically novel substances, chemically unrelated to the benzodiazepines, possess preclinical profiles suggestive of potential anxiolytic utility (Figure 16.3) (Gershon & Eison, 1987).

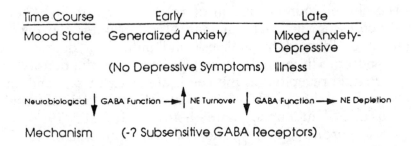

Figure 16.2 A Neurobiological Hypothesis Addressing the Temporal Relationship of Anxiety Preceding the Onset of Depressive Illness *Source: Paul, S. M. (1988). Anxiety and depression: a common neurobiological state?* Journal of Clinical Psychiatry, 49,(Suppl. 10); 13–16.

Pyrazolopyridines

Tracazolate, a pyrazolopyridine, displays anxiolytic-like activity in animal models, with a potency one-quarter to one-half that of chlordiazepoxide. Although tracazolate weakly inhibits pentylenetetrazol- and bicuculline-induced convulsions, it potentiates the anticonvulsant and anticonflict actions of chlordiazepoxide. In rodents tracazolate appears to exhibit less potential for undesirable interactions with CNS depressants and demonstrates a greater separation between sedative and therapeutic doses than does chlordiazepoxide (Patel & Malick, 1982). Unlike the benzodiazepines, tracazolate enhances (^{3}H) flunitrazepam binding in rat brain (Meiners & Salama, 1982); in common with the benzodiazepines, it antagonizes bicuculline-induced convulsions and enhances [^{3}H] GABA binding. Whereas [^{3}H] GABA binding is enhanced by tracazolate via an increase in the number rather than the affinity of GABA receptors (Patel & Malick, 1982; Meiners & Salama, 1982), the reverse accounts for its enhancement of [^{3}H] flunitrazepam binding.

Similar enhancements of benzodiazepine binding have also been observed with two related pyrazolopyridines-cartazolate and etazolate. Cartazolate, a structural relative to tracazolate, has been found effective as an anxiolytic in preliminary clinical trials (Sakalis, Sathananthan, Collins, et al., 1974). Like tracazolate, cartazolate lacks sedative effects, and only weakly antag-

Preclinical Profiles of Selected Non-Benzodiazepines

Class	Drug	Effects
Pyrazolopyradines		
	Tracazolate	■ Anxiolytic effects
	Cartazolate	■ Non-sedating
	Etazolate	■ Less interaction with CNS depressants
Imidazol Derivatives		
	Fenobam	■ Anxiolytic activity
		■ Minimal sedation
		■ Little interaction with alcohol
		■ Decrease in locomotor activity
Quinoline Derivatives		
	PK 8165	■ Blind to benzodiazepine receptors
		■ "Pure anticonflict" drugs
	PK 9084	■ No sedation
		■ No ataxia
	CGS 9896	■ Anxiolytic effects similar to those of benzodiazepines
	MK 801	
	DU 27725	
	DU 27716	■ Interaction with brain benzodiazepine receptors
	Amperozide	
Azaspirodecanediones		
	Buspirone	■ Anxiolytic effects similar to those of diazepam
		■ Low incidence of sedation
		■ Little interaction with alcohol or other medications

Figure 16.3 Preclinical Profiles of Selected Non-Benzodiazepines
Source: Adapted from Gershon, S., Eison, A. S. The Ideal Anxiolytic Psychiatric Annals *17(3): 160, 1987.*

onizes pentylenetetrazol convulsions. Unlike diazepam, it fails to prevent convulsions induced by electroshock and strychnine (Beer, Chasin, Clody, et al., 1972). All three pyrazolopyridines restore behavior suppressed by punishment in animal conflict procedures and exhibit inhibition of adenosine-stimulated [³H] cyclic AMP formation in guinea pig cortical preparations in vitro (Beer, et al., 1972; Psychoyos, Ford, & Phillipps, 1982).

Imidazole Derivatives

Data from animal studies suggest that fenobam, an imidazole derivative, possesses anti-anxiety activity without muscle relaxant or sedative-hypnotic activity, and also displays minimal interaction with alcohol (McNeil Pharmaceuticals, 1974). Administration of a single dose of fenobam produces a dose-dependent decrease in spontaneous locomotor activity in rats (Rastogi, Lapierre, & Singhal, 1980).

In clinical trials, fenobam was found to be an effective anti-anxiety agent when compared to placebo. It is reportedly safe, with minimal side effects and no excessive sedation (Lapierre & Oyewumi, 1982). In a double-blind, placebo-controlled clinical study, fenobam was as effective as diazepam and superior to placebo in relieving anxiety symptoms in neurotic outpatients (Pecknold, McClure, Appeltauer, et al., 1982). According to those investigators, fenobam's anti-anxiety effects appear to result from psychostimulation rather than from the sedative action observed with diazepam.

Quinoline Derivatives

The quinoline derivatives PK 8165 and PK 9084 are chemically unrelated to the benzodiazepines, yet selectively inhibit [^{3}H] diazepam binding. They demonstrate greater potency for brain than for kidney benzodiazepine binding sites. Unlike the benzodiazepines, PK 8165 and PK 9084 have been suggested to be "pure anticonflict drugs" whose anticonflict and anticonvulsant effects are dissociated. Thus, both agents increased punished responses in the rat conflict procedure, but did not antagonize pentylenetetrazol- or bicuculline-induced convulsions. Also, unlike the benzodiazepines, PK 8165 and PK 9084 did not produce ataxia or sedation even at doses five to 20 times greater than those effective in the conflict procedure (LeFur, Mizoule, Burgevin, et al., 1981).

OTHER NON-BENZODIAZEPINES

Some nonbenzodiazepine compounds, which have pharmacologic effects similar to the benzodiazepines, interact selectively with brain benzodiazepine receptors. CGS 9896, a novel pyrazoloquinoline, is a potent inhibitor of [³H] flunitrazepam binding in rat brain and protects mice against bicuculline- and pentylenetetrazol-induced seizures (Gee & Yamamura, 1982). CGS 9896 is as potent as diazepam in the Cooke-Davidson anticonflict model, but unlike diazepam lacks sedative effects (Yokoyama & Glenn, 1982).

Other non-benzodiazepines possess anticonflict activity, including the anticonvulsant, MK-801 (Clineschmidt, Williams, Witoslawski, et al., 1982). Zopiclone suppresses aggressive behavior but does not possess muscle relaxant or anticonvulsant activity (Effland & Forsch, 1982). The piperazine derivatives DU 27725 (Oliver, 1981) and amperozide (Effland & Forsch, 1982) exhibit anti-aggressive activity without sedative properties or motor impairment. The phenylpiperazine DU 27716, which is chemically and pharmacologically similar to DU 27725, inhibits hypothalamically-induced aggression in rats as well as isolation-induced, group, territorial, and intermale aggression in rodents (Oliver, 1981; van der Poel, Olivier, Mos, et al., 1982). Other nonbenzodiazepines such as melperone abolish experimental anxiety in normal human subjects (Molander, 1982).

Ace Inhibitors: (Angiotensin Converting Enzyme Inhibitor)

Captopril is a competitive inhibitor of the peptidyl dipeptide hydrolase that converts angiotensin I (AI) to angiotensin II (AII), hydrolyzes des-ASP-angiotensin I to angiotensin III and inactivates the vasopressor peptide bradykinin. Widely used synonyms for the enzyme are converting enzyme, angiotensin converting enzyme (ACE), and kininase II.

It is possible, that some of the activity of these agents (captopril) may be due to accumulation of bradykinin. Alteration of other peptide/protein systems (including opioid peptides, vasopressin, substance P, enkaphilin) may play a role in the mediation of the effects of captopril in various target organs, one of which is the brain.

This agent has been shown to have significant behavioral effects in animal test systems.

Captopril pretreatment causes an alteration of apomophine-induced stereotopy and this does not appear to be due to a displacement of apomorphine from the dopamine receptor site. The observed results may be explained by captopril-induced alterations in endogenous modulators of the dopamine receptor site. Costall and Naylor (personal communication) have also studied a series of ACE inhibitors and found that several display positive actions in a series of tests predictive of anxiolytic activity.

Buspirone

An azaspirodecanedione, buspirone (Buspar) is both structurally and pharmacologically distinct from the benzodiazepines. It possesses a nontraditional pharmacologic profile and spectrum of activity and may represent the first of a novel class of psychotherapeutic agents. Its behavioral profile includes:

- A "taming" effect in rhesus monkeys and inhibition of monkey aggressive response to poleprod (Tompkins, Clemento, Taylor, et al., 1980);
- Inhibition of conditioned avoidance responses in the rat (Riblet, Taylor, Eison, et al., 1982);
- Reduced shock-elicited fighting in mice (Table 16.2) (Riblet et al., 1982).

Buspirone's anxiolytic potential is demonstrated in anticonflict activity; it attenuates shock-induced suppression of drinking in the rat (Riblet et al., 1982) and of feeding in both rat and monkey (Geller & Hartman, 1982). However, buspirone does not exhibit the ancillary pharmacologic properties of the benzodiazepine anxiolytics. It lacks anticonvulsant activity against pentylenetetrazol, picrotoxin, bicuculline, and strychnine-induced seizures, as well as seizures induced by maximal electroshock (Riblet et al., 1982). Further, buspirone lacks sedative-hypnotic

Table 16.2 Effects of Buspirone

Behavioral Profile of Buspirone
• "Taming" effect in rhesus monkeys
• Inhibition of conditioned avoidance in rats
• Reduced shock-induced fighting in mice
• Conflict attenuation

Abuse/Dependency Potential of Buspirone
• No interaction with alcohol
• No euphoria (dysphoria at high doses)
• No sedation (except at high doses)

Source: From Gershon, S., Eison, A. S. The Ideal anxiolytic. *Psychiatric Annals* 17(3), 156–170, 1987.

and muscle-relaxant properties and does not potentiate the depressant effects of alcohol or hexobarbital (Riblet et al., 1982).

Buspirone neither stimulates nor inhibits [^{3}H] benzodiazepine binding in vitro and does not influence the actions of GABA or halide ions on [^{3}H] benzodiazepine binding. It binds to dopamine receptors, but does not interact with receptor ligands for several other neurotransmitters (Riblet et al., 1982). Electrophysiologic and biochemical studies suggest buspirone possesses dopamine autoreceptor antagonist activity (McMillen, Matthews, Sanghera, et al., 1983) and influences the effects of both dopamine and GABA upon midbrain dopamine neurons (Sussman, 1988) and acts on 5HT1A receptors.

Buspirone appears to lack the potential for physical dependence or abuse. In monkeys trained to self-administer cocaine, buspirone does not serve as a positive reinforcer and fails to sustain self-administration. It neither possesses discriminative stimulus properties in rats nor substitutes for oxazepam or pentobarbital in appropriately trained animals (Balster & Woolverton, 1982). Similarly, buspirone does not produce signs of physical dependence in animals following chronic administration (Allen, 1980) and, unlike diazepam, does not block pentobarbital withdrawal-induced convulsions (Riblet et al., 1982).

Several controlled clinical studies have shown buspirone's anxiolytic potency to be comparable to that of diazepam (Goldberg & Finnerty, 1979; Goldberg & Finnerty, 1982; Rickels, 1981; Rickels, Weisman, Norstad, et al., 1982; Feighner, Merideth, & Hendrickson, 1982). Whereas diazepam appeared more effective in reducing the somatic symptoms of anxiety, buspirone appeared more effective in reducing symptoms indicative of cognitive and interpersonal problems, including anger-hostility (Rickels et al., 1982). Also, buspirone relieves depression associated with anxiety (Goldberg & Finnerty, 1982).

In clinical evaluations, buspirone exhibits a low incidence of sedative and other side effects (Goldberg & Finnerty, 1982; Newton, Casten, Alms, et al., 1982). When compared with diazepam, buspirone produces less psychological impairment (Lader, 1982) and in tests of driving skills produces placebo-like or improved performances (Moskowitz & Smiley, 1982). Alcohol fails to alter either the psychologic or acute psychomotor effects of buspirone, whereas lorazepam-induced impairments are enhanced by alcohol administration (Mattila, Aranko, & Seppala, 1982). Unlike that of diazepam, buspirone's side effect profile is not altered by the concomitant use of other medications, except haloperidol (Gershon, 1982). In recreational sedative abusers, buspirone appears to lack abuse potential; it fails to produce euphoria or sedative effects at low doses (10 mg) and causes physical and mental dysphoria and sedation at high doses (40 mg) (Table 16.3) (Cole, Orzack, Beake, et al., 1982).

Buspirone is completely and rapidly absorbed, reaching peak plasma levels 60 to 90 minutes after ingestion (Gammans, Mayol, & Labudde, 1986). Food does not interfere with absorption. Indeed, postprandial administration of buspirone results in a decreased degree of first pass metabolism, increasing the amount of unmetabolized and pharmacologically active drug (Gammans et al., 1986). There are no active metabolites of buspirone that contribute significantly to observed pharmacological effects. Both hepatic and renal disease decrease buspirone clearance (Gammans et al., 1986).

While there is a paucity of reports, there are several recent publications that have indicated that Buspirone may be effica-

Table 16.3 Buspirone: Anxiolytic Profile

	Buspirone	Benzodiazepines
Antiaggression	+	+
Conflict	+	+
Conditioned avoidance	+	+
Anticonvulsant	−	+
Sedation	−	+
Muscle relaxation	−	+
Functional impairment	−	+
Interaction with central nervous system depressants	−	+
Abuse potential/physical dependence	−	+

Adapted from Eison A. S., & Temple D. L. (1986). *American Journal of Medicine,* 80(3B):1.

cious in late-life anxiety (Napoliello, 1986; Singh & Beer, 1988). In an unpublished but controlled study in forty (M/F:10/30) elderly patients (> 65 years of age) with a primary diagnosis of anxiety (ICD-9 anxiety neuroses $n = 20$, ICD = 9 Depressive Neurosis $n = 20$), Claus Bohm (personal communication) found that buspirone in a range of 5–30mg over four weeks when compared to placebo, reduced mean Hamilton anxiety (A) and Hamilton Depressive (D) scores by more than 50% ($p < .01$) A > D). Moreover, recent reports indicate a possible efficacy of this agent in agitated and disinhibited demented elderly (Colenda, 1988; Tiller, Dakis, & Shaw, 1988). Other non-benzodiazepine Buspirone analogues (i.e., Gepirone) (Eison et al., 1986) continue to be developed and they, too, seem to be efficacious, nonsedating, and well tolerated.

Comparisons of the profiles of benzodiazepine, non-benzodiazepine agents, as well as antidepressants as anxiolytics provide useful information for further drug development. Drug development, however, is also dependent on a knowledge of those mechanisms that underlie anxiety, and of those that subserve its reduction by anxiolytic drugs or thymoleptic agents.

PROFILE OF THE IDEAL ANXIOLYTIC

Neuropharmacologic Perspective

Although various receptors, neurotransmitter systems, and endogenous ligands have been exclusively implicated in mediating the actions of anxiolytic drugs by some, both laboratory and human data suggest that receptor alterations in any one system or pathway cannot account entirely for the genesis of anxiety. Were just a single system involved, one might propose that the ideal anxiolytic agent would specifically, selectively, and potently counteract aberrant activity at the anxiogenic locus. As explained by Gray (1978) non-benzodiazepine and non-barbiturate drugs that are anxiolytic but do not have side effects have enabled us, using a series of comparisons, to "triangulate" anxiety. This approach is valuable in developing hypotheses concerning putative neural substrates and mechanisms of anxiolytic drug actions. Although the precise neuronal mechanisms of the nonbenzodiazepine, buspirone have not yet been identified, this drug clearly is anxiolytic without producing the side effects common to many anti-anxiety agents. Such compounds provide the impetus to continue the search for the ideal anxiolytic.

Clinical Perspective

Were one to model the concept of the actions of an ideal anxiolytic on anxiety after Koch's criteria for establishing an organism in the etiology of a given disease, one could reasonably propose that the ideal anxiolytic or the processes initiated by its administration must:

- Be effective in all types of anxiety disorders;
- Be identifiable during anxiolysis in treated patients and detectable at its sites of action;
- Antagonize anxiety, however induced, on every occasion.

In a more practical sense, as proposed by Lehman (1979) the ideal anxiolytic agent (and all other drugs) should be safe, reliable, and effective. It should not demonstrate acute toxicity, cause allergic reactions, or elicit untoward physiologic effects with chronic administration, and should not be lethal in large doses. Further, it should not impair psychomotor performance or interact with CNS depressants. Finally, it should not induce physical or psychologic dependence or cause withdrawal phenomena.

To be effective, the ideal anxiolytic should *selectively* decrease anxiety without causing sedation or other mental or psychologic effects, such as impairment of cognitive performance or aggressive or hostile feelings and behavior. Such behavior has occasionally been attributed to the benzodiazepines (Lader, 1981) in the past.

Another important consideration is safe, effective, and selective reduction of anxiety in extremes of the life cycle, who are more vulnerable to untoward effects. The side effect profile is an important aspect of a drug's utility, since compliance weakens if side effects are numerous or pronounced.

Until we understand the etiology of anxiety, we cannot assess how selective anxiolytic drugs are in terms of their mechanisms. However, clinically effective agents can be compared in terms of side effect profiles. For example, buspirone has been demonstrated to be both effective and safe. In a battery of driving skill tests designed to assess levels of psychomotor performance, buspirone did not inhibit, and in fact improved, performance (Moskowitz & Smiley, 1982). Neither the psychologic nor the acute psychomotor effects of buspirone are altered by alcohol ingestion (Mattila, Aranko, & Seppala, 1982). Buspirone also does not potentiate the depressant effects of alcohol or hexobarbital in animals (Riblet et al., 1982). Moreover, the concomitant use of other medications, including benzodiazepines (Tollefson & Montague-Clouse, 1988) does not appear to alter buspirone's side effect profile (Gershon, 1982).

In clinical and animal models, neither chronic (Allen, 1980) nor acute administration of buspirone elicits physical dependence or abuse, and the drug fails to substitute for benzodiazepines or barbiturates in rat (Balster & Woolverton, 1982). In recreational drug abusers, buspirone lacks euphoriant effects at therapeutic doses and may induce dysphoric effects at higher doses (Cole et al., 1982).

In summary, buspirone is effective in the treatment of anxiety and lacks the side effects that may hamper treatment with established anxiolytics and hypnotics. Compared with the benzodiazepines, buspirone produces less psychologic impairment and appears more effective in reducing anger-hostility (Rickels et al., 1982; Lader, 1982). It also appears to alleviate depression associated with anxiety (Goldberg & Finnerty, 1979). Comparative controlled pharmacologic studies for the organic anxiety disorders however, have yet to be reported.

CONCLUSION—THE IDEAL

Unfortunately, the ideal geriatric anxiolytic has yet to be developed. In the absence of such an agent, as well as in the absence of controlled studies of the comparative pharmacotherapy in the elderly, the authors will, nevertheless, offer some guidelines for the management of late life anxiety. In the process a prototype will be implicated. These guidelines are based on the experiences of the authors and the principles previously stated. For new lifetime onset, first time, persistent anxiety, with no previous history of affective illness or family history of such, and after the treatment of organic factors, the authors recommend a trial of buspirone. The trial of buspirone should be undertaken for at least one month with the target of anxiety relief. If the anxiety symptoms seem overwhelming before the elapse of the month, buspirone may be supplemented with a short acting benzodiazepine, such as lorazepam, oxazepam, or alprazolam on a temporary basis until a therapeutic dosage for a therapeutic time period is achieved. Indeed, Tollefson (1988) has recently reported on the efficacy and safety of sequential alprazolam supplemented with buspirone. On the other hand, if for a new lifetime onset anxiety disorder there is a suggestion of an affective component, i.e., diurnal energy disturbance or of a family history of affective disorder, then a six-week therapeutic trial of a secondary amine tricyclic antidepressant, nortriptyline, or desipramine may be undertaken. In the authors' experience, the warning of "start low, go slow, but go all the way," should be well heeded. In our experience nortriptyline is an antidepressant drug of choice in the elderly. The availability of low dose pills (10 mg), its low incidence of side effects, and the value of therapeutic blood levels in depressive disorders persuade us to support its use. Again, for nontolerable anxiety during this initial period the addition of a short acting benzodiazepine may be temporarily efficacious.

For both, persistent nonaffective anxiety and persistent affective anxiety, alternative pharmacotherapy should be considered. In addition, after a nonsuccessful buspirone trial, an antidepressant trial (as outlined above), may be undertaken. Alternative or adjunctive psychotherapy should always be considered. For patients with histories of primary anxiety disorders predating their elderly years, buspirone here too, is an agent of choice.

As we have already emphasized, there have been no published comparative controlled late life anxiolytic trials. Buspirone's reported efficacy and safety in late life anxiety, its efficacy in elderly dysinhibition (and possibly, therefore, dementia), (Colenda, 1988; Tiller, Dakis, & Shaw, 1988), its ideal side effect profile especially in the elderly, the suggestion of its efficacy as an antidepressant makes it potentially of value for late life anxiety. Controlled elderly trials with buspirone need be undertaken and especially also as antidepressants (Goldberg & Finnerty, 1979). Unfortunately, the biggest drawback to buspirone continues to be its lack of an immediate anxiolytic effect, unlike the benzodiazepines. Indeed, Rickels (1988) recently reported an efficacy and side effect comparison study between clorazepate and buspirone in chronically anxious patients. While three-quarters of the clorazepate patients experienced withdrawal symptoms as compared to no buspirone patients, 45% (versus 26% clorazepate patients) of the buspirone patients discontinued treatment during their first four weeks of treatment. In addition, evidence exists that prior benzodiazepine sustained use may make a buspirone trial less valuable (Rickels, 1982). Recent reports, though very preliminary, of a possible risk of tardive dyskinesia in those exposed to Buspirone must be further investigated (Strauss, 1988). Future drug development should maintain the benefits of Buspirone and its analogues and incorporate the immediacy benefits of the benzodiazepines without their problems (dependency, sedation, memory incoordination, etc.).

SUMMARY

Pathologic anxiety has been a longstanding and pervasive problem for the physician. Moreover, its frequency is apparently increasing, placing new emphasis on the need for rational therapy. Recent emphasis on the understanding and treatment of the mental health needs of the elderly and more sophistication with regard to psychiatric nomenclature, especially with regard to the anxiety disorders, highlights this effort for rational therapy.

As the mechanisms responsible for the generation of anxiety as well as for the actions of diverse classes of drugs that reduce anxiety become known, it will be possible to develop modes of pharmacological intervention that better approach the ideal. Both receptors (benzodiazepine) and neural systems (GABA), serotonin, norepinephrine, dopamine, septohippocampal, as well as endogenous ligands have been implicated in the mediation of anxiety. Further, both drug-induced and stimulation-induced models have been utilized to explore proposed neural substrates.

While efficacious against anxiety, tricyclic antidepressants and benzodiazepines exhibit side effects and ancillary properties unrelated to anxiolysis. The new generation of pharmacologically novel substances, the non-benzodiazepines, include such compounds as tracazolate, fenobam, PK 8165, CGS 9896, buspirone, DU 27716, and melperone. From a neuropharmacologic perspective, non-benzodiazepine and nonbarbiturate drugs, as well as antidepressants that are anxiolytic but possess few side effects, will enable us by successive stages, to approach the ideal anxiolytic.

Clinically, it is suggested that the ideal anxiolytic should have a greater short term onset. It should also selectively decrease anxiety without causing sedation or other mental or psychologic effects such as impairment of cognitive or psychomotor performance or aggressive or hostile feelings or behavior. Additionally, it should not interact with CNS depressants or induce physical or psychologic dependence. Agents that address these issues will be very useful in the management of anxiety.

COMMENTARY

1. Sedation may be desirable for some elderly patients, especially since elderly people may be increasingly anxious at night.

2. For some older people the ideal anxiolytic is that pill which works after a single dose. The only such pills that are available that produce such an effect are drugs that are sedative. Sedative drugs are usually perceived as immediately helpful. This raises an important question. Should anxiolytics be produced that are immediately sedating but may produce undesirable consequences with continued use as opposed to developing drugs that are purely anxiolytic and do not have sedating properties, but may take several weeks to produce the therapeutic effect? There is at present no drug which produces the immediate effect after one dose, and yet is nonsedating. Although it is theoretically possible to have a drug that is both immediately anxiolytic without any sedating effects, no such drugs are currently available. An alternative strategy is to use a pure anxiolytic nonsedating drug which may take several weeks to produce a full effect, and also use a short acting hypnotic for sedation until the anxiolytic begins to work. This would decrease the risk of administration of a potentially hazardous sedating drug. Unfortunately, for elderly patients, using more than one drug may only worsen a frequent problem of polypharmacy.

3. It is possible to have drugs that are initially stimulating that go on to be anxiolytic in effect.

4. There are no good data indicating that varapamil has any psychotropic effect.

5. There is an occasional increase in irritable, socially unacceptable behavior with benzodiazepines. This may be seen in the elderly as well as in young adults.

ACKNOWLEDGMENTS

We would like to extend our thanks to Arlette Miara and Kay Wyko for their help in the preparation of this chapter. This chapter is a modification/revision of an article previously published in S. Gershon & A. S. Eison (1987). The Ideal anxiolytic. *Psychiatric Annals, 17*(3), 156–170.

REFERENCES

Allen, L. E. (1980). Physical dependence study using buspirone and diazepam in rats. Mead Johnson Research Center. Biological Research Report No. 8094.

Baldessarini, R. J. (1980). Drugs and the treatment of psychiatric disorders. In A. G. Gilman, L. S. Goodman, & A. Gilman (Eds.), *Pharmacological Basis of Therapeutics, Edition 6* (pp. 339–375). New York: MacMillan Publishing Co.

Balster, R. L., & Woolverton, W. L. (1982). Intravenous buspirone self-administration in rhesus monkeys. *Journal of Clinical Psychiatry, 43*(12, Sec 2), 34–37.

Beer, B., Chasin, M., Clody, D. E., et al. (1972). Cyclic adenosine monophosphate phosphodiesterase in brain: Effect on anxiety. *Science, 176*, 428–430.

Burch, T. D., & Ticku, M. K. (1980). Ethanol enhances [^{3}H]-diazepam binding at the benzodiazepine-GABA-receptor-ionophore receptor complex. *European Journal of Pharmacology, 67*, 325–326.

Clineschmidt, B. V., Williams, M., Witoslawski, J. J., et al. (1982). Restoration of shock-suppressed behavior by treatment with (+)-5-methyl-10, 11-dihydro-5H-dibenzo [a,d] cyclohepten, -5,10-imine (MK-801), a substance with potent anticonvulsant, central sympathomimetic and apparent anxiolytic properties. *Drug Development Research, 2*, 147–163.

Cole, J. O., Orzack, M. H., Beake, B., et al. (1982). Assessment of the abuse liability of buspirone in recreational sedative users. *Journal of Clinical Psychiatry, 43*(12, Sec 2), 69–74.

Colenda, C. (1988). Buspirone in treatment of agitated demented patient. *Lancet*, May, *21*, 1169 (Letter to the Editor).

Donovan, B. T. (1988). *Humors, hormones and the mind: An approach to the understanding of behavior* (pp. 166–169). London: Mac-Millan Press, Ltd.

Drugan, R. C., Maier, S. F., Skolnick, P., et al. (1985). An anxiogenic benzodiazepine receptor ligand induces learned helplessness. *European Journal of Pharmacology, 113,* 453–457.

Edwards, J. G. (1981). Adverse effects of antianxiety drugs. *Drugs, 22,* 495–514.

Effland, R. C., & Forsch, M. F. (1982). Anti-anxiety agents, anticonvulsants and sedative hypnotics. *Annual Reports in Medicinal Chemistry, 17,* 11–19.

Eison, A. S. et al. (1986). Serotonergic mechanisms in the behavioral effects of buspirone and gepirone. *Pharmacology, Biochemistry and Behavior, 24,* 701–707.

Eison, M. S. (1989). The new generation of serotonergic anxiolytic: Possible clinical roles. *Psychopathology, 22*(supplement 1), 13–20.

Feighner, J. P., Merideth, C. H., & Hendrickson, G. A. (1982). A double-blind comparison of buspirone and diazepam in outpatients with generalized anxiety disorder. *Journal of Clinical Psychiatry, 43*(12, Sec 2), 103–107.

Gammans, R. E., Mayol, R. F., & Labudde, J. A. (1986). Metabolism and disposition of buspirone. *American Journal of Medicine, 80*(Suppl. 5B), 41–51.

Gee, K. W., & Yamamura, H. I. (1982). A novel pyrazoloquinoline that interacts with brain benzodiazepine receptors: Characterization of some in vitro and in vivo properties of CGS 9896. *Life Science, 30,* 2245–2252.

Geller, I., & Hartman, R. J. (1982). Effects of buspirone on operant behavior of laboratory rats and cynomologus monkeys. *Journal of Clinical Psychiatry, 43*(12, Sec 2), 25–32.

Gershon, S. (1982). Drug interactions in controlled clinical trials. *Journal of Clinical Psychiatry, 43*(12, Sec 2), 95–98.

Gershon, S., & Eison, A. S. (1987). The ideal anxiolytic. *Psychiatric Annals, 17*(3), 156–170.

Goldberg, H. L., & Finnerty, R. J. (1982). Comparison of buspirone in two separate studies. *Journal of Clinical Psychiatry, 43*(12, Sec 2), 87–91.

Goldberg, H. L., & Finnerty, R. J. (1979). The comparative efficacy of buspirone and diazepam in the treatment of anxiety. *American Journal of Psychiatry, 136,* 1184–1187.

Gray, J. A. (1982). Precis of the neuropsychology of anxiety: An enquiry into the functions of the septo-hippocampal system. *Behavioral and Brain Sciences, 5,* 469–534.

Gray, J. A. (1978). The neuropsychology of anxiety. *British Journal of Psychology, 69,* 417–434.

Greenblatt, D. J., Shader, R. I., & Abernethy, D. R. (1983). Current status of benzodiazepines. *New England Journal of Medicine, 309,* 354–358.

Harvey, S. C. (1980). Hypnotics and sedatives. In A. G. Gilman, L. S. Goodman, & A. Gilman (Eds.), *Pharmacological Basis of Therapeutics, Edition 6* (pp. 391–447). New York: MacMillan Publishing Co.

Insel, T. R., Ninan, P. T., Aloi, J., et al. (1984). A benzodiazepine receptor-mediated model of anxiety: Studies in nonhuman primates and clinical implications. *Archives of General Psychiatry, 41,* 741–750.

Kandel, E. (1983). From metapsychology to molecular biology: Explorations into the nature of anxiety. *American Journal of Psychiatry, 140,* 1277–1293.

Lader, M. (1981). Benzodiazepine dependence. In R. Murry et al. (Eds.), *The misuse of psychotropic drugs.* London: Gaskell Press. (Royal College of Psychiatrists Special Publication Number 1).

Lader, M. (1982). Psychological effects of buspirone. *Journal of Clinical Psychiatry, 43*(12, Sec 2), 62–67.

Lader, M. (1982). Summary and commentary. In E. Usdin, F. Skolnick, J. F. Tallman, et al. (Eds.), *Pharmacology of benzodiazepine* (pp. 53–60). New York: MacMillan Press.

Lapierre, Y. D., & Oyewumi, L. K. (1982). Fenobam: Another anxiolytic? *Current Therapy Research, 31,* 95–101.

LeFur, G., Mizoule, J., Burgevin, M. D., et al. (1981). Multiple benzodiazepine receptors: Evidence of a dissociation between anticonflict and anticonvulsant properties by PK 8165 and PK 9084 (two quinoline derivatives). *Life Science, 28,* 1439–1448.

Lehman, H. E. (1979). Tranquilizers: Clinical insufficiencies and needs. Quoted in Future Prospects of Anxiolytic Drugs in S. Fielding & H. Lal (Eds.), *Industrial Pharmacology* (V. 3, p. 403). Mt. Kisco, New York: Futura Publishing.

Mattila, M. J., Aranko, K., & Seppala, T. (1982). Acute effects of buspirone and alcohol on psychomotor skills. *Journal of Clinical Psychiatry, 43*(12, Sec 2), 56–60.

McMillen, B. A., Matthews, R. T., Sanghera, M. K., et al. (1983). Dopamine receptor antagonism by the novel antianxiety drug, buspirone. *Journal of Neuroscience, 3,* 733–738.

McNeil Pharmaceuticals. (1974). Pharmacological profile of McN 3377-98: A potential anti-anxiety agent. Pharmacological report No. 256 (740125) *McNeil International Report* January 25, 1974.

Meiners, B. A., & Salama, A. I. (1982). Enhancement of benzodiazepine and GABA binding by the novel anxiolytic tracazolate. *European Journal of Pharmacology, 78,* 315–322.

Molander, L. (1982). Effect of melperone, chlorpramazine, haloperidol and diazepam on experimental anxiety in normal subjects. *Psychopharmacology, 77,* 109–113.

Moskowitz, H., & Smiley, A. (1982). Effects of chronically administered buspirone and diazepam on driving-related skills performance. *Journal of Clinical Psychiatry, 43*(12, Sec 2), 45–55.

Napoliello, M. J. (1986). An interim multicentre report on 677 anxious geriatric out-patients treated with buspirone. *British Journal of Clinical Practice,* February, 71–73.

Newton, R. E., Casten, G. P., Alms, D. R., et al. (1982). The side effect profile of buspirone in comparison to active controls and placebo. *Journal of Clinical Psychiatry, 43*(12, Sec 2), 100–102.

Nutt, D. J., & Linnoila, M. Neuroreceptor science: A clarification of terms. *Clinical Psychopharmacology, 8*(6), 387–388.

Oliver, B. (1981). Selective antiaggressive properties of DU 27725: Ethological analyses of intermale and territorial aggression in the male rat. *Pharmacology, Biochemistry and Behavior, 14*(Suppl. 1), 61–77.

Patel, J. B., & Malick, J. B. (1982). Pharmacological properties of tracazolate: A new nonbenzodiazepine anxiolytic agent. *European Journal of Pharmacology, 79,* 323–333.

Paul, S. M. (1988). Anxiety and depression: A common neurobiological state? *Journal of Clinical Psychiatry, 49*(Suppl. 10), 13–16.

Paul, S. M., Marangos, P. J., & Skolnick, P. The benzodiazepine GABA-chloride ionophore receptor complex: Common site of minor tranquilizer action. *Biological Psychiatry, 16,* 213–229.

Pecknold, J. C., McClure, D. J., Appeltauer, L., et al. (1982). Treatment of anxiety using fenobam (a non-benzodiazepine) in a double-blind standard (diazepam) placebo-controlled study. *Clinical Psychopharmacology, 2,* 129–133.

Petty, F., & Sherman, D. (1981). GABAergic modulation of learned helplessness. *Pharmacology, Biochemistry and Behavior, 15,* 567–570.

Psychoyos, S., Ford, C. J., & Phillipps, M. A. (1982). Inhibition by etazolate (SQ 20009) and cartazolate (SQ 65396) of adenosine-stimulated [^{3}H] cAMP formation in 2-[^{3}H] adenine-prelabeled vesicle prepared from guinea pig cerebral cortex. *Biochemical Pharmacology, 31,* 1441–1442.

Rastogi, R. G., Lapierre, Y. D., & Singhal, R. L. (1980). Some behavioral and neuropharmacological aspects of fenobam: A new anti-anxiety drug. *Recent Advances in Canadian Neuropsychopharmacology, 2,* 26–35.

Riblet, L. A., Taylor, D. P., Eison, M. S., et al. (1982). Pharmacology and neurochemistry of buspirone. *Journal of Clinical Psychiatry, 43*(12, Sec 2), 11–16.

Richardson, J. W., & Richelson, E. (1984). Antidepressants: A clinical update for medical practitioners. *Mayo Clinic Proceedings, V. 59.*

Rickels, K. (1982). Benzodiazepines in the treatment of anxiety. *American Journal of Psychotherapy, 36,* 358–370.

Rickels, K. (1981). Recent advances in anxiolytic therapy. *Journal of Clinical Psychiatry, 42*(Sec 2), 40–44.

Rickels, K. (1978). Use of antianxiety agents in anxious outpatients. *Psychopharmacology, 58,* 1–17.

Rickels, K., Schweizer, E., Csanalosi, I., et al. (1988). Long-term treatment of anxiety and risk of withdrawal: Prospective comparison of clorazepate and buspirone. *Archives of General Psychiatry, 45,* 444–450.

Rickels, K., Weisman, K., Norstad, N., et al. (1982). Buspirone and diazepam in anxiety: A controlled study. *Journal of Clinical Psychiatry, 43*(12, Sec 2), 81–86.

Sakalis, G., Sathananthan, G, Collins, P., et al. (1974). SQ65396: A non-sedative anxiolytic? *Current Therapy in Research, 16,* 861.

Schofield, P. R., Darlison, M. G., Fujita, N., et al. (1987). Sequence and functional expression of GABA receptor shows a ligand-gated receptor super-family. *Nature, 328,* 221–227.

Sethy, V. H., & Hodges Jr., D. H. Alprazolam in a biochemical model of depression. *Biochemical Pharmacology, 31,* 3155–3157.

Sherman, A. D., & Petty, F. (1982). Additivity of neurochemical changes in learned helplessness and imipramine. *Behavioral Neural Biology, 35,* 344–353.

Sherman, A. D., & Petty, F. (1984). Learned helplessness decreases [^{3}H] imipramine binding in rat cortex. *Journal of Affective Disorders, 6,* 25–32.

Singh, A. N., & Beer, M. (1988). A dose range-finding study of buspirone in geriatric patients with symptoms of anxiety. *Journal of Clinical Psychopharmacology, 8*(1), 67–68.

Strauss, A. (1988). Oral dyskinesia associated with buspirone use in an elderly woman. *Journal of Clinical Psychiatry, 49*(8), 322–323.

Sussman, N. (1988). Diagnosis and drug treatment of anxiety in the elderly. *Geriatric Medicine Today, 7*(10), 37–51.

Suzdak, P., Schwartz, R. D., Skolnick, P., et al. (1986). Ethanol stimulates gamma-aminobutyric acid receptor-mediated chloride transport in rat brain synaptoneurosomes. *Proceeds of the National Academy of Science, USA, 83,* 4071–4075.

Tiller, J. W. G., Dakis, J. A., & Shaw, J. M. (1988). Short-term buspirone treatment in disinhibition with dementia. *Lancet,* August, *27,* 510 (Letter to the Editor).

Tollefson, G. D., & Montague-Clouse, J. (1988). Alprazolam plus buspirone in treatment of anxiety. *American Journal of Psychiatry, 145*(3), 379–380 (Letter to the Editor).

Tompkins, E. C., Clemento, A. J., Taylor, D. P. et al. (1980). Inhibition of aggressive behavior in rhesus monkeys by buspirone. *Research Communications in Psychology, Psychiatry, and Behavior, 5,* 337–351.

van der Poel, A. M., Olivier, B., Mos, J., et al. (1982). Antiaggressive effect of a new phenylpiperazine compound (DU 27716) on hypothalamically-induced behavioral activities. *Pharmacology, Biochemistry and Behavior, 17,* 147–153.

Yokoyama, N., & Glenn, T. (1982). CGS 9896 and CGS 8216: Potent benzodiazepine receptor agonist and antagonist. 184th ACN National Meeting Abstracts, Division of Medicinal Chemistry, Abstract 58.

CONCLUSION

Carl Salzman

It is apparent from the wealth of research and clinical information presented in the preceding chapters that the concept of anxiety as a discrete state independent of other disorders or from the natural consequences of aging is considerably less clear in older people than in younger adults. Anxiety in the elderly has always been considered to be essentially equivalent to anxiety in younger adults, both in etiology, as well as in clinical presentation. However, only a handful of research studies have focused on anxiety in the elderly, and very few clinicians have sought to define and describe experience of anxious older people. The conclusion to be drawn from the clinical and research observations as recorded in this volume, is that anxiety in the elderly is an exceedingly complex experiential phenomenon that shares certain aspects with younger adults, but also may substantially differ from younger adults. As the authors in this volume further suggest, it is becoming critical for clinicians to understand that anxiety may present differently in the elderly, and that treatment may differ from younger adults as well. It is also becoming essential for researchers to redefine the clinical state of anxiety as it applies to the elderly so that more precise inquiry can be made into its etiology, pathogenesis, and, of course, its treatment. If there is one observation that virtually every contributor agrees upon, it is that anxiety as a pure affective state does not appear frequently in older people, but is usually mixed together with other affective states, and confounded by numerous aspects of late life experience, including illness, medication, normal aging, increased social and psychologic stress, approaching death, as well as early life experiences and psycho-social characteristics. The following synthesis is an attempt to summarize what has been learned about anxiety in the elderly as presented by the contributors to this volume.

I. Definition, description, and prevalence
   A. Anxiety exists in the elderly, although the causes may be somewhat different than in younger adults, and the incidence and prevalence may also differ.
   B. The prevalence of anxiety in the elderly is lower than for middle-aged adults, although under reporting of anxiety may be more common. Anxiety-related disorders such as phobias, panic, and obsessive compulsive disorders, are less prevalent in late-life than in younger adult life. Anxiety attacks (as well as panic attacks) occur less frequently in the elderly, although anxiety as a symptom occurs relatively frequently.
   C. Anxiety in the elderly may be of several types.
      1. Depletion anxiety concerns the loss of external supplies rather than serving as a signal of psychological conflict. Depletion anxiety is analogous to separation anxiety.
      2. Death anxiety, the fear of dying is not specific to the elderly. If older people have death anxiety, it may be less frequent and less severe in those older patients who have retained a sense of purposefulness about life.
      3. There is a high comorbidity between anxiety and other psychological syndromes. Anxiety commonly accompanies other medical and psychiatric illness.

4. There is a high comorbidity with depression. However, anxiety may be clinically differentiated from
   depression in the following manners.

Anxiety	Depression
a. Loss of self-confidence	a. Guilt, worthlessness
b. Difficulty falling asleep	b. Anhedonia, and decreased motivation
c. A sense of apprehension	c. Anergia

5. Anxiety may overlap with appropriate fears and concerns about life (such as getting mugged, going out in
   bad weather, finances).

D. There are very few elderly patients with pure agoraphobia or OCD, but more careful survey data are needed.

E. Anxiety is often a part of general medical disorders in
   the elderly.

1. Anxiety symptoms may be difficult to distinguish
   from physical illness, and may be usefully divided
   into somatic symptoms and psychic symptoms.
   Symptoms of both psychic anxiety and somatic anxiety exist in patients with chronic depression with an
   especially close relationship between psychic anxiety
   and chronic depression in geriatric patients. There is
   also consensus that physical symptoms are both part
   of anxiety as well as a cause of it.

2. GI symptoms are especially prevalent, and may overlap with true hypochondriasis.

3. Anxiety may be a side effect of medications given for
   medical disorder.

4. Anxiety may be associated with an increased morbidity from physical illness. Treatment of anxiety accompanying physical illness may therefore improve recu-
   peration.

5. Anxiety may be a predictable part of many physical
   illnesses, especially cardiovascular, respiratory, endocrine, and infection.

6. Anxiety and dementia also frequently co-exist in a complicated relationship. Anxiety may aggravate dementia, and dementia may be associated with anxiety as the symptoms progress in severity. As with the co-existence of anxiety and depression, co-existence of anxiety and dementia has been insufficiently studied.
7. There is also a relationship between anxiety in the elderly and alcohol consumption. Data suggest that rates of abstention, as well as rates of excessive alcohol use, may be high in the elderly age groups. Alcohol use may be both a cause as well as result of anxiety. However, not all alcohol use or abuse in the elderly may be the result of anxiety.

II. The impact of aging on the biologic etiology of anxiety
   A. The neurobiologic substrates of anxiety in the elderly are not well understood and such understanding is complicated by normal age-related changes in the central nervous system as well as by changes associated with illness, or the development of a dementia.
   B. Neurotransmitters, especially norepinephrine and GABA, as well as neurohormones such as glucocorticoids, that change with age may be associated with some of the symptoms that define anxiety in old age. Any cause and effect relationship between change in CNS function and anxiety remains to be determined by future research.

III. Treatment
   A. There are numerous treatments of anxiety-type symptoms in the elderly including interpersonal psychotherapy, behavioral techniques, and pharmacotherapy. Elderly patients sometimes respond surprisingly well to nonpharmacologic treatments, especially when the clinician is flexible and adapts the treatment technique to the older patient. Research efforts need to continue to explore these techniques.
   B. Pharmacologic treatment needs to be informed by age-related changes in drug disposition (pharmacokinetics) as well as an awareness of altered central nervous system sensitivity. These changes include:

1. Age alters benzodiazepine pharmacokinetics. A decrease in metabolic clearance of benzodiazepines that undergo hepatic microsomal oxidative reactions. The consequence of this decreased clearance is a prolonged half-life rather than an increased serum or peak plasma concentrations.
2. During chronic administration, drug accumulation is a direct result of this decreased clearance.
3. Decreased protein binding is not a clinically relevant factor when prescribing benzodiazepines to the elderly. Even though there is a decrease in free fraction, there is no change in free concentration.
4. There is an increased pharmacodynamic (receptor site) sensitivity to benzodiazepines in the elderly, regardless of changes in pharmacokinetics. This may result from a decreased coupling of benzodiazepine to the receptor rather than decreased affinity or decreased receptor number.
5. Although pharmacologic treatment may bring about symptomatic relief, it may also be associated with considerable toxicity in the elderly.
C. Cognitive toxicity of benzodiazepines in the elderly.
 1. The elderly may be more sensitive to the adverse effects of all psychotropic drugs on task performance. In research studies there is a clear single dose impairment, but this impairment may not exist after multiple doses so that the data regarding adverse effects from chronic drug administration are equivocal. It is possible that benzodiazepines exacerbate the symptoms of mild-moderate dementia, but these changes are reversible when the drug is withdrawn.
 2. Both single and multiple doses of benzodiazepines induce cognitive impairment, especially memory loss.
 3. Nighttime doses induce daytime psychomotor impairment, decreased attention, and decreased memory.
 4. There are no data suggesting differences in cognitive toxicity among benzodiazepines or between classes of benzodiazepines.

D. Behavioral treatment.
   The use of progressive muscle relaxation as a technique
   is especially helpful for the anxious elderly. It can be
   combined with controlled breathing, and with other
   techniques such as thought stopping, cognitive restructuring, muscle relaxation, and positive imagery. Further
   research is essential, since there are a number of problems associated with using these techniques in the elderly. These include:
   1. Decreased cognition in the elderly makes under-
      standing the techniques difficult.
   2. Behavioral techniques are best for specific fears;
      there is less experience using these techniques with
      generalized anxiety.
   3. The elderly may not evaluate their symptoms as psy-
      chological in nature.
   4. There is an insufficient number of mental health pro-
      fessionals to provide these behavioral treatment
      techniques.
   5. Anxious elderly patients may see family doctors
      rather than psychiatrists.
E. Psychotherapy may be a very useful treatment approach for elderly patients and for those with mild anxiety; it may be considerably less toxic than medication.
   1. Anxiety rarely if ever, presents alone in the elderly; it
      is commonly associated with depressive affect.
   2. Flexible therapeutic techniques are necessary, pro-
      viding time for slower paced talking and recollection.
   3. Treatment techniques are not necessarily aimed at
      problem or even symptom resolution *per se*—sharing
      of worry, affect, and apprehensions may be thera-
      peutic.
   4. Anxiety about illness or even approaching death can
      be lessened by gentle but frank and open discussion.
IV. Looking ahead
   A. Looking ahead, it is evident that increased attention by
      clinicians as well as researchers should be devoted to
      defining and understanding the experience of worried

older people. Whether or not a specific diagnostic category of anxiety needs to be retained in order to understand this experience in older people and create improved treatment modalities, or whether redefinitions are necessary is an important topic for future research. Meanwhile, treatment techniques continue to develop and further research is recommended.

B. Continued epidemiologic research focused on the incidence and prevalence of anxiety-like symptoms needs to be conducted with careful attention paid to hidden presentations of the states of worry through alcohol use, physical symptoms, decline in mental function, or older patient's denial of distress.

C. Adequate research on the definition of treatment of anxiety in the elderly is hampered by the relative dearth of appropriate anxious patients. Again, it must be emphasized, that anxiety in the elderly rarely exists alone, but more usually exists in combination with depression or dementia. Agitation on the other hand is a more prominent symptom that requires treatment in this age group. Additional problems complicating future research efforts include more precise recognition and definition of anxiety that is secondary to medical illness, drug treatment, or polypharmacy. It is suggested that more aggressive efforts are needed in order to recruit adequate research subjects to study this problem.

D. There is a lack of consensus about types of new rating scales that would be useful in geriatric anxiety research.
   1. Discrimination between anxiety and depression is desirable, but there must also be a recognition that symptoms of both categories are so interwoven that a comprehensive dysphoria scale may also be necessary or even preferred.
   2. Measurement of change in the elderly is difficult. There may be a need to construct new scales based on words used by older patients themselves.

E. A variety of new chemical structures has been developed in order to treat symptoms of anxiety. Of these new structures buspirone seems to be well adapted to use with the elderly. New compounds that share anti-anxiety efficacy of buspirone but that have a more immediate onset of action would be desirable.

It is encouraging that the contributors to this volume have been able to clarify both the existence of anxiety in the elderly as well as problems in its definition, presentation, treatment, and future research needs. It is hoped that these contributions will stimulate future work and lead to further clarification and understanding of the problems of the older person and perhaps, to a future volume of increased knowledge concerning anxiety in the elderly.

Index

313